Also by Ellie Taylor:

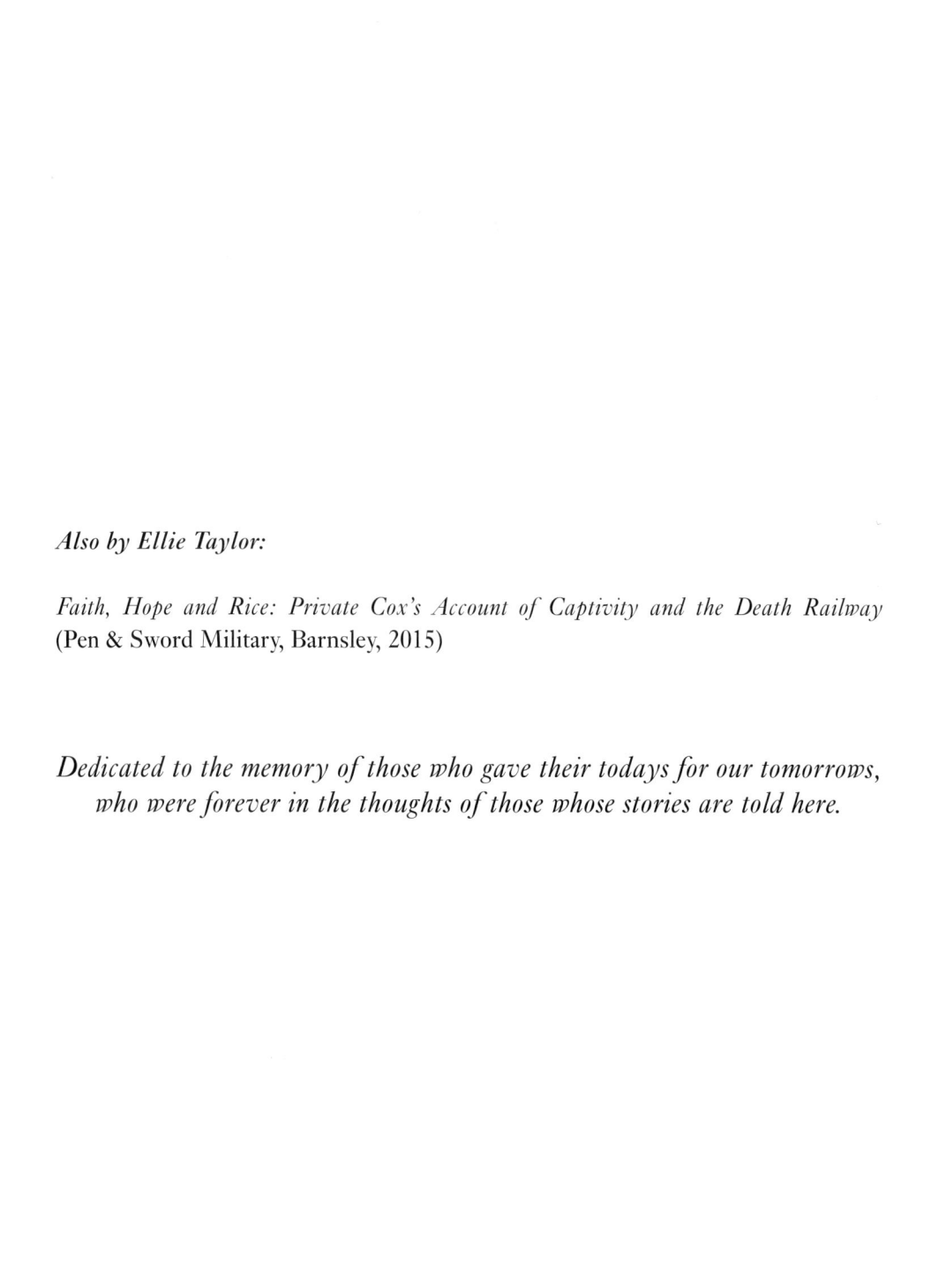

Faith, Hope and Rice: Private Cox's Account of Captivity and the Death Railway (Pen & Sword Military, Barnsley, 2015)

Dedicated to the memory of those who gave their todays for our tomorrows, who were forever in the thoughts of those whose stories are told here.

A CRUEL CAPTIVITY

Prisoners of the Japanese – Their Ordeal and the Legacy

Ellie Taylor

Pen & Sword
MILITARY
AN IMPRINT OF PEN & SWORD BOOKS LTD.
YORKSHIRE – PHILADELPHIA

First published in Great Britain in 2018 by
Pen & Sword Military
An imprint of
Pen & Sword Books Ltd
Yorkshire – Philadelphia

Copyright © Ellie Taylor, 2018

ISBN 978 1 52673 261 3

The right of Ellie Taylor to be identified as Author of this work has been asserted by her in accordance with the Copyright, Designs and Patents Act 1988.

A CIP catalogue record for this book is
available from the British Library.

All rights reserved. No part of this book may be reproduced or transmitted in any form or by any means, electronic or mechanical including photocopying, recording or by any information storage and retrieval system, without permission from the Publisher in writing.

Typeset by Aura Technology and Software Services, India
Printed and bound in England by TJ International Ltd, Padstow, Cornwall.

Pen & Sword Books Limited incorporates the imprints of Atlas, Archaeology, Aviation, Discovery, Family History, Fiction, History, Maritime, Military, Military Classics, Politics, Select, Transport, True Crime, Air World, Frontline Publishing, Leo Cooper, Remember When, Seaforth Publishing, The Praetorian Press, Wharncliffe Local History, Wharncliffe Transport, Wharncliffe True Crime and White Owl.

For a complete list of Pen & Sword titles please contact

PEN & SWORD BOOKS LIMITED
47 Church Street, Barnsley, South Yorkshire, S70 2AS, England
E-mail: enquiries@pen-and-sword.co.uk
Website: www.pen-and-sword.co.uk

Or
PEN AND SWORD BOOKS
1950 Lawrence Rd, Havertown, PA 19083, USA
E-mail: Uspen-and-sword@casematepublishers.com
Website: www.penandswordbooks.com

Contents

Acknowledgements   vii
Prologue   viii

Chapter 1	Prelude to Captivity	1
Chapter 2	Corporal Robert Arthur Hall	11
Chapter 3	Lance Corporal Henry Thomas Doughty	19
Chapter 4	Captain Albert Edgar Symonds	27
Chapter 5	Lance Bombardier Francis John Docketty	35
Chapter 6	Driver John Overton	43
Chapter 7	AC1 Harold Joseph Prechner	51
Chapter 8	Private Norman McCandless Finlay	61
Chapter 9	Able Seaman William Coates Nicholls	71
Chapter 10	AC2 Rosslyn Morris	79
Chapter 11	Private Alfred Frederick Davey	87
Chapter 12	Gunner William Henry Hall	97
Chapter 13	Gunner William Harold George Pick	105
Chapter 14	Signalman Lewis Pope	113
Chapter 15	Corporal William Taylor	123
Chapter 16	Sergeant Robert John Rutherford	131
Chapter 17	Private Eric Gordon Barnes	141
Chapter 18	Detective Crown Sergeant William Gordon Wilson	149
Chapter 19	Gunner George John Gagen	157
Chapter 20	Fusilier James Swordy	166
Chapter 21	AC1 John Stuart Robertson	176

Chapter 22	Private Raymond William Charles Wyatt	183
Chapter 23	Lance Corporal John Dunlop Petrie	191
Chapter 24	In the Shadow of Captivity	199

Select Bibliography 203

Index 205

Acknowledgements

I owe a debt of gratitude to many people for the help they have given me with this book. I began to write it armed with plenty of enthusiasm but only limited knowledge of the whole question of Far East captivity, based mainly upon those aspects of it which had affected my father, who spent the majority of his time as a prisoner of war at various camps along the Thai-Burma railway. Researching the stories of twenty-two men who were held at an array of different camps in locations across South East Asia has been a steep learning curve, one which I would have found impossible to negotiate without the help of those whose years of experience in this field has equipped them with in-depth knowledge of the plight of those who had the misfortune to become prisoners of the Japanese. First and foremost, huge thanks go to Keith Andrews, Chief Researcher at COFEPOW (Children of Far East Prisoners of War), for the many hours spent undertaking research on my behalf and for his patience in answering what must have seemed an endless list of questions. Many thanks also to Andrew Snow of the Thai-Burma Railway Centre, for making available information about the men who were transported to Thailand and Burma to work on the Death Railway. My thanks also to Ronnie Taylor, for generously sharing so much of the knowledge he has gained over many years of research in the field of Far East captivity. Thanks also for help given to me in various ways by: Margaret Martin of the Java FEPOW Club 1942, Stephen Walton of the Imperial War Museum, Tony Banham, Martyn Fryer, Paul Carter, Walter Tuttlebee, Shirley Barnes, Anthony Spero, Keith Bettany, Theresa Loong and former Far East prisoners of war Paul Loong and William Mundy.

Lastly, my thanks also go to those without whose willingness to trust me with so many precious memories of much loved fathers and grandfathers, this book would not have been possible: Christine Beer-Hall, Colin Docketty, David Henry Doughty, Marie Edwards (nee Overton), Sarah Edwards, Susan Gagen, Stephen Gagen, Felicity G. Gelder, Florence Graham, Stella Henderson, Helen Hough, Jane Lewis, Sheila Lewis, Keith Nicholls, Graham Petrie, Alan Pick, Jennifer Pickup, Sarah Pilbeam, Martin Prechner, Beverley Pudney, Barbara Roberts, Ian Robertson, John Rutherford, Janice Skilton, Peter William Taylor, Gillian White and Alison Young.

Prologue

The handwriting on the pages of the photo album was a little faded but still clear enough to read. One photo in particular caught my eye, an image taken in September 1945 from the deck of the MV *Britannic* as she passed through the Suez Canal, homeward bound for Liverpool. The accompanying annotation recalled the hospitality shown during the voyage to a group of returning Far East prisoners of war who were on board that ship, sailing home after three and a half years in captivity.

> Quite a fuss was made of us – extra nourishing food, Guinness each morning at eleven, best seats at the films!

The last words of the annotation made for poignant reading:

> There was no fuss waiting at home. We were yesterday's story!

How desperately sad that this group of men, and thousands like them, who had endured the very depths of human suffering at the hands of their Japanese captors, should feel so overlooked and unappreciated. Worse still, perhaps, the passage of time has shown that having survived an ordeal which killed countless thousands, the shadow of captivity would hover over these men for many years to come.

Chapter 1

Prelude To Captivity

O ther than the fact that most of those whose stories feature in this book came from humble beginnings and had experienced the kind of impoverished childhoods which had befallen many who grew up in the years of the Depression, there would appear to be little that would have united them had their paths not collectively gone on to cross that of the Imperial Japanese Army. Prior to the outbreak of war, some had already made the decision to enlist in His Majesty's Forces, motivated by a desire to escape the poverty of their upbringings or to see more of the world. Most, however, had not. Of these, some had become tradesmen after having served apprenticeships, some had followed in their fathers' footsteps and joined family businesses, others remained in the jobs they had first acquired upon leaving school. Ordinary men going about their ordinary lives, none of whom could have envisaged what lay ahead of them when they vowed to fight for their country. The declaration of war against Germany saw those lives begin to change, particularly in the case of those whose call-up papers heralded an entirely different chapter in life, when military training intervened and took them away from home, a tiny foretaste of what was to come. However, it was the subsequent entry into the war of Japan which brought about irrevocable changes to the men's lives, and which ultimately united them in a battle to survive against the odds as prisoners of the Japanese.

Towards the end of 1941, those men who weren't already serving in the Far East were among the thousands who boarded ships at Liverpool or Gourock, not having been told where they were going for reasons of security but suspecting they were headed for the Middle East. For most, their first port of call was Halifax, Nova Scotia, where, at a time when the United States had yet to enter the war, they were transferred to American vessels for the next stage of their journey eastwards. Many of the young men setting off towards the other side of the world were no more than nineteen or twenty years old and some had never before left British shores. An understandable anxiety accompanied them on their voyage. Harold Prechner, attempting to sound upbeat but clearly feeling homesick and concerned about what the future held, wrote a heartfelt letter to one of his sisters after several weeks at sea.

> Cigarettes are obtainable in any quantity (one brand only) at a ridiculously low price, also milk and plain chocolate in half pound slabs, if you want it! Up

'til recently we had oranges given to us and could also buy them in any quantity we desired...However, give me England without any of these things, every time. I think, had I been an orphan with no friends or relatives, I might have enjoyed this trip, but the thought of being away for so long and the uncertainty of the future is not exactly conducive to happiness.

Japan's entry into the war on 7 December 1941 and the accompanying escalation of the threat to British interests altered the destiny of those whose stories feature here, determining that the destination to which they were now heading was the Far East. Alf Davey later ruefully recalled the moment onboard ship when he and his comrades were informed that they were headed for Singapore. 'They said, "you're going to an island fortress. You'll be alright."' As history has recorded, this was most certainly not the case. The men who sailed towards the supposedly impregnable island in early 1942, though armed with months of training and, theoretically at least, combat ready, could not have envisaged what lay ahead at the hands of an enemy whose savagery shocked seasoned veterans. Within weeks – or, in some cases, days – of their arrival, they faced the prospect of becoming prisoners of war. One of the men, Driver John Overton, at no small personal risk, kept a diary. His early entries reflected the ferocity of the Japanese attack on the island.

February 6: enemy started shelling our camp. One casualty, on guard. February 7: enemy made first landing on island, under constant shell fire, on ammo detail at night. February 8: went to Jurong on petrol detail. Shelled the whole time. February 9: enemy made second landing on island, chaos amongst troops and civilians. Fierce fighting took place.

The speed and intensity of the battle and the subsequent surrender of Allied forces was no less shocking for those who had been in Singapore for some time, the stark realisation that they were powerless to fight on and were now at the mercy of the Japanese later recalled by Bertie Symonds:

Above all things, there was a shared sense of shame, a feeling of bewilderment and humiliation. Dirt and sweat had become commonplace and in a country where the heat and humidity demanded several changes of clothes and numerous showers each day, few of us had any opportunity to wash properly for many days, far less to change our clothes, and this fact alone seemed to degrade us.

The statistics associated with Far East captivity have the power to shock – over 130,000 Allied military personnel were captured by the Japanese, of whom some

60,000 were put to work on the construction of the Thai-Burma railway – vast numbers which do much to convey a tragedy of huge proportions. However, behind those statistics lay the stories of sons, husbands and fathers, many of whom had, until a couple of years earlier, been farmworkers, factory workers, coalminers, bricklayers, men who had signed up to fight for their country but who, as prisoners, found themselves fighting their greatest battle against disease, held captive by an enemy who refused to recognise the rules of the Geneva Convention and treated them barbarically, with the result that twenty-five per cent of those held captive did not survive. The idea for this book was generated by a comment my father made whilst working on an account of his own experiences of captivity in the Far East. Writing a postscript in 1990 to the notes he had originally written in 1946, he commented, 'nearly forty-five years later, I can look back and know that for me, and for many others like me, the war did not end in August 1945. Parts of it remained to be coped with and still do, to this day.' Following the eventual publication of his story, in *Faith, Hope and Rice* in 2015, I began to reflect more closely on that comment and wondered to what extent the physical and psychological scars he had borne as a consequence of his captivity were representative of those borne by other former Far East prisoners of war. Response to the book's publication provided the beginning of an answer and, with it, the impetus to tell the stories of others who had also been held captive by the Japanese.

The stories of the twenty-two former Far East prisoners of war which appear in this book are the result of my having extended an invitation to families of former FEPoWs to tell me about fathers and grandfathers for whom the suffering associated with captivity had not ended with the celebrations of VJ Day. In several respects the twenty-two appear to be fairly representative of the approximately 50,000 British servicemen taken captive in the Far East; the proportion who served in the Army, the Royal Navy or the Royal Air Force roughly correlates to the overall number in those branches of the services who were taken prisoner, as does the proportion who were sent to work as slave labour on the largest of the Japanese's construction projects, the Thailand-Burma railway. Also included are two men who, although civilians, were treated by the Japanese as military prisoners as a consequence of their having fought to defend British interests against the invading Japanese. A sadder correlation is provided by the fact that, just as surviving Far East prisoners of war are a rapidly diminishing group, of the twenty-two men whose stories feature in these pages, only one of them remained alive at the time of researching and writing this book and, sadly, he also has now died. There is no indication that any of the men knew each other, the only exception being two who served in the same battalion, though after the first few months of their captivity they were held in different locations. There were, however, occasions when the twenty-two may have crossed paths with each other; some sailed on the same ships to the Far East; many undoubtedly shared the same overcrowded camp conditions in Singapore or Java in the early days of their captivity before they were dispersed to various parts of Japan's newly acquired empire and, in the case of those who were sent to work on the Thai-Burma railway, several of the men were, at one time or another, at the same camps.

With all but one of the twenty-two men having died by the time I began working on this book, it has largely fallen to sons, daughters and grandchildren to contribute much of the information on which the stories that follow are based. Some of that information includes the men's own written accounts of their experiences, some very brief, others quite lengthy, together with letters written to loved ones. Some men recorded their thoughts in the days and weeks immediately before their captivity began, some did so whilst still held captive or shortly afterwards, and others waited years before putting pen to paper, their own words providing much of the narrative of their stories. In the case of those men who waited decades before recording their thoughts, it appears to have been far less a case of their having struggled to remember the detail of their experiences than one of their having been unable to forget.

Not all of the men left written testimony of their experiences, or did so only very briefly. Partly as a consequence of this, the level of detail in the stories that follow varies, but this is also partly due to the fact that some official records are incomplete, the available information fragmented. However, in many cases the men's movements from one camp to another were recorded in meticulous detail. These records, together with archive material, accounts given by fellow prisoners, information given to the authorities by the men themselves shortly after their liberation and anecdotal evidence from families combine to shed light on the nature of their ordeals. Whilst some spoke openly about this part of their lives, others did not, seldom mentioning their years in captivity, not least, perhaps, because all returning prisoners had been ordered not to talk about their experiences when they arrived home.

> If you had not been lucky enough to have survived and had died an unpleasant death at the hands of the Japanese, you would not have wished your family and friends to have been harrowed by lurid details of your death. This is just what will happen to the families of your comrades who did die in that way if you start talking too freely about your experience. It is felt certain that now you know the reason for this order you will take pains to spare the feelings of others.

How uncomfortably that order sits against the haunting words of the Kohima Epitaph: '*When you go home, tell them of us and say, for your tomorrow, we gave our today.*' Although some, including my father, chose to ignore the order not to talk of their experiences, brusquely entitled, 'Guard Your Tongue', others took it quite literally and spoke only very rarely about their ordeal for the rest of their lives; some chose to talk about it only after the passage of many years, whilst others did so only in the 'safe' environment of a FEPoW gathering, where, among fellow ex-prisoners, there was no need to attempt to explain the inexplicable or describe the indescribable. Although there are no statistics in relation to the number of men who chose, for whatever reason, not to talk about their years in captivity, it is generally accepted that this represents a very large proportion of those taken prisoner – in effect, a silent majority. Their silence is in no way indicative of their experience of captivity having been any less horrific than that of those who spoke up and, therefore, their stories are no less valid. Not only did they suffer the same deprivations and degradations, the same sense of helplessness and, sometimes, hopelessness during their captivity as those who found themselves able to talk about what they had been through, but their silence added an extra component to the struggle to adjust to civilian life following their return.

This book does not pretend to be a comprehensive account of all aspects of Far East captivity. Though the men whose stories feature were held at various locations across South East Asia, from Japan to Java, from Thailand to Hong Kong, from Burma to the Spice Islands and beyond, many others were held elsewhere. However, regardless of location, their captivity was characterised by degradation, starvation, brutality and the wholesale neglect of their most basic needs as human beings; those who survived did so having experienced disease on an epic scale and having witnessed the deaths of many of their comrades. Neither does this book seek to examine in any depth the physical and psychological conditions with which the men were left to contend, often with little help. Rather, what this book sets out to do is to tell the stories of twenty-two men who had the misfortune to be held as prisoners of war

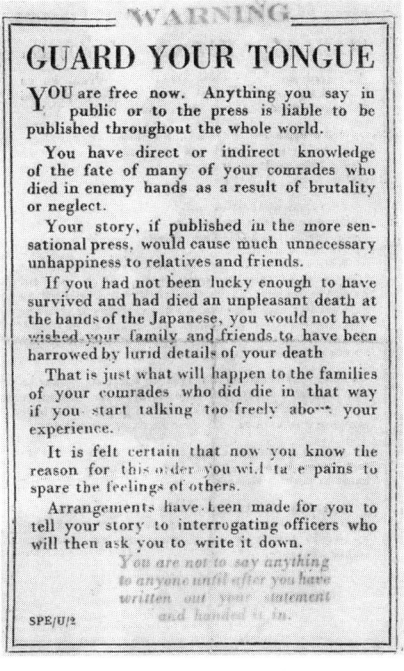

The printed order given to all returning Far East prisoners of war discouraging them from talking about their captivity.

Map of South East Asia showing the various locations at which the PoWs were held.

of the Japanese, looking not only at their particular experiences of captivity but also at how their lives played out after their return from the Far East and the extent to which their war, like my father's, did not end in August 1945.

It has been a privilege to have been allowed to record the stories of these brave men, and I am very grateful to all those who entrusted me with so much personal information about dearly loved fathers. Throughout the men's stories I have referred to them using the names by which they were most commonly known among their families. Whilst every effort has been made to represent both them and their experiences accurately from information given to me by the families, as well as that which has been unearthed through research, any errors in the narrative are mine.

These then are the stories of twenty-two men whose destiny it was to endure a cruel captivity at the hands of the Japanese.

The Captives

Corporal Robert Arthur Hall: Royal Air Force, AMES 250
Sumatra, Burma, Thailand, Singapore

Lance Corporal Henry Thomas Doughty: Royal Army Ordnance Corps
Singapore, Thailand

Captain Albert Edgar Symonds: Indian Army Ordnance Corps & Indian Electrical & Mechanical Engineers
Singapore

Lance Bombardier Francis John Docketty: 5th Searchlight Regiment, Royal Artillery
Singapore, New Britain

Driver John Overton: Royal Army Service Corps
Singapore, Thailand

AC1 Harold Joseph Prechner: Royal Air Force, RTO
Java, Singapore

Private Norman McCandless Finlay: 2nd Battalion East Surrey Regiment
Singapore, Thailand, Philippines

Able Seaman William Coates Nicholls: Royal Navy, Post Division
Bangka, Japanese Naval ships, Singapore

AC2 Rosslyn Morris: Royal Air Force, No. 605 Squadron
Java, Japan

Private Alfred Frederick Davey: 4th Battalion Royal Norfolk Regiment
Singapore, Thailand

Gunner William Henry Hall: 135th Field Regiment, Royal Artillery (East Anglian) (Hertfordshire Yeomanry) (TA)
Singapore, Thailand

Gunner William Harold George Pick: 77th (Welsh) HAA Regiment, Royal Artillery (TA)
Java, Ambon, Singapore

Signalman Lewis Pope: Royal Corps of Signals
Singapore, Thailand

Corporal William Taylor: 6th Battalion Royal Norfolk Regiment
Malaya, Singapore, Thailand

Sergeant Robert John Rutherford: 9th Battalion Royal Northumberland Fusiliers
Singapore, Japan

Private Eric Gordon Barnes: 2nd Battalion Argyll & Sutherland Highlanders (Princess Louise's)
Malaya, Thailand, Japan

Detective Crown Sergeant William Gordon Wilson: Royal Naval Dockyard Police, HK
Hong Kong

Gunner George John Gagen: 148th Field Regiment, Royal Artillery (Bedfordshire Yeomanry) (TA)
Singapore, Thailand

Fusilier James Swordy: 9th Battalion Royal Northumberland Fusiliers
Singapore, Thailand, Japan

AC1 John Stuart Robertson: Royal Air Force, No. 211 Squadron
Java, Japan

Private Raymond William Charles Wyatt: 5th Battalion Bedfordshire and Hertfordshire Regiment
Singapore, Thailand

Lance Corporal John Dunlop Petrie: 3rd Battalion Singapore Straits Volunteer Force
Singapore, Thailand

A note about camp names on the Thai-Burma Railway:
Many of the camps on the Thai-Burma railway were known by alternative names and had various pronunciations and spellings. In addition, because of the difficulties of pronunciation, the PoWs devised their own names for some of the camps, i.e. Wang Pho was commonly known as Wampo. For this reason, throughout I have referred to

Map of the Thai-Burma Railway showing the location of camps at which those whose stories are featured here were held. (There were many other camps along the 415 kilometre railway)

the camps using the Macpherson naming standards, the naming convention accepted by the Centre for Research, Allied PoWs under the Japanese, and devised by Neil MacPherson and Rod Beattie of the Thailand–Burma Railway Centre. In order to avoid confusion, where I have quoted from the written accounts of those men who used their own forms of names for camps, I have replaced those names in line with those used in the naming standards, and with the camp names shown on the map. Camps at the Burma end of the railway were often referred to by their distance from the base camp at Thanbyuzayat. For instance, Anankwin, forty-five kilometres from Thanbyuzayat, became known also as the 45-km Camp.

Chapter 2

Corporal Robert Arthur Hall

Royal Air Force, Air Ministry Experimental Station (AMES 250)

There was little sign in Bob Hall's early life of the perceived rebelliousness which would one day be responsible for his inclusion in a group of men whose collective name became a byword for courage and bravery. Born in 1918 in Bristol, as a child Bob would spend as much time as he could at the docks, fascinated by the ships which arrived from far-off countries with exotic-sounding names. Little did he realise that within a couple of decades he would experience voyages at sea which were the stuff of nightmares rather than of dreams. A studious child, Bob showed little inclination to follow his parents into factory work and, having been awarded a scholarship to the grammar school, was promised a grant by the council to enable him to go to Bristol University to study chemistry. When war was declared he was working in an office to help fund his studies but immediately put aside his plans and volunteered to join up. A childhood ailment which had left him with a burst eardrum caused his application to be rejected initially but the following year, before he was able to take up his place at university, he received his call-up papers and enlisted in the Royal Air Force.

After completing his basic training, in 1940 Bob was posted to RAF Uxbridge in Middlesex, where he was trained on the latest radar technology at the newly formed Air Ministry Experimental Station (AMES 250), a mobile radar unit. Whilst there he was promoted to corporal and then, in March 1941, amid concern about the worsening situation in the Far East, was posted to Singapore. The unit set up a base at Tanah Merah Besar to the east of the island and covered the approaches to Singapore over a sector from the north via the east to the south-south-east. It was radar operators at AMES 250 who detected the aircraft which dropped the first bombs on Singapore in the early hours of 8 December 1941 and who, two days later, picked up the sinister shadows over the ocean which, in a crushing blow to British forces, resulted in the sinking of HM Ships *Prince of Wales* and *Repulse*, with massive loss of life. Towards the middle of February 1942, with Singapore under heavy bombardment and defeat seemingly imminent, RAF personnel were ordered to destroy their equipment to prevent it falling into enemy hands and to then leave the island. So it was that on 13 February, two days before the fall of Singapore,

Bob and the rest of the unit were evacuated on the *Tien Kwang*, headed for Java. The following day, both the *Tien Kwang* and another ship that was fleeing Singapore, the *Kuala*, were sunk just off Pompong Island, resulting in many deaths, including those of women and children.

Together with some of the other survivors from the *Tien Kwang*, Bob eventually made it to the east coast of Sumatra, over eighty miles away. The group then crossed to Padang on the west coast, using what had become an established evacuation route for those escaping from Singapore. The intention had been for the men to then cross to Ceylon, particularly those with knowledge of the latest specialist radar equipment, whom the Japanese would have been keen to interrogate, but a shortage of boats meant that for many, including Bob, this was not possible. Unable any longer to avoid capture, on 17 March 1942 Bob was one of approximately 150 RAF personnel taken prisoner by the Japanese at Padang. The manner of their hurried departure from Singapore and the subsequent sinking of their ships had left them with little more than the clothes they stood up in as they contemplated an uncertain future at the hands of an enemy whose reputation had preceded them. Any lingering doubts Bob may have harboured about the capacity of the Japanese for brutality were cruelly dispelled when his best friend met his death at the hands of the *Kempeitai* (Japanese secret police) after throwing a punch at a guard who was torturing a fellow prisoner.

Bob was taken to a Dutch army barracks, the first of many Japanese prisoner of war camps he would experience, where he spent the following six weeks or so. In mid April the Japanese instructed the British commanding officer, Captain Morley, Royal Artillery, to provide a party of 500 men for transportation to an unknown destination where they would be put to work on railway construction, and Bob was among those selected. It was later revealed that the criteria used for selection included a perceived propensity to cause trouble, based on the previous behaviour of the men during the two months since they had become prisoners of war, something which would, perhaps, increase their chances of surviving whatever lay ahead. The party – twenty officers and 480 'other ranks', drawn from all three services – became known as the British Sumatra Battalion. The battalion went on to earn a reputation for their strength of spirit in the face of adversity and their fierce loyalty to each other, due in no small part to the leadership qualities of their commanding officer, Captain Dudley Apthorp, Royal Norfolk Regiment. After his eventual return from the Far East, Bob was one of many men who, in later life, remained largely silent about their experiences in captivity, giving their families little indication of all that they had been through. When Bob's daughter, Stella, later learned of his inclusion in the battalion and the selection criteria behind it, the perception of her father as having been something of a rebel was one she found quite difficult to grasp. 'I hadn't thought of my dad as a troublemaker.'

On 9 May 1942, the self-styled British Sumatra Battalion were taken by train a hundred miles or so to the north before continuing their journey by road to Medan in Northern Sumatra, arriving at Uni Kampong, a Dutch internment camp, three days later. On 15 May, Bob and his comrades were ordered to board a steamer, the ironically named *England Maru*. This ship, and others like it, which had not been built for the transport of human cargo, had been converted for the purpose by the addition of tiers of wooden decking in the holds, into which as many prisoners as possible were unceremoniously crammed. These vessels became known by all who had the misfortune to experience them, as 'hellships'. On board the *England Maru*, the only sanitation provided was in the form of a crude wooden *benjo*, or toilet, slung over the side of the ship, but the prisoners' access to the deck was severely limited, and the overcrowded and insanitary conditions in the holds were made worse by the ship remaining at anchor for over twenty-four hours in overpowering heat before the voyage even got underway. Given the conditions in which the men were forced to exist for the nine days of their voyage it is little wonder that, by the time they disembarked at Mergui in Burma on 25 May, several of them were critically ill with dysentery. Within a month of their arrival, twelve members of the battalion were dead. Meanwhile, the remainder, suffering from malnutrition and vitamin deficiency, existing on a diet consisting mainly of poor quality rice and whatever they managed to source from their surroundings or acquire from the native Burmese, were put to work on the construction of new runways at an aerodrome. On 10 August, Bob and his comrades were marched to the docks to board the *Tatu Maru*. Though the prisoners were spared the discomfort of the hold for this voyage, so overcrowded was the deck that there was insufficient room for any but a few to sit down at any one time. When they reached the estuary of the Tavoy river the following day, the men were transferred to the overcrowded holds of two smaller vessels. Disembarking several hours later, they were marched to their next camp near Tavoy where, once again, many were assigned to work on an aerodrome.

Bob's next move came on 21 October 1942, when the battalion were taken by barge to Moulmein and from there bundled into metal trucks and taken by rail to Thanbyuzayat, the base camp for the Burma end of what would become the Thailand-Burma railway. The Japanese had already built camps every five kilometres along the route the railway was to take and, just as at the Thailand end of the railway, accommodation consisted of bamboo and attap thatched huts. Within days of their arrival, all but the sickest men in the battalion – the only British unit to work at camps on the Burma end of the railway – were moved to Hlepauk. (The camps located at the Burma end of the railway were also referred to by their location in kilometres from the base camp, hence Hlepauk was also known as the 18 km camp). Bob and his comrades were immediately put to work and issued with the primitive tools with which they and thousands of their fellow prisoners would spend the following sixteen months building embankments, cuttings and bridges, and hacking a path for the railway through virgin jungle and solid rock. The battalion remained at this camp until the beginning of January 1943, when they were transported by truck to Tanyin, the 35 km camp. Despite their isolation, from time to time the men were able to get news of the world beyond the confines of the many camps at which they were held. As Bob later noted: 'We got news throughout from various sources, natives and Nips included, but most importantly, from our own hidden radios, run on batteries, at great risk to the fellows concerned. The news was a great moral help at times.'

Over the course of the following ten months, the men were moved from one camp to another every few weeks, first to Thetkaw, the 14 km camp, where they worked in teams laying railway track, and where the Japanese increased the pressure upon them by forcing them to work in shifts around the clock.

Increased pressure brought increased sickness among the prisoners, with Bob among the many not only suffering from various diseases but also having acquired tropical ulcers, which had often begun as no more than a tiny scratch but, due to general debility and the absence of any medical supplies, quickly became infected.

PoWs at work on a large embankment in Burma. (Photo by kind permission of the Thai-Burma Railway Centre)

Bob later noted that he had suffered 'about thirty-five doses of malaria, but after the first twenty or so I seemed to acquire a natural resistance, which reduced the effects'. A move to Kunhnitkway, the 26 km camp, followed, and then another to Anankwin, the 45 km camp, where the prisoners were put to work unloading and loading rails, sleepers and – most importantly – rations, which at least afforded opportunities to acquire much needed extra food. At the beginning of May came a move to Rephaw, the 30 km camp, where the battalion remained until the middle of July. The next move was to Taungzun, the 60 km camp, where the prisoners were put to work rebuilding bridges damaged by the monsoon rains. As the end of 1943 approached, nearly eighty of the original party of 500 had died either from disease or from the combined effects of starvation, lack of medical supplies and exhaustion.

In November, when the battalion was on the move to Changaraya, Bob was one of several who, due to sickness, got no further than Aungganaung, the 105 km camp, and on 12 January 1944 was one of 250 men who were sent down to Kan'buri hospital camp, some fifty kilometres from the base camp at the southern end of the railway, where conditions were significantly better. Having acquired a leg ulcer that had stubbornly refused to heal for many months and suffering multiple bouts of malaria, Bob remained at Kan'buri for the rest of his captivity and it was from there that he was finally liberated after the Japanese surrender in August 1945.

Bob was among the first of the prisoners in Thailand to begin his journey home. After being transported to Rangoon he sent a telegram to his parents at the end of August informing them of his freedom and wrote a letter to them three days later. With quiet understatement he told them, 'during imprisonment I had an average time of it for those who survived.' The reality was, of course, that serious illness had become the norm, his words painting a bleak picture of the conditions he and his fellow prisoners had endured and the subsequent toll on their health.

PoW Des Bettany's depiction of death on the Thai-Burma Railway. (Photo by kind permission of Keith Bettany, www.changipowart.com)

I've been free of fever since January. I never made acquaintance with dysentery or cholera, thank the Lord. Owing to the poor food and hard work it was difficult to put on weight, and after the railway was finished we came down to a good base camp in Siam from Burma ... and I still only weighed 49 kilos (7st 10lb). There have been cases of men actually going down as low as four to five stone and still recovering, despite lack of medical supplies! In Siam, however, I speedily improved. The Nips in '44 and '45 seemed to get the wind up about us, as it became apparent that we weren't going to lose the war outright, and improved our food and conditions immensely ... . Another big trouble was leg ulcers. Several hundreds, if not thousands, have had amputations. I had one on my right leg which kept me off work more or less for nine months.

Bob arrived at Southampton docks on board HMS *Corfu* on 7 October 1945. Once he was back upon English soil, Bob returned home to Bristol and endeavoured to resume the life he had been forced to abandon. After a battle with the council, who had withdrawn their offer of a grant, Bob finally took up his place at university and was still a student when he met Norma, a former WAAF who had been based at Bomber Command HQ during the war. They married in 1949 and the next few years saw the arrival of a son and a daughter, as well as Bob's graduation with an MSc in research chemistry, after which he became a research chemist with ICI and the family moved to West Kilbride, Ayrshire.

Unlike many who returned from the Far East, Bob saw no recurrence of the malaria which had felled him time and again in Burma, often commenting that he thought he must now be immune to it. The greatest impact that his captivity appeared to have had upon his physical health at that time appeared to be the damage done to his hearing. He attributed this to the numerous beatings about the head he had received from the guards. Far more in evidence than

Bob Hall and his daughter Stella on a beach holiday in 1956.

anything physical, however, were the clear signs of his having been psychologically scarred. Stella explained, 'it's true to say that my mum, brother and myself all bore the brunt of his mental state. He was often tense and irritable and prone to occasional outbursts of temper.' She added that her father appeared to have been badly affected by the feelings of utter helplessness engendered by his experiences in captivity, which had served to intensify deep-rooted feelings of insecurity and caused him to lash out at those closest to him. Although at pains to point out that there was also a lighter side to him, she added that when he returned from the Far East,

> he was extra driven and intolerant of what he regarded as failings in his family and others in general ... . I think he had coped by convincing himself that he'd eliminated all possible weaknesses in himself.

Though Bob went on to have a successful career with ICI and was instrumental in the development of several new products, he retired early in the 1970s to look after Norma when she became terminally ill.

Having seldom spoken of his past experiences, towards the end of his life Bob visited a local museum which featured an exhibition on the subject of Far East captivity. Stella explained.

> I left him alone upstairs, where he spent a long time looking at everything – the banned sketches, the letters, a small piece of rail, even a Japanese flag, captured from a Jap officer on liberation. When he came back down he just said, 'some of the chaps were discovered with radios and ...' making a gesture across the throat. Although I didn't press him to say more, I did get the feeling that he was glad to have seen it, and something had just lifted from him.

Bob Hall and his wife Norma in 1968.

Bob Hall with his daughter Stella at her wedding in 1975.

Nevertheless, it is perhaps indicative of the extent to which his experiences in the Far East continued to play on his mind that when Bob became hospitalised with a serious illness for the last two weeks of his life, according to Stella, 'he was semi-conscious much of the time and would keep saying, "PoW days" over and over. I think it was a form of nightmare.'

It was not until after Bob's death in 1995, at the age of seventy-seven, that the true impact upon his physical health of his time as a prisoner of war became known. The cause of his death was given as polyarteritis nodosa, a rare autoimmune disease, his post mortem report making a connection between the damage which had been done to his organs and the deprivations and diseases from which he had suffered during his captivity. Said Stella of the disease which her father would not have contracted had it not been for the callous neglect of his Japanese captors, 'they reckoned that his PoW illnesses made this possible, so I guess they got him in the end.'

Chapter 3

Lance Corporal Henry Thomas Doughty

Royal Army Ordnance Corps (RAOC), Light Aid
Detachment 55 Infantry Brigade

So traumatised was Harry Doughty by something that he had been forced to do during his captivity that he could not bear to tell anyone about it for over fifty years. When he finally confided in his son, he did so only after having received an assurance that what he said would not be repeated until after his death. The passage of time had done nothing to dim his memories nor lessen the pain they continued to cause him.

Harry was one of thousands of young men whose lives were propelled along a different path to that originally intended as a consequence of the outbreak of war in 1939. Born in 1919 in Selly Oak, Harry was just five years old when his father died, plunging the family into poverty as his mother struggled to raise him and his five siblings on her own. After leaving school at the age of fourteen, Harry took a job as a tea boy at the Cadbury factory in Birmingham and had worked his way up to the position of storeman by the time he received his call up papers in 1940. Leaving behind him the only job he had ever known, Harry enlisted in the Royal Army Ordnance Corps at Chilwell. As he underwent army training, he was posted first to Colchester and then to Tidworth where, following events at Dunkirk, plans for his unit to be sent to Europe were shelved in favour of preparation for an invasion. Further moves followed, to Manchester, Norwich, Hawick and then Lichfield, where, shortly after being promoted to lance corporal, he discovered that he was to be posted overseas.

After travelling to Liverpool, on 29 October 1941 Harry boarded the HMT* *Orcades* and

Harry Doughty in 1940.

---

* HMT = Hired Military Transport, i.e. a merchant ship requisitioned to carry military personnel.

sailed across the Atlantic to Halifax, Nova Scotia, where he was then transferred to the American vessel the USS *West Point* as part of a convoy headed towards an as yet unconfirmed destination. As a result of Japan's entry into the war in early December 1941, that destination became Singapore, but the *West Point* first took Harry and his comrades to India, where they spent two weeks undergoing intensive training in preparation for what lay ahead of them. It was to be many years before Harry ever spoke about events following his arrival in Singapore but when he did so, and also decided to write an account of his experiences, the memories remained clear.

> We were bombed by Japanese aircraft as we went through the Malacca Straits, the channel between Java, Sumatra and Singapore. We docked at Singapore in late January 1942. We were attached to 55 Infantry Brigade, giving assistance in light aid for their vehicles. On the dockside at Singapore we had the job of starting the motor vehicles as they were unloaded from the ship. We then drove them away from the bombings which were going on. All our tools and equipment had gone to the Middle East, where we were due to go originally. In order to gain some tools we decided to go to Seletar airfield but found no personnel there. The airfield was full of bomb craters and the aircraft destroyed. On entering a large building it was obvious that this was the RAF dining room. The long tables contained full plates of food untouched. It appeared the airmen had to do a quick evacuation.

With no Allied aircraft to defend them, Harry's unit then came under heavy bombardment by the Japanese.

> We were constantly mortar shelled. Japanese aircraft were constantly flying over on reconnaissance, causing us to open fire with Bren gun and rifle fire .... . Singapore was supposed to be an island fortress. It had two large naval guns pointing out to sea. The Japanese came down the mainland.
> (There appears to have been a general perception among many of the men that the guns Harry refers to were not capable of engaging targets on the mainland, when in fact all but one of them could traverse, and did so with considerable effect on the Japanese.)

On 15 February 1942, a little over two weeks after having disembarked from the *West Point*, Harry became a prisoner of war.

> Our commanding officer ordered us to lay down our arms. He said hostilities should cease. We destroyed our weapons and ammunition. A day or two later we marched with our kit, escorted by the Japanese, destination Changi barracks.

> This march was pretty horrifying with the tropical heat, lack of water and food. We marched over the debris of war, burnt out vehicles, overhead power lines down, trees and soldier victims of war lying in the road and across hedgerows.

Harry spent the following four months at Changi, during which he, like many others, experienced the dire consequences of being held captive by an enemy who had complete disregard for the health and welfare of their prisoners. With the camp under British administration, over the following weeks an ordered existence of sorts was fashioned from the very basic means at the prisoners' disposal.

> We rigged up a field kitchen to cook our meals. Working parties were organised, some PoWs going with the Japanese for cleaning up operations in Singapore, while others would go outside the wire fence under Japanese guard for burials in a selected area. Other working parties were arranged under guard to go outside the wire to collect firewood and seawater for cooking purposes. With the tropical heat and the amount of perspiration loss, salt was considered essential in our food.

The lack of nutritious food and medical provisions rapidly resulted in widespread disease and numerous deaths. As Harry commented, 'the sound of the bugler's Last Post was a constant sound for our men.' This was a picture of wholesale neglect which was repeated at prison camps throughout South East Asia.

In the middle of 1942, the Japanese began to transport large parties of men to Thailand to work on the construction of a railway that would provide an alternative supply line for their troops. Harry was among the first to be sent, leaving on 18 June 1942 with the June Mainland Party, under the command of Major R.S. Sykes, RASC. The men were completely unaware of the nature of the project awaiting them. The move was portrayed by the Japanese as being of benefit to the prisoners, which could not have been further from the truth.

> We had heard rumours that the Japanese were going to move us up country where there was good food and recreational facilities. We left Changi and went to the railway station, where there was a train with a long line of goods trucks. We were ordered into these steel trucks, thirty men per truck. We still did not know where we were going. Some of the lads were suffering with stomach upsets and had to revert to putting their backsides out of the door entrance to the trucks as we travelled. We did eventually have three prearranged stops on the journey. These were for food (rice) and toilets (trenches dug out of soil). Having travelled the full length of Malaya, we finally arrived at our destination, Ban Pong, Thailand. We marched with our kit to a base camp containing huts made

> of bamboo poles and attap roofing …. As this was part of the monsoon season, the camp was adrift with water. The latrines had been dug too close to the huts.

Over the following months, thousands more would pass through this camp as they joined the huge workforce, but for many it would be a one way journey. After an overnight rest, Harry and his comrades were marched to Nong Pladuc, where they were put to work constructing bamboo and attap huts, a process which would be repeated at camps the length of the railway.

> The huts were very long, the roof sloping to about two feet from the ground. This gave a very small amount of light with extra light visible from both open ends. Bamboo platforms were built on each side of the hut, leaving a gangway about two yards wide. On the platforms, split and flattened bamboo was tied down. Each man lay side by side to sleep. These beds were infested with bed bugs and the whole area was a feeding ground for insects and mosquitoes.

Months of poor quality food had left the prisoners with little resistance to infection and disease, as Harry was to discover. 'After several days I had my first bout of tropical fever. On reporting sick to our own medical officer, it was medicine then back to duties. We still had some medical supplies at that time.'

From Nong Pladuc, the party was then marched to Kan'buri and once more put to work.

> We built more huts and unloaded tools and lengths of railway lines. Right from the start at Changi and then the other camps, we had roll calls whereby we had to

Kan'buri camp, Thailand. (Photo by kind permission of the Thai-Burma Railway Centre)

call our numbers out in Japanese. These roll calls – and sometimes hut searches – could be made without prior notice at any time of the day. Very often we were kept to attention for long periods in the heat of the day. Some of the lads collapsed.

The Japanese made a point of trying to harness any particular skills possessed by their prisoners and it was whilst Harry was at Kan'buri that, having learned he was an accomplished carpenter, they exploited his talents in a way which was to haunt him for the rest of his life. His son explained:

> he was ordered under penalty of death to make wooden Samurai swords as he was a skilled carpenter. What he didn't know was that the Japanese soldiers used these to practise their beheading technique. It was only later in his captivity that he fully understood what he had made them for.

In October 1942 Harry was among a group of men marched upcountry to Kannyu, an area of extremely difficult terrain from which the cutting later known as Hellfire Pass was excavated.

> We were split up into parties, each with a guard, and got aboard some barges …. My boatload of PoWs went into the jungle to build huts. I was left with two Japanese guards for a while. I became their cook and butcher. I did not know the first thing about butchering but the situation made you learn very quickly. I used to sleep on the ground in the cookhouse area near the firewood pile. Large rats used to run over me. I later joined the main party, building huts, cutting bamboo, felling trees, clearing the jungle and carrying earth to build up the railway embankment. We worked from early morning and returned at night. While we

PoW Des Bettany's sketch of prisoners building the Thai-Burma Railway.

were doing this work, other prisoners of war were being force-marched up and through the jungle to work in the camps and on the railway.

The true extent to which the Japanese considered their prisoners to be expendable became clear once work on the construction of the railway was deemed to be falling behind schedule, from which time onwards the word 'speedo' echoed in the ears of all who were unfortunate enough to have been forced to work the length of the 415-kilometre track. Not only were men who were considered fit enough to work put under intense pressure, but so also were those who were seriously ill.

Japanese engineers demanded a certain number of men from the camp for each day's work, irrespective of the number of sick men, and to make up the day's quota the Japanese often forced totally unfit men from their hospital beds to make up the number. The engineers were issuing orders to complete several metres of the railway or sections of bridges or spans in a certain time scale. The pressure was on, so the word familiar to us from the engineers or guards was 'speedo, speedo'. This also encouraged them to dish out more brutal beatings.

Recalling the particular brutality of the Korean guards at this and other camps, Harry added:

to supplement the Japanese guards, Korean auxiliaries were engaged to help out. The Koreans were considered by the Japanese to be lower in class, hence, the Koreans were more brutal than some of the Japanese to the prisoners.

In December 1942, Harry moved to Tarsao hospital camp and remained there for seventeen months, during which time disease and exhaustion had clearly taken their toll.

I lost count of the number of times I went down with malaria. We had very little, if any, medical supplies. Occasionally we might get a small dose of powdered quinine. I also had several bouts of dysentery, including amoebic dysentery, and I developed a small lump in my groin, which was cut out without anaesthetic.

In May 1944, Harry was moved down the line to Tha Muang, where he remained until the following September when he was sent back upcountry to Tha Mayo. Two months later he was moved down the line again, this time to Tampi. Construction of the railway had been completed in October 1943 but Harry was one of many prisoners who remained in the camps in order to undertake maintenance work. By 1944, Allied air raids had become frequent and, when the train on which Harry was travelling in order to carry out ballast work on the track was targeted, he was fortunate to survive.

Allied aircraft bombed the train and the railway.... We panicked, ignored the guards and took off hell for leather into the jungle. I found a large fallen tree, under which I managed to crawl for protection from the bombing and machine gunning. Afterwards, with my nerves shattered, I returned to the train. It was just as if you had taken all the rivets out of it. We lost a lot of our men plus some Japanese and their horses, which were in one of the trucks. You would not think you could see anything like it. It was a terrible, bloody night. We remained near the track until morning, when we had the grim task of recovering and burying the bits and pieces of our colleagues.

Harry's next camp move, in June 1945, finally took him away from the railway to Pratchi in eastern Thailand near the border with French-Indo China (now Cambodia), where the prisoners were tasked with building a road from Pratchi to Mergui on the coast of Burma. The road was intended to provide the Japanese with an escape route from advancing Allied forces. In their urgency to have it built quickly, many prisoners were, quite literally, worked to death. Harry had been at Pratchi a little over two months when he and his fellow prisoners awoke one morning to find that the Japanese had left the camp. Shortly afterwards came the discovery that the war had ended.

We were driven out of the camp in lorries to Bangkok and the following day we boarded a Dakota aircraft. This aeroplane had no seats so we sat on the floor. We flew over the railway that we had worked on.

Upon arrival in Rangoon, Harry was admitted to hospital until he was considered fit enough to travel and then began his journey home, arriving at Liverpool docks on board the SS *Orduna* on 18 October 1945, nearly four years after he had sailed off to war.

Once back in England Harry returned home to Birmingham to pick up the threads of his life, but captivity had left its mark upon him. Like many who returned from the Far East, he found himself tormented by nightmares, but he was also left with a number of physical reminders. In addition to suffering from recurrent bouts of malaria and digestive problems, the beri beri he had contracted in Thailand had left him with numbness in his feet, which he referred to as 'dead feet', and for which he was later classed as disabled. Numerous beatings had left him with severe hearing problems, which eventually led to deafness, and he also required extensive dental treatment as a result of prolonged vitamin deficiency. It was whilst Harry was receiving dental treatment shortly after his return from the Far East that he met his future wife, Joan, who worked at one of the dental clinics he attended. They married in 1948 and went on to have three children.

Meanwhile, given the problems with his health, it was fortunate for Harry that his former employers at Cadbury's had kept his job open for him. He resumed work there shortly after his return to England and remained there until he retired, during which time he progressed to being a senior manager in charge of the warehouses.

Harry's children grew up knowing very little about their father's ordeal or the reason he often struggled with his emotions and appeared somewhat distant. As his son, David, recalled,

Dad threw himself into his work and, as a child, I didn't really bond well with him. He used to go off on his own fishing or spend the entire weekend working on his cars or on his own.

Harry Doughty and his wife Joan when they married in 1948.

Over the years it became a source of anxiety to David that, 'at every Remembrance Sunday he would be in tears but would never explain why'. It was not until his father was in his seventies that, prompted by David, he began to talk about his experiences as a prisoner of war and eventually revealed the way in which his carpentry skills had been used against his fellow prisoners. Even though refusal to have complied with the demands of the Japanese would have resulted in his own death, the episode left Harry so tormented by feelings of guilt that, according to David, 'he eventually told me in strictest confidence with the understanding that this information would not be released until after his death. He felt very upset about doing that. He was in tears as he told me about it'.

Harry died in 2011, at the age of ninety-two. Said David, 'I can't imagine how he remained sane, having to live a further sixty-five years with the images and memories he had of his time as a prisoner of war. The mental scars remained with him until his death.'

Chapter 4

Captain Albert Edgar Symonds

Indian Army Ordnance Corps & Electrical & Mechanical Engineers (IEME)

'Do I still hate them? No, not really. As the years pass, I simply accept that these things happen,' wrote Bertie Symonds, as he reflected upon his time as a prisoner in the hands of the Japanese. They were, he added, years which were characterised by 'long periods of back-breaking work and, most of all, the nagging hunger and homesickness and the feeling of fear and uncertainty which was with us almost all the time'. They were also years that led to untold heartbreak and changed the course of his life.

Bertie was born in Portsmouth in 1916, one of four children whose father served in the Royal Navy, and home was wherever their father happened to be posted until 1925 when the family settled in Southsea. After graduating from Birmingham University with a degree in engineering, Bertie had joined his father's Austin motor dealership but, having enlisted in the Territorial Army whilst at university, decided instead to pursue a career in the military. His application for a permanent commission was accepted shortly before the outbreak of war and as a lieutenant in the Hampshire (Fortress) Royal Engineers, he was posted to one of the three large Victorian sea forts located in the Solent and settled down to life in Hampshire with his wife and young daughter. He then took what was to be a life-changing decision by applying for a transfer to the Indian Army. Having heard that there was a shortage of engineer officers in India, he was lured by the promise of early promotion, the potential to earn more money and, most of all, by the distinct possibility of his young family being able to join him. Within months, he found himself in Bombay and, in October 1941, promoted to captain, was posted to Singapore. Less than two months

Bertie Symonds during his service in the Indian Army.

later he witnessed the first bombs falling upon the island and would not see his family again for another four years, with devastating consequences.

Bertie's recollection of the events which unfolded in February 1942 remained very clear when, later, he wrote an account of his experiences.

> To this day, I still recall with amazement the situation that existed during those last two days, the 14th and 15th February .... I had acquired a government printed newspaper at Kallang Aerodrome – probably one of the last – across the front of which, in heavy type, was the statement, 'Singapore must stand – Singapore shall stand'. It went on to report the battle situation on Friday night and Saturday morning, with the comment, 'Japanese Suffer Huge Casualties'. What a pathetic lie! Almost all of us were unhappily aware of the desperate situation in which we were placed and we knew with certainty that the next twenty-four hours might be our last.

Following the surrender of Allied forces to the Japanese, Bertie was one of many who were ordered to make their way to Changi. Rather than walk, he and his fellow officers climbed aboard a Chevrolet water tanker they had chanced upon, loaded it with kit and supplies and headed to the main road, only to find it blocked by a sea of humanity.

> The highway was filled with a straggling column reaching out of sight in both directions. Soldiers, civilians, women, all heading towards Changi – the civilians to internment in the jail, the service personnel to Roberts Barracks. Looking back, it is difficult to describe our feelings as we waited at that crossroad – shame at our predicament, embarrassment that we had transport, while they, many already dragging their feet, were walking ... but the vacant looks from men shuffling past made me acutely aware of the luxury of even a water tank.

Having arrived at Changi, Bertie and his comrades found accommodation in a garage previously used for army vehicles, which at least offered some shelter, whereas many were forced to sleep out in the open. Recalling the appalling price paid by the most vulnerable amongst them in the earliest days of their captivity, he noted that:

> life was more wretched than it ever needed to be. Among the elderly and the sick, malnutrition soon began to claim its victims. Many of those who had fought a losing battle through the steaming jungle right down to Singapore Island entered the camp with hideous wounds and tropical ulcers and... were

among the first to suffer and many to die. And for those fresh out of home with no acquired immunity, there was malaria.

The refusal of the Japanese to provide the lifesaving drugs which were known to be available to them illustrated from the outset their complete indifference to the fate of their captives, an attitude which was to persist throughout the years of captivity.

With the camp under British administration, Bertie noted:

> it took us just a day or two to realise that the camp command intended to maintain the fullest military discipline … . They were determined to preserve a full chain of command and a strict officer/other rank relationship.

This was, he noted, an attitude which 'awarded us the officer's considerable privileges, which others and I felt were not right or acceptable in the present circumstances'. Unwilling to align himself with the view that officers should not work, Bertie volunteered to take charge of a working party of thirty NCOs. Having been taken to the outskirts of the city, the party's first task was to search for and then commandeer trucks which, until just a few weeks earlier, had been driven by British soldiers but were now the property of the Japanese. The party was then put to work on the construction of a Shinto shrine, commemorating the Japanese war dead, at the golf course at Bukit Timah. Bertie and the other drivers in the party spent their days driving trucks loaded with building materials from Singapore docks to the construction site. During this time he and his comrades were housed in a native *kampong*, or village, close to the golf course and it was whilst here that Bertie had his first brush with illness when he contracted dengue fever. The care he was shown by the village headman whilst he was ill was in direct contrast to the callous neglect shown by the Japanese to those in their charge, whatever the state of their health. 'The majority of the guards were brutal and most seemed to enjoy making life as difficult as possible for the men working under them.' He added:

> our loading and unloading was usually accompanied by shouts of 'speedo' and 'damme' and 'Nippon number one, British soldier number ten', and the dropping of a shovel or a pause to wipe the sweat from one's eyes often became a signal for a hail of blows across our shoulders with that favourite weapon of the Nippon guard, a pick axe handle.

The arrival one day of a senior Japanese officer accompanied by a British interpreter/liaison officer prompted an intervention of fate which may well have increased Bertie's chances of surviving a captivity during which so many perished.

The interpreter explained that the Japanese army required a number of pictures to be painted, depicting scenes of the last days of the battle, which would be hung in the new Japanese War Museum (formerly the Raffles Museum) and that they required someone with artistic skills for this. The interpreter recognised Bertie as having been a fellow engineering student at Birmingham University and, recalling that he had been something of an artist, suggested him for the role. Bertie's commanding officer initially refused to assist in any way with this idea but then agreed on the grounds that, since Bertie would be given a degree of freedom to move around, this would provide an opportunity to perhaps pick up valuable news from the Malays and Chinese. 'The following day they took me into Singapore to buy paints, paper and the rest. I was given a very official armband covered in Nippon characters and a printed pass.' Bertie spent the following days sketching and painting but, before long, despite having been given permission to visit various sites of battle, came into conflict with one of the guards who, unimpressed by his armband, became incensed when Bertie refused to paint a picture of him.

> He apparently decided that a few blows with his rifle butt on my back would help me to produce what he wanted. When I did not respond, he transferred his attention to my head and face, and made a sorry mess of both my nose and mouth, all the time shouting 'damme' and 'no good na' and other unintelligible remarks.

This was far from being an isolated incident, as Bertie later noted: 'beating, bashing and torture had become a normal part of a prisoner's life.'

In October 1942, he learned that a large party of prisoners was to be sent to Thailand and that his name was on the list to go, only to then be informed that it had been removed.

Bertie Symonds' sketch depicting Changi Jail, Singapore, and the guards' ill treatment of prisoners.

It seemed that I had not yet completed all the pictures required by Nippon Headquarters and I was to stay back until I had done so. Perhaps it is not too much to say that this painting job, which at first I did not want to do, may well have saved my life.

The party Bertie had narrowly missed accompanying was destined to work on the construction of the Thai-Burma railway. Many among the party would not return.

On 31 December 1942, Bertie was sent back to Changi and initially allocated to work in the gardens. However, shortly afterwards, when the officer who had been in charge of the camp workshops became too ill to continue with the job, Bertie was appointed to replace him.

I began to realise just how lucky I was. I now had a regular job with an acceptable measure of responsibility which, to some extent, related to my normal army duties …. This was in profound contrast to the majority of men in Changi, whose lives revolved around mindless hard labour from early morning to evening.

Though orders had been given at the capitulation to destroy anything which could have been of use to the Japanese, the contents of the workshops had remained untouched and the extensive facilities therein were harnessed in multiple ways.

In a community the size of Changi, as a need arose, someone was found with the knowledge or ability to produce what was required … rubber sandals, rope, nails, the list was endless and it included making coffins.

Bertie went on to note that, as time wore on, an increasing number of desperately sick men returned from the groups that had been sent to Thailand, the demand for coffins far out-stripping supply as overwork, malnutrition and disease took their toll. He continued to run the workshops for the duration of his captivity, at the heart of an enterprise which saw prisoners employing remarkable ingenuity to fashion everyday but, nonetheless, vital objects from the most basic materials.

We acquired barrack room lockers … which we cut, shaped and welded into dixies, mugs, baking trays, buckets and pails. We produced toothbrushes and brooms using the same palm fronds that we used for attap. Clogs were made from motor tyres and from soft rubber wood, and with the latex from the rubber trees we repaired boots and shoes.

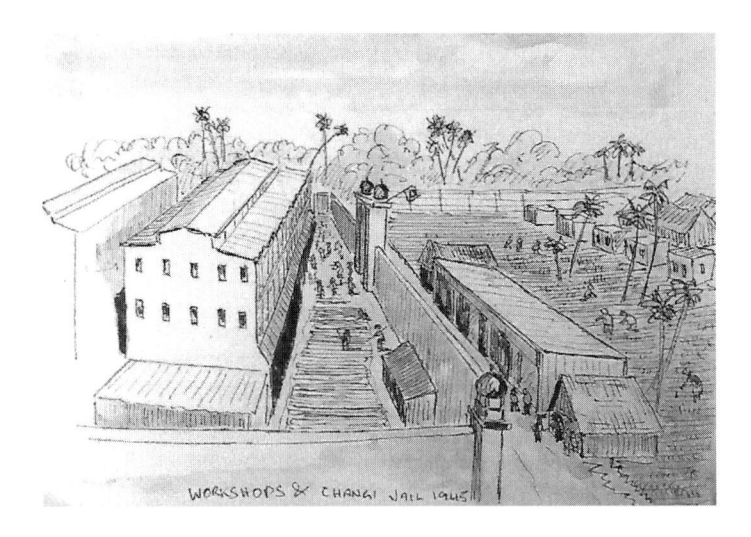

Bertie Symonds' sketch of the Workshops and Changi Jail, Singapore.

Bertie also set up a shop for the repair and maintenance of hospital equipment and was particularly proud of having helped the doctors to design a press that extracted the juice from lalang grass. It had been discovered that, if taken in sufficient quantities, the juice had a positive effect in the treatment of deficiency-related diseases such as pellagra. The privileges afforded by Bertie's officer status did not preclude him from contracting various tropical diseases nor prevent him from suffering from vitamin deficiency. In addition to dengue fever and several bouts of dysentery, he noted, 'I also had my share of tropical ulcers and several nasty spells of a most painful deficiency disease which affected my mouth and tongue but which was relieved by liberal doses over several weeks of the doctor's repulsive lalang grass juice.' In June 1945, Bertie also contracted amoebic dysentery, for which, again, no drugs were available.

When, in 1944, the Japanese gave the order that all prisoners were to move to the confines of Changi jail, the workshops were quickly dismantled and relocated and continued to produce a steady stream of much needed equipment, those in the workshops providing much of the labour and ingenuity which went into making the jail more habitable. It was in the early months of 1945, recalled Bertie, that:

> we became aware of a change in the attitude of the Korean guards. Those in the workshops now attempted to ingratiate themselves with us … . We were sceptical about this change in character. They had, all the years we had known them, been more Japanese than the Japs, they were more strident in speech, more callous and more cruel, if this were possible, than their masters and I could look back over the past years to countless beatings by the Koreans in the workshop, always for the most trivial, if for any reason at all.

He went on to add that they suddenly began to produce various items of food and – albeit too late for many – drugs, 'all the things the Japs had declared non-existent for three years'. Recalling how he learned that his ordeal would soon be over, Bertie noted:

> during the night of 6th August, I was suddenly awakened, disturbed by a rising crescendo of noise from inside the jail, voices talking and shouting .... In our own hut we lay awake talking, wondering, apprehensive, not knowing that a short time before, our pirate radio operators in the jail and in the officers' lines had heard the BBC Overseas radio announce that an atomic bomb had been dropped on Hiroshima.

After the eventual liberation of the camp, Bertie boarded the *Britannic* and sailed via India for England, arriving at Liverpool docks on 21 October. He returned home to the heartbreaking news that his wife wished to begin a new life in America with a US Marines' officer whom she had met in Bertie's absence and to take their young daughter with her. 'Like so many other people in the services caught up in the war in the Far East, I suppose I had simply stayed away too long,' he later noted. With nothing left for him at home, he decided to remain in the Indian Army, returned to India in January 1946, and was promoted to the rank of major the following June. However, unable to see a future for himself after the partition of India and Pakistan, he returned permanently to England in May 1947, shortly after which he met Betty at a social event in Portsmouth. They married in 1948 and their daughter arrived five years later. Meanwhile, as he set about the task of returning to civilian life, Bertie was put in touch with a local businessman who owned a company which built and sold commercial vehicles, and worked there in various capacities from salesman to company director until he retired in his seventies.

In forging a new life for himself after the havoc wrought by his years away, Bertie had, as far as possible, put the war and his captivity behind him, but its effects could still be felt. Shortly after his return to India in 1946, he had suffered a recurrence of the amoebic dysentery which he had contracted during his captivity and spent two months in hospital in Bombay. This left him with a legacy of bowel problems and, following his return to England in 1947, he was admitted to a military hospital

Bertie Symonds and his wife Betty when they married in 1948.

in Millbank, London, for three weeks. He subsequently suffered from irritable bowel syndrome, which required frequent hospital treatment, for the rest of his life and was awarded a small pension in recognition of the fact that this condition had been acquired during his captivity. A further bequest from those years arrived in the last decade or so of Bertie's life when he was diagnosed with solar keratosis, a condition caused by extended exposure to the sun, which, according to his daughter, Sarah, manifested itself in ulcerated spots and plagued him for the rest of his life.

It became apparent when Bertie was in his seventies that, despite nearly fifty years having passed since his return from the Far East, he continued to harbour a great deal of anger about his experiences as a prisoner of war. According to Sarah, her father's GP advised him 'to let some of his anger out rather than bottle it up'. After being referred to a psychiatrist at the Royal Naval Hospital Haslar, in Gosport, which specialised in treating military personnel, he was advised to 'exorcise his past by writing his memoirs'. Until this time Bertie had shared little about his experiences in captivity but, with a clarity of mind that the passing of the years had done little to diminish, he discovered that writing about those years provided a release for his anger.

At the age of ninety-six Bertie was diagnosed with vascular dementia and was admitted to residential care. He had suffered from nightmares for some time but, said Sarah:

Bertie Symonds with his wife Betty in 1990.

> from this point on, the nightmares and links back to being a prisoner of war became much more obvious …. When he was woken in the night he would think it was the Japanese prison warders coming to take him to be tortured. It was very real to him.

How cruel that whatever else dementia erased from Bertie's mind, it left intact the memories of the horrors he suffered during captivity which remained with him until his death in 2015 at the age of ninety-nine.

Chapter 5

Lance Bombardier Francis John Docketty

5th Searchlight Regiment, Royal Artillery

Frank Docketty was twenty-five years old when he became a prisoner of war. He would later reflect on the irony of the fact that had he not contracted malaria – a life-threatening disease – some nine months after being captured by the Japanese, he would certainly not have lived to see his twenty-sixth birthday. That he did so was, perhaps, not purely down to chance but also a result of his having had the mental strength to survive an ordeal which must have seemed all but hopeless to those who experienced it.

The hardships of Frank's upbringing, whilst undoubtedly not perceived as a blessing at the time, may well have played their part in equipping him for what he was to face in years to come. Born in Silvertown, Essex, in 1917, Frank and his sister and two brothers had a peripatetic childhood, one in which dire poverty saw the family move from Woolwich in South East London to Kent, then back to London again and from there to Surrey. Eager to learn a trade and make something of his life, Frank had just completed an apprenticeship as a bricklayer by the time war broke out in 1939. Having already enrolled in the local unit of the Territorial Army, he was sent to Longmoor Camp in Hampshire to undergo training on searchlights. His unit, 316 Battery, was then transferred to the Royal Artillery and posted to Tangmere aerodrome in Sussex, where they later became part of the 5th Searchlight Regiment, operating anti-aircraft guns. Amid heightening tension in the Far East in the autumn of 1941 the regiment was ordered overseas and Frank found himself on board the HMT *Largs Bay*, which arrived in Singapore on 6 November 1941. Little over a month later, as the Japanese rapidly advanced towards Singapore following their invasion of Malaya, Frank was among those fighting to defend the island. The intensity of the Japanese attack and the confusion of the ensuing battle caused Frank to become separated from his section. Recalling his desperate struggle to find his way back to them, he noted in 1946:

> I headed blindly into the jungle, hastened by a cowardly fear of which I am ashamed. I was clawing at dense foliage, immune to any sense of feeling, terror stricken ... . I came to a clearing of uniformly placed rubber trees and went

dashing across without thought. I was running across the flank of the Japs, all I knew at the time was the dreaded cracking of rifles ...

He added that having finally found his way back to his battery:

> I was wet through from sweat, mud and blood. An officer put me with three others who were suffering from shell-shock and after a while I was given a Bren gun by the major and pushed into a slit trench. By this time, I was in my shirt-sleeves and fired at anything. Spent cartridges piled up against my arm, but I couldn't feel a thing.

It was during a lull in hostilities that Frank realised that his arm had been badly burnt by the cartridges. Shortly afterwards came the capitulation of British forces and the beginning of three and a half years of captivity for Frank.

Two days later Frank joined the thousands who had converged upon Changi, where he spent the following eight months until 18 October 1942, when he was among a group of 600 prisoners, all members of the Royal Artillery, who had been selected for transportation elsewhere. After having been marched to the docks, the prisoners, under the command of Lieutenant Colonel J. Bassett, 35th Light Anti-Aircraft Regiment, were crammed into the holds of a ship Frank remembered as having been called the *Masta Maru*. They were forced to endure the suffocating heat of the holds for three days before the Japanese allowed the covers to be removed shortly before they called at Sourabaya, Eastern Java, to take on supplies, by which time several of the men, including Frank, had contracted dysentery. After nineteen days at sea the ship finally reached its destination, Rabaul, on the volcanic island of New Britain, Papua New Guinea, dysentery having by then claimed the life of one of the prisoners. The following day the men began marching through ankle-deep volcanic ash towards Kokopo, a European missionary settlement, and were bundled into trucks for the last part of the journey. Towards the end of November the men learned that the fittest – or least sick – among them were to be moved. Had Frank not been seriously ill with malaria at the time, it is almost certain that he would have been among the 517 who were passed fit enough to travel to the island of Ballalae in the Solomon Islands, where they were to be put to work constructing an airstrip. Frank was one of eighty-two men left behind at Rabaul who, having been declared unfit for work, were considered expendable in eyes of the Japanese, and treated as such thereafter.

For the next two and a half years Frank and his fellow prisoners led a very isolated existence. Neither letters from home nor Red Cross parcels found their way to them, and none of them had access to a secret radio which might otherwise have reminded them that a world existed beyond the cruelty, death and disease of their island prison camp. The only medical officer among the group of 600 who had left Singapore had been sent to Ballalae Island, so, for those left on Rabaul, this role was taken on by one of the prisoners who had experience as a medical orderly and who also happened to be a Methodist preacher. Indeed, in the absence of drugs which would otherwise have saved many lives, there was often little he could do for the men other than offer spiritual comfort. By the end of January 1943 diphtheria, malaria, amoebic dysentery and beri beri, combined with acts of Japanese brutality, had claimed the lives of ten men. With the exception of a sergeant who, at great personal risk, repeatedly supplied the prisoners with modest amounts of quinine tablets, the Japanese continued to refuse to provide their increasingly sick captives with medicines to ease their suffering.

In February 1943 Frank and his fellow prisoners were moved to a small valley near Tobera airfield, which, as the death toll among them continued to rise, came to be known by the men as Death Valley. By the end of the following month only forty-five of them remained alive. All were suffering from malaria, beri beri or dysentery, and in some cases all three, as well as having painful tropical ulcers on their legs. However, increasing ill-health proved no barrier to being savagely beaten by the guards, often for no reason. In the months which followed, although Allied bombing of the nearby airfield became more frequent, any boost this gave to the men's morale was countered by yet more deaths among the group, and Frank later told Colin that there were times when they feared that death would claim them all, particularly after the departure in early 1944 of the one guard who had shown any sympathy for their plight. Fellow prisoner Alf Baker, who later wrote of his experiences, noted that when Frank fell seriously ill in early 1944 with malaria and dysentery, rather than be given any medical attention by the Japanese, he was given a beating for not working.

The beach at New Britain on which the PoWs slept before their transfer to Watom Island, photographed in 2002. (Photo courtesy of Colin Docketty.)

38   A Cruel Captivity

In February 1944, with the group's number reduced to twenty-one, the prisoners were ferried across to Watom Island and split into small groups.

Though the prisoners were forbidden, on pain of serious punishment, to have any contact with the Tolai natives with whom they shared the island, Frank clearly thought this a risk worth taking, as he later explained to his son, Colin.

> Whenever he could, he spoke with the natives, who helped him survive by telling him what he could eat and sometimes delivering food to his tent whilst he was asleep. Dad said that their actions probably saved his life.

The natives showed him which roots, bugs and spiders could safely be eaten, strengthening his will to survive, though the lack of any medical provision sometimes called for desperate means. In the absence of any recognised treatment for leg ulcers, Frank improvised his own treatment, as he later explained to his son.

> He used to make candles for the Japs out of coconut oil from the copra and noticed that this oil had a healing property, as some of it spilt onto his leg ulcer

The main tunnel on Watom Island on which Frank Docketty worked, with Tolai natives, photographed in 2002. (Photo courtesy of Colin Docketty)

by accident. He then put his whole lower leg into hot oil and miraculously fixed his ulcer.

Frank was among those put to work digging tunnels into the mountain, which were apparently intended by the Japanese to enable them to move from place to place in the event of an Allied invasion. The work was relentless, shovelling fallen rock and earth and then carrying the rubble out of the tunnel whilst continually being harangued by the guards.

Frank then became involved in an incident which could easily have resulted in his execution, when one of the guards fell to his death from some rocks after grappling with him when he refused an order to return to work. As it was, Frank was held in isolation from his fellow prisoners for the remainder of his time in captivity. 'In Dad's words, a guard placed the point of a sword into his back and pointed him at the jungle and pushed him forward,' said Colin. Located some distance from his comrades, Frank was again put to work digging tunnels, accompanied by two guards, his only other human contact being that of a couple of the natives, who took great risks befriending him. Having discovered that Frank was a strong swimmer, the Japanese then also tasked him with diving for a particular kind of shellfish for them. This he did for some time but, following a close encounter with a shark, he refused to go back in the water, despite being viciously beaten and, as further punishment, was thereafter held in an enclosure with pigs and chained up at night. Using the opportunity to steal the pigs' food, he later commented that it was better than the rations he had been provided with.

Allowed no contact with his fellow prisoners, it was from the natives that Frank learned that his ordeal would soon be over, as he recalled shortly after his return from the Far East.

> After yet another day of toil working for the eternal 'master', Tokolup (a native) came to me and said in his way that the war was over and that soon I would be free. This was amazing to me; in fact I didn't believe him. This island native had heard such important information before the Japanese around me! He had listened to the drums from the mainland and that is what they had said …. The Japs at this stage obviously had no knowledge concerning this information and behaved in the same way as previously, not showing any care or respect for their prisoners.

Frank noted that, after another three days or so, a Japanese sergeant major told him that the war was indeed over, prompting a change of attitude.

> He then gave me a cigarette, some bananas and a pair of boots. I hadn't worn boots for so long, I felt awkward in them. He was obviously embarrassed at the

situation and appeared to not be able to do enough for me. I was worried for my safety from other Jap soldiers and witnessed one commit *hari kari*. He found a shady spot and laid a white cloth on the ground. On it he laid several items of personal value, including his sword, then he knelt at the edge of the cloth and said a little 'prayer', then he drew a knife from its scabbard, which he then plunged deep into his stomach area. Then with a forceful 'north, south, east, west' action, he passed out and fell onto the cloth with the knife still in place. A few comrades then came and took a corner of the cloth each and carried him away.

Days later, Frank was reunited with those of his comrades who had survived. 'By this time, they had all been able to shave and cut each other's hair to the scalp. I, however, still had hair past my shoulders and a beard on my chest.' Frank added, 'the Japanese then approached us and said that we had to say that we had been well treated …. They produced a document for us to sign, but nobody did.'

On 7 September, when Frank's time in captivity finally came to an end, he was one of only eighteen prisoners of the original 600 transported to Rabaul to have lived to see freedom. It was later discovered that of the 517 prisoners who had been shipped to Ballalae Island, those who hadn't already died from disease or ill-treatment, or as a result of Allied bombing, had been massacred by the Japanese in mid-1943. Frank and the other seventeen survivors of Rabaul were rescued by the Royal Australian Navy and put on board HMAS *Vendetta*, where they were medically examined and supplied with Australian naval uniforms. They were then taken to the Australian General Hospital (AGH) at Jacquinot Bay, and a week later to the AGH at Lae, in Papua New Guinea. Frank was emaciated and suffering from vitamin deficiency and his legs were adorned with tropical ulcers. Upon his eventual discharge from hospital, Frank was transferred to the AGH staff within the Australian Army, and was enlisted at Melbourne, where he remained until he returned home to England on the SS *Orontes* at the end of 1946.

After spending the previous five years in the tropics, Frank had difficulty adjusting to the cold English climate and, upon hearing of a scheme to entice tradesmen to emigrate to Australia, decided to draw upon his skills as a bricklayer and applied to be one of the so-called 'ten pound Poms'. Within weeks, the same ship that had taken him to the Far East back in 1941, now took him to Australia. The *Largs Bay* arrived in Freemantle on 2 January 1947, whereupon Frank became the first of the 'Poms' to descend the ship's gangplank, a photo of the scene appearing in the *Sydney Morning Herald* the following day. Shortly afterwards Frank was joined in Australia by May, the girlfriend he had first left behind when he had been posted overseas some six years earlier. Frank and May returned to England for family reasons four years later, were married in 1952 and their son was born the following year.

Although Frank had clearly begun in earnest to make a new life for himself following his ordeal in captivity, his past experiences continued to affect him. The nightmares which he experienced ever since his return from the Far East persisted for many years, as did recurrences of the malaria from which he suffered in captivity. In addition, he was left with impaired vision due to the effects of vitamin deficiency, permanent weakness in one of his legs as a result of tropical ulcers, and was found to be suffering from strongyloidiasis (a tropical worm infection), known at that time as 'hookworm'. He required hospital treatment for this condition, for which he was eventually awarded a small pension, until the 1970s.

Frank Docketty and his wife May when they married in 1952.

Colin grew up very much aware of Frank having been a prisoner of war, partly because he heard his father's nightmares for himself, but also because Frank talked about his experiences. Thus, as a young boy, Colin was told about the natives who his father believed had saved his life, and so learned the origins of his intolerance of food wastage. 'As a child I was never allowed to leave anything on the plate. My mother used to sometimes spirit away troublemaking items from my plate, just to keep my father happy.' Despite persistent problems with his health, Frank employed the same singlemindedness he had learned during his years in captivity to establish a thriving business as a builder. However, according to Colin, his survival against the odds in Rabaul appeared to have bequeathed to him something of a 'devil may care' attitude towards working in potentially dangerous situations. 'This never seemed to bother him, as he would say he was living on borrowed time as it was, and was not only grateful, but surprised, to still be alive.' Frank's health began to fail seriously, however, in 1980 when he suffered the first of two heart attacks.

Although, unlike many former captives of the Japanese, Frank often talked about his time as a prisoner of war, his early attempts to write about his experiences shortly after he had returned from the Far East proved too distressing for him to continue.

Frank Docketty around 1985.

According to Colin 'he started to write about some of the atrocities performed by the Japs when he was affected so badly that he realised he didn't want to "go there" again.' He did, however, enjoy the camaraderie of FEPoW gatherings, in particular, meeting up in the late 1980s with some of those who had shared the dark days of captivity in Rabaul and Watom Island, the only ones truly able to understand the particular horror of those years and their lasting impact upon those who survived. Said Colin, 'his life was changed forever by those experiences and there wasn't really a day which went past without some mention of his years in captivity.' Poignantly, it was after having returned home from a FEPoW function in March 1990 that Frank died from heart failure at the age of seventy-two, his years as a prisoner of war remaining with him right to the end.

Chapter 6

Driver John Overton

Royal Army Service Corps (RASC)

When John Overton – or Jack, as he was known – boarded the Polish ship MS *Sobieski* at Gourock on 29 October 1941, he had no way of knowing that it would be another four years before he would again see his wife and meet for the first time the child she was expecting. After meeting Ida at a local dance, they had married in June 1939 and had begun their life together in Little Minsterley in Shropshire. Jack had been born at Church Farm, Hope, near Minsterley, in 1912 and he and his five siblings had been raised there by their father after their mother had died following childbirth. With the family smallholding the only income, Jack had been unable to take up the offer of a scholarship to the local grammar school. He worked on several farms and then took a job as a driver at the local creamery, where he remained working until he was conscripted into the Royal Army Service Corps as a driver in September 1940. Now, little more than a year later, he found himself sailing across the Atlantic into the unknown. Following their arrival at Halifax, Jack and his comrades were transferred to the American vessel USS *Mount Vernon* to continue their voyage eastwards via Cape Town and Mombasa, events in the Far East having dictated that their destination was to be Singapore.

Although Jack seldom spoke in later life about his years in captivity, from the moment of his arrival in Singapore on 13 January 1942 he kept a diary, sometimes recording his thoughts daily, at other times more sporadically,

Jack Overton in 1945.

some entries very brief, others much more detailed. Following his repatriation, he added more notes to this record of his experiences. Upon arrival in Singapore, Jack's unit was taken to Tanglin Barracks, moving a few days later to Holland Village and, on 4 February, to Payalebar. His diary entries for the final days of the battle for the island capture some of the chaos and confusion of those times.

> 13 February: reports of surrender heard. Contradicted soon afterwards. REs, RAs and RASC and every available man went to make stand at Bukit Timah.
>
> 14 February: on ration detail at Polo Club. Terrific shelling, lucky to get back safely to Chancery Lane at 10pm. Went in dugout to sleep, called out 2.30am to go on ammo detail.
>
> 15 February: got to Alexandria Ammo Dump early morning … couldn't get near. Part of it on fire and going up. Told to get back before daylight, enemy opened up shelling before we got started.

This was followed by a particularly poignant entry recording the death of a fellow soldier and friend.

> Poor old Sam got killed unloading ammo. We held a little service, made a cross and collected flowers for his grave. Not many dry eyes while we remembered him. Died with a smile on his face. God comfort his mother in her loss, for he was a great lad.*

At the time Jack wrote these words, he could not have imagined how very many deaths would follow during the course of the next three and a half years. He added, 'it is only a matter of time before we have to surrender. Everyone very upset. Great loss of life amongst troops and civilians.'

After being taken into captivity, Jack continued to write his diary, despite the risk of severe punishment from the Japanese had his notes been detected. A week after beginning life within the confines of Changi, the privations of captivity under the Japanese had become only too clear: '23 February: food problem not too good, drinking water scarce', as had the consequences of the overcrowded and insanitary conditions: '27 February: dysentery pretty bad, reported sick.' Although with the camp under British administration the prisoners had relatively little contact with

---

* Many years later, Jack's granddaughter, Sarah, managed to trace Sam's family and let them know of this diary entry. They had, until then, been unaware of what had become of him and were immensely grateful to have finally found out.

the Japanese, some of Jack's diary entries, together with notes which he made about his captivity, illustrate the level of discipline imposed upon prisoners by their own commanding officers, and his personal feelings about this.

> During one of my trips to get rations from Singapore I took 1lb of sugar out of Japanese rations, was reported to the British Officer in charge and was put under close arrest. The Japs didn't know anything of this as it was entirely in British hands. I went before the CO ... and was sentenced to ten days FP* and twenty days Jap pay stopped, which I served in a small compound in the middle of a mangrove swamp with no protection against mosquitoes and on half rations, which wasn't enough to satisfy the gnawing hunger and, for picking up a coconut which had blown down, was awarded an extra fourteen days detention. If the British public knew what things happened in a PoW camp under our own administration they would be disgusted.

After nine months at Changi, on 2 November 1942 Jack was moved to Thailand with 'P' Party, under the command of Lieutenant Colonel H.A. Fitt, 18th Battalion Reconnaissance Corps. Jack noted:

> we left Changi for the unknown. We entrained at Singapore, thirty-five to forty in a small railway van. After a nightmare journey of five nights and four days we arrived at Ban Pong, Thailand. We were marched from the station to a transit camp which was in a deplorable state, sludge and water knee deep, no drinking water and the food terrible. We were allowed to buy bananas and other foods off the Thais if we had money. After two days we were transported in lorries to Kan'buri, thirty miles away, stayed overnight then marched to Chungkai, our first jungle camp.

His diary entry for 10 November added: 'we were taken to work on the railway and soon got to know the Jap word of "*kura*", which is the lowest form of address.'

Jack noted of his time at Chungkai:

> bad food, hard work and bad general conditions soon started to take its toll of the men. Men with dysentery were made to work, with the result they got worse. Men going to latrines at night would be greeted with '*kura*' from the Jap sentry who would be standing out of sight, with the result the poor fellows would be beaten and kicked for not saluting and made to stand to attention

---

* FP stands for Field Punishment, which was a brutal form of punishment that usually had the PoW standing, or tied, up in the full glare of the sun.

perhaps half the night and had to evacuate their bowels where they stood. We worked from daylight to dark … .Beatings were frequent and work hard.

Jack remained at Chungkai until 16 January 1943, when he was assigned to a party who were moved upcountry under the command of Captain Akaster, RAOC. 'We had orders to move farther up jungle. We were attached to a group of Japanese REs who were bridge-building.' Jack's notes suggest that here he had the good fortune to encounter a member of the Imperial Japanese Army who showed a degree of concern for the prisoners.

The Jap sergeant in charge was the nearest approach to a Japanese gentleman it has been my lot to meet …. We had very few slappings and better food. Our first bridges were at Wang Takhain, where we built twelve, then moved on to Ban Khao, where we built three bridges. The work was very hard. We had to cut down big timber in the jungle and haul it out with ropes, shape it into required lengths and shapes. We had to use antiquated pile-drivers, making anything from 400 to 500 pulls on the ropes without a break. After completing the three bridges we moved on into the jungle to a place called Non Pradai. We marched eighteen kilometres with full kit including Jap kit, cookhouse utensils and sacks of rice. We reached Non Pradai footsore and weary. I had dysentery at the time and was feeling all in …. Next day we were taken into the middle of the jungle and ordered to build a bridge over a ravine.

Jack noted that having completed the bridge ahead of schedule, the following March the party returned to Chungkai, supposedly for a rest, but the men were put to work breaking up stones to be used as ballast for the railway. 'Our "rest" was hanging over a seventy-foot quarry on ropes.' On 3 April, Jack's party was then moved to Wang Pho, of which he noted:

Wang Pho quarries and viaducts will always remain a grotesque nightmare for me and hundreds more. The Japanese beastliness and cruelty during this period was horrible. Many a poor fellow who was sick and unable to do the heavy work was beaten and kicked into unconsciousness. Many were struck over the head with iron bars, but a thick bamboo was their favourite weapon. Working thirty-six hours without a break was quite common.

At the end of April, Jack was moved again, to Arrow Hill, and put to work unloading rails and sleepers, and at the end of May was sent farther upcountry to Wang Yai where, he noted, 'no drinking or washing water available unless it rained. Water had to be carried six kilometres from the river for cooking purposes.' After yet another move, to Tampi, in August 1943, he noted:

we were put in the middle of a Tamil camp where cholera had broken out, food was horrible and sickness was heavy. Here I went down with a heavy dose of malaria but after five days had to report for work again …. We were compelled by the Japs to bury Tamils who were dying of cholera.

The following September, with the prisoners under immense pressure to complete the railway, the party was sent still farther north to Prang Kasi where, Jack noted:

we had to work night and day. We had to work with elephants moving huge logs for bridge building. If the elephant couldn't move the log, fifteen British soldiers were sent to do it and were helped along by a Jap with bamboo. Here again, the food was horrible and, coupled with hard work, no clothes or footwear, the situation was desperate.

Weeks later, construction of the railway having been completed, Jack and his comrades were moved to Kinsaiyok. Jack's diary entry for 25 October 1943 noted, 'taken to the jungle while the Japanese big shots performed the opening ceremony of the line. At 5pm we were put on a steam train and journeyed back to Wang Yai.' After liberation, Jack gave details of sabotage he had performed at this and earlier camps, noting that, 'during the time at Wang Yai, I destroyed drums of diesel, oil and petrol …. The amount of damage was considerable.'

It was whilst at Wang Yai that Jack received his first letters from home, one of which informed him that he had become a father, prompting the following diary entry. 'My pal and myself celebrated the occasion by spending what few cents we had on two jam tarts, which we got from the black market.' (As befits the sharing of such a significant moment, Jack and his 'pal', Eric Gibbons, were to remain great friends for the rest of their lives.) Less than a month later, on 17 November 1943, Jack was moved to Nong Pladuc, and put to work on the construction of a new camp, the purpose of which was:

to accommodate men coming down from the jungle. There were pitiful sights and hospitals and billets were crowded to suffocation. Many poor fellows were too weak to help themselves and many never recovered. Two or more every day were carried to their last resting place … .Medical supplies were very short, bandages had to be made out of any material available, saved, washed and used over again.

From January 1944 onwards, as his health deteriorated, Jack required repeated hospital treatment himself. In addition to suffering repeated bouts of malaria throughout the year, he had cellulitis and by December 1944 had also contracted bacillary dysentery. He remained at Nong Pladuc until early 1945, when he was taken by train to Ubon, in north-east Thailand. By May the camp held over 3,000 prisoners who had been drafted in to work on the construction of an airstrip.

On 14 August 1945, although oblivious to the dropping of the atomic bombs, Jack was nonetheless aware from the behaviour of the guards that something significant was afoot. 'Ihara's Nips dashing around', he recorded in his diary, noting the following day, 'first half day for weeks. Emperor's broadcast.' Three days later the normal routine of camp life and the allocation of the men to working parties having been disrupted, he noted, 'everyone thinks the war is over, nothing official.' Due to Ubon's remoteness from the location of most of the camps in Thailand, it was not until 18 August that Jack and his comrades were told the news they had been longing for.

> Announced on roll call that the war in Greater East Asia was ended. Everyone very quiet and orderly, seemed too good to be true .... Concert in evening. British, American and Dutch national anthems sung, first time in three and a half years. Scene very touching.

No longer inhibited by the need to keep his diary secret, Jack made daily entries from then onwards until he embarked upon his journey home, recording everything from the elation shown by the men at the sight of their own planes.

> 20 August: four-engined plane came over, everyone waving and cheering. Dropped leaflets to tell us the Japanese had surrendered unconditionally, to stay in camp, be careful what we eat and that help would arrive as fast as humanly possible

One of two books in which Jack Overton wrote his diary, this one containing entries from 14 August 1945 onwards.

to the way the men occupied themselves while they waited to begin their journeys home: '26 August: international football match. England 1, Holland 0, Colonel Toosey (who had arrived at the camp that day) presented cup and two dollars for winners, one dollar for losers, a personal gift.' By mid-September, Jack's diary entries reveal the frustration he was no doubt feeling at having not yet begun the long journey home: '14 September: told we shall very likely be moving on Sun 16, position rather obscure. 17 September: no news of moving yet'; but, on 24 September, Jack finally left Ubon for Bangkok. Even then, bad weather intervened and it was another three days before he flew to Rangoon. 'Brought to Rangoon Field Military Hospital by ambulance. Good bed, food and surroundings.' The following day he underwent a medical examination, was passed fit to travel and shortly afterwards boarded the SS *Orbita*. Jack finally sailed into Liverpool docks on 9 November 1945, able at last to return home on 10 November to be reunited with Ida and to meet his daughter for the first time.

Jack's daughter, Marie, has clear memories of her father's homecoming, and of the road outside the family home being decorated to welcome him. 'In later years I was told how much of a hero the local boys thought him but I really don't think he was aware of that, as life had to get back to some sort of normality.' To this end, Jack soon returned to his former driving job at the local creamery, where he remained until the 1960s, before going on to work at the local stone quarry. He and Ida had another daughter in 1947 but despite his efforts to consign the events of the previous three and a half years to the past, his years in captivity had long-term effects for both him and his family. As a consequence of his captivity, Jack missed the first years of his elder daughter's life, affecting their relationship, as Marie explained.

> The lack of father/daughter feeling was due to the wartime separation. Of this I have no doubt. I have a sister who was born in 1947 and who had a very much closer relationship with our father. This is understandable as he had her from a newborn rather than a three and a half year old toddler!

Like many of those who returned from the Far East, Jack was also affected by persistent nightmares and by a recurrence of the malaria he had contracted in captivity, both of which hampered his attempts to move on with his life. Marie clearly recalls her father's repeated bouts of malaria. 'I do remember him having bouts of malaria for a long time after the war and can still see how the bed would shake, and can still see the quinine tablets in a Zube tin.' Jack was subsequently admitted to the specialist FEPoW unit which had been established at the Liverpool School of Tropical Medicine to receive treatment and undergo

Jack and Ida Overton at their daughter Marie's wedding in 1969.

tests, but, added Marie, 'although he did suffer from bouts of malaria and horrid flashback nightmares, he wasn't considered for a pension'. According to Marie, her father very rarely talked about his experiences, but it appears that this in no way blunted his memories of captivity nor the emotions associated with it. Marie recalled a rare moment when her father had mentioned his time as a prisoner of war. 'This would have been twenty-five years after he came home. Dad was asked how they all knew the war had ended. He did describe the moment, and broke down.' Neither did the passing of the years temper Jack's feelings towards the Japanese. According to Marie 'his experiences left him a very bitter man to the end of his life.'

Jack Overton with his wife Ida, daughter Marie and granddaughter Sarah in 1971.

Jack died in 1997, aged eighty-five. During the long years of his captivity Ida had written to him every day – letters which, for the most part, were returned to her undelivered. Those letters, symbolic of all that Jack had missed whilst in Japanese hands, were kept safe, tied up in a bundle and tucked away. And there they remained, unopened, their contents potentially too sorrowful, perhaps, for Jack to ever explore, in much the same way that having recorded his thoughts many years earlier, he then chose to remain largely silent about his experiences in the Far East, rather than exposing himself to the pain that talking about them may have generated.

Jack Overton with his granddaughter Sarah in the mid 1970s.

Chapter 7

AC1 Harold Joseph Prechner

Royal Air Force, Radio Telephone Operator

When he returned from the Far East towards the end of 1945 to a country still in the grip of rationing, the inconveniences this presented were of little consequence to Harold Prechner, given the level of deprivation he had endured whilst a prisoner of war.

> To me, the discomforts, the shortages, mean nothing. Life is luxurious compared with my existence of the past few years, and if I could only feel a sense of real security, I should be quite happy.

With these words, written in January 1946 to a woman he had never met, Harold began to unburden himself about the years he had spent as a captive of the Japanese in a way that he had felt unable to with his own family in the weeks since he had arrived home, when the euphoria of freedom had developed into melancholy in his struggle to adjust to life after captivity.

Harold and his twin brother, Cecil, were born in 1906. Together with their three sisters, they were brought up in the East End of London, where their father had established a thriving business as a builder and was proud to have been able to send his sons to the respected Worshipful Company of Grocers School in Hackney. Tragically, he was killed in a motorbike accident when Harold and his brother were ten, leaving their mother to bring up the five children alone. Following the outbreak of war,

Harold Prechner in 1941.

Harold enlisted in the Royal Air Force in December 1940 as a radio telephone operator. After a period of training in Blackpool, he was stationed at RAF North Weald in Essex, where he received promotion to AC1 in November 1941, shortly before learning that he was to be posted overseas, an experience which would take him away from his family for nearly four years.

Cecil had also enlisted in the RAF but, unlike his brother, would remain in England for the duration of the war. On 8 December 1941, Harold boarded the SS *Athlone Castle* and sailed from the Clyde to an undisclosed destination. Writing to one of his sisters during the voyage, he signed off his letter with the words 'I may not be able to write again for some time, but will do so at the first opportunity.' It would be August 1943 before Harold's family received a telegram informing them that he had been taken prisoner by the Japanese, and several more months before they actually heard from him.

The *Athlone Castle* arrived in Durban, South Africa on 8 January, 1942. Almost a week later, their destination now confirmed as Singapore, Harold and his comrades transferred to the SS *City of Canterbury* and arrived at Keppel Harbour on 11 February. However, with the island under heavy bombardment by the Japanese, the ship was immediately diverted to Java, arriving at Batavia (now Jakarta) on 15 February. Days later, Harold found himself stationed at an RAF unit at Pamekasan on the island of Madura, off the east coast of Java, where he was among those who operated a mobile radar unit. Within two weeks of their arrival they were ordered to leave in order to escape the advancing Japanese. Recording these events shortly after his repatriation to England, Harold wrote:

> we received orders to make for the port of Tjilitjap, South Central Java, and to destroy our mobile radar units before doing so. We executed this order by taking the units into a field outside Sourabaya and hurling hand grenades at them .... After a long and tense journey by lorry, with nothing to eat but our iron rations, we arrived at Tjilitjap, which shortly afterwards was dive-bombed for about two hours, causing complete havoc and destruction.

Harold and his comrades then made their way by lorry to Purwokerto, where they were split into two groups and ordered to head for Bandoeng. The group Harold was assigned to boarded a train for the journey, and soon found themselves under attack by the Japanese.

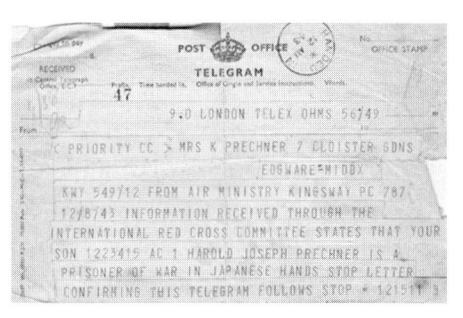

Telegram dated 12 August 1943 informing Harold Prechner's family that he was a prisoner of war of the Japanese.

> Exhausted, having had little sleep for about two days, I had already fallen into a deep sleep when I was rudely awakened by what seemed to be 'all hell let loose'. I quickly realised on coming out of my initial stupor that we were being attacked … with machine guns and mortars. Miraculously, our wagon had not been hit. We were then told to disembark and I then discovered the extent of the havoc that had been wreaked. One part of the train was in flames and there were many dead and wounded.

After leaving the train, the remaining men made their way to Tasikmalaya, crossing a river where a bridge had been blown up by the Dutch in the mistaken belief that the approaching survivors were Japanese troops. Harold was able to pull himself across on a cable which had been rigged from the opposite bank.

> This meant being partly immersed for a while and, having seen by the light of the moon crocodiles thrashing about, I felt a bit apprehensive, to put it mildly. The last man had hardly arrived when we heard machine gun fire from the bank we had just left. The Japs had caught up and not having one rifle between us, we were very fortunate.

Clearly feeling lucky to still be alive, he noted, 'I am thankful to whatever divine Providence there is that I was spared that night. I shall always remember with sorrow the young lives that were lost and, with horror, the tragic events of that night.' The group eventually reached Tasikmalaya, where, following the capitulation of the Dutch on 8 March 1942, Harold noted, 'I found myself a prisoner of war under representatives of a barbaric and sadistic race of sub-humans, known as Japs.'

Harold spent the following two months at Tasikmalaya, where conditions were rather better than those he was to face at many of the other camps to which he was moved in the following months and years. On 18 May 1942, he was among those who were transported by train back to Sourabaya, to the Lyceum, a former school. Held in tiny classrooms, the extent of overcrowding was such that the prisoners had to take it in turns to sleep as there was insufficient space for them all to lie down at the same time. Fed on a diet of rice pap three times a day, Harold was put to work unloading ships at the docks. He later noted of his time here, 'terrible conditions'. Brief notes such as this, written in Changi in August and September 1945 following the news of the Japanese surrender, provide a chronology for the almost three and a half years Harold was a prisoner of war and offer a glimpse of life in each of the camps at which he was held. At the beginning of June 1942, Harold was among those assigned to a group of 200 men the Japanese had demanded be sent to Semarang on the north coast. The men were tasked with extending the runway

One of the huts in which the PoWs lived at Semarang, Java, photographed in the 1980s by one of those who had been held captive with Harold Prechner.

at the aerodrome at Kalibanteng – backbreaking work for men whose fitness was rapidly diminishing.

Supplied with only meagre rations of food, the men supplemented their diet with whatever they could buy from the natives in exchange for their few personal possessions. Of this time Harold noted, 'Long days of hunger and slavery in tropical sun. I certainly proved myself tough. At end of period, about seventy-five out of 200 working, and I was one of them.' That there were no deaths during the eight months the prisoners spent at this camp was partly due to the leadership shown by their senior officer, Wing Commander O.G. Gregson, who often took beatings from the Japanese in the process of defending his men and for whom Harold had enormous respect. Of equal significance to their survival of so tough a period of their captivity was, perhaps, the part played by the medical officer within the group, Dr Richard Philps, who agreed to secretly treat the Japanese guards for sexually transmitted diseases in return for being allowed to visit a pharmacy at the local hospital where, despite the obvious risks involved, a Dutch doctor provided small quantities of lifesaving drugs with which to treat the prisoners.

By the beginning of February 1943, with work on the airstrip completed, the men were sent back to Sourabaya, a twelve-hour journey in tropical heat, locked inside steel trucks. Jaarmarkt was a former fairground which now housed thousands of prisoners, prompting Harold to record, 'food better, but what a concentration camp. Guards very brutal under the "Bull".' Within a couple of months of his arrival at Jaarmarkt, Harold became seriously ill and was transferred to hospital in Tjimahi, central Java.

Ironically, his illness may well have saved his life, since it prevented him from being among those prisoners selected for transportation to the island of Haruku, in the Spice Islands, the death rate among whom was tragically high. Of the camp in Tjimahi to which he was moved upon his release from hospital Harold noted, 'what a paradise after Jaarmarkt'. At the beginning of June 1943, Harold was moved again, this time to a camp in Bandoeng. 'Guards pretty rough – "Mad Harry" the worst. I hope he meets his punishment one day,' wrote Harold. He remained here until November 1943, after which he was moved to a succession of camps in Tjimahi and Batavia, about which he noted little, and then, in February 1944, to Adek. 'Very bad. Guards worst lot in my experience. Nervous tension bad all the time.' At the beginning of May, Harold was moved to Macasura, which prompted a 'fairly good', with food rations improving and where the prisoners were given farming duties. However, this upturn in events was not to last as, on 8 January 1945, Harold

The hospital at Tjimahi, Java, to which Harold Prechner was transferred in 1943.

was among a party of 1,000 prisoners who were put on board an OSK Ferry and transported to Singapore. His comment, 'awful nights on boat', appears something of an understatement of the typically overcrowded and insanitary conditions so characteristic of hellship voyages, which many former prisoners later stated were among the worst experiences of their captivity.

Arriving in Singapore three days later, Harold's next stop was River Valley Road Camp, where he was to remain for over three months, becoming more emaciated by the day. 'Rations cut in March. Semi-starvation. God, how weak I became, only two meals? per day.' Matters were clearly not improved when, on 10 April, he was moved to Keppel Harbour camp. 'What a hell camp. Starvation and slavery.' From here, in mid-June, Harold was sent to Changi jail, where he remained for the rest of his captivity. On 11 August 1945, Harold heard official confirmation that the war had ended and some of his notes became more detailed. As befits someone who had been taken to the brink of starving to death, he described meals and improvements in rations in some detail.

21 August: first meat arrived. We asked for increased rations of rice. 325 g was granted.

25 August: English bugle reveille for first time. Breakfast – milk pap, rissole. Tiffin – hash. Dinner – fresh meat stew, fresh meat patty, tinned meat hash, rice, 2 cups.

28 August: issue of 6 oz of Kraft cheese. Will wonders never cease! Allied plane dropped leaflets in Japanese and later in English telling us war is over! Great excitement …. We were told to stay put and not make ourselves ill by eating too much solid food!

29 August: first official news bulletin just went through amplifier. Short wave radio now in camp. All PoWs in Singapore to be flown to Rangoon! (roll on).

31 August: three four-engined planes dropped forty-six canisters and various bales on Changi airfield. Receiving and transmitting set dropped. Now listening to broadcast news from S.E. Asia Command Station, Ceylon. British Fleet should be here Sunday or Monday (2nd or 3rd September) and then real freedom for us.

3 September: Most of the Jap guards gone. Liberators dropping comforts etc. daily on Changi Aerodrome. Much stomach trouble in camp. 12 pm.

> Hoisting ceremony of US, UK and Dutch flags. Great emotional cheering ....
> Japs very docile. Their turn is coming very soon now.

As well as recording the joy of freedom and the relief from near-starvation, Harold's notes also hint at the damage wrought by years of vitamin deficiency. 'Much beri beri in camp. Have slight touch in feet and legs for several days.'

On 6 September, Harold wrote a letter to his sister, his first as a free man.

> My heart is so full in writing this, my first unrestricted letter for years and as a free man, that I cannot fully express my thoughts and emotions .... I cannot really grasp yet that the war is all over and that very soon I shall probably be leaving for home. Events of the past few days have been so crowded and exciting that they will forever live in my memory.

By 11 September Harold was understandably impatient to leave the land of his incarceration, writing, 'hope to God I shall be (leaving) soon'. In the meantime, however, he apparently chose to ignore the advice not to overeat:

> 12 September – Mountbatten arrives for Victory Parade today. Another good dinner from the Navy: soup, mashed potatoes, peas etc., steak and kidney pudding, currant tart and custard. The old stomach is being subject to great strain.

Finally, on 15 September, Harold began his journey home, noting: 'The Great Day. Left Changi to board the [HMT] *Tegelberg*, a Dutch ship. Never shall I forget.'

The *Tegelberg* arrived at Liverpool docks on 11 October 1945 and shortly afterwards Harold made his way back to the family home in North London. So horrified was his youngest sister at the treatment he had endured that she offered her services as a trained secretary to the UK prosecution team at the Tokyo War Crimes trials the following year and was employed as private secretary to Comyns Carr QC, the leading UK prosecutor. Harold felt it was poetic justice indeed that his own sister should be involved in seeking to bring retribution upon the heads of those Japanese guilty of war crimes. Despite the appalling conditions in which he had been forced to exist on a near starvation diet for much of the time in captivity, once back home Harold's health recovered well, the only obvious physical legacy of his years in the Far East a skin complaint which required treatment at the specialist FEPoW unit of Queen Mary's Hospital, Roehampton, until the 1950s. Of more concern to those around him was his mental state. Not only was he plagued by dreadful nightmares, but he was also subject to fits of depression. It was as a response to his depression

58 A Cruel Captivity

Harold Prechner with his wife Fay when they married in 1948.

that it was suggested he write to Fay, the cousin of a member of Harold's extended family, who lived in New York. Thus began a transatlantic correspondence which lasted two and a half years and evolved into something much deeper, Harold clearly having met his soulmate.

Fay arrived in England in August 1948 and she and Harold were married the following October, settling down together in Southgate, London, where Harold

Harold Prechner with his wife Fay, son Martin and sister Lilian in 1950.

worked as an estate agent. The following years saw the arrival of a son and a daughter and, to all intents and purposes, it appeared that Harold had put the past behind him.

However, it transpired that the past was not entirely content to be forgotten, with repercussions not only for him but also for his family, not least his son, Martin. 'As a child, I vividly remember being awoken at night by my father's screaming, from the depths of some nightmare back in the camps of Java.' Only partially reassured by a vague explanation of the war being in some way to blame for this, Martin also remembers, as a seven-year-old passenger in a car being driven by his father, witnessing behaviour which inspired real fear.

> A large black limousine drew alongside our little Ford Prefect. The limo had darkened windows and was flying the Japanese flag on the front wing – clearly the Ambassador or some other dignitary. Harold, who was normally so calm and reserved, suddenly went berserk and tried to drive the limo off the road, shouting insults and swearing at the occupants. They accelerated away and we had to stop so my mother could calm him down, all very frightening for me and my sister in the back of the car.

Asked if his father had ever voiced his feelings towards the Japanese, Martin explained, 'he would not have anything made in Japan in the house. When, as a teenager, I wanted to buy a Sony tape recorder, my mother had to undertake long and delicate negotiations on my behalf before he relented.'

Only in later life did Harold overcome a reluctance to talk about his experiences as a prisoner of war, having been persuaded by Fay to join a local branch of the FEPoW Association. According to Martin, 'amongst his fellow FEPoWs, he could really open up, and only they could fully understand his torment because they all suffered in similar ways.' In his sixties Harold was diagnosed with a heart condition, after which his health steadily deteriorated. In 1981, after contracting pneumonia, Harold died at the age of seventy-five. Although towards the end of his life he had found solace in the company of others who had shared the horrors of captivity, his attitude towards the Japanese did not soften. Said Martin, of his father, 'Forgive and forget? I don't think he ever forgave the Japs, and he certainly never forgot.'

Chapter 8

Private Norman McCandless Finlay

2nd Battalion East Surrey Regiment

When Norman Finlay left his home in Crook, County Durham, and headed for London at the age of seventeen it wasn't the first time he had run away, but this time he was quite determined that he wasn't going to go back until he was ready. Born in 1919 in Scotswood, Newcastle upon Tyne, his childhood had become unsettled following his mother's death when he was eleven years old and his father's subsequent remarriage. Despite the fact that his stepmother was very kind, and the two half-brothers he had recently acquired adored him, Norman ran away on several occasions, leaving behind his two sisters, only to be brought back by his father, an engineer for the fire service. This time was to be different, however. Having lied about his age, Norman enlisted in the East Surrey Regiment and was posted to the 2nd Battalion, thereby embarking on a path that would see him away from home for considerably longer than he could have envisaged.

After a period of basic training on home soil, in October 1937 Norman was posted to the Sudan. This was followed in 1938 by a move to Shanghai, where the East Surreys were on protection duties but, following the outbreak of war, they were sent to Singapore for combat training and then, at the beginning of 1941, to northern Malaya. Of the many British servicemen who were to face the Japanese in combat in the following weeks, those in the East Surreys were amongst the better prepared. Nevertheless, after the

Norman Finlay around 1945.

Japanese invaded Malaya in early December 1941, the battalion suffered heavy casualties, their much depleted ranks amalgamating with those of the Leicesters to form the British Battalion towards the end of December. The speed and intensity of the Japanese advance down the Malayan peninsula eventually forced the battalion to retreat to Singapore at the end of January 1942. Norman later shared one of his abiding memories of the Japanese having landed on the island during the first week of February with his daughter, Sheila.

> My father recalled a noise like tanks approaching, but what it turned out to be was hundreds of Japanese soldiers riding bicycles that had no tyres on. The noise they could hear was the sound of the wheels grinding on the roads.

My own father, Fred Cox, served with Norman in the East Surreys and noted the intensity of the Japanese attack, his recollection of the closing stages of the battle suggesting that several of their comrades were killed as the battalion played their part in trying to repel the Japanese.

> For a while we were able to hold them off, but they came again …. More and more men were failing to come back from the patrols. The chap who had been at the side of me earlier hadn't made it back; now there was just an empty space.

Two days after the ceasefire that signalled the Allied defeat, Norman, along with the rest of the battalion, marched through the streets of Singapore to Changi. In later life he spoke sparingly about the time he spent in captivity, according to Sheila, just snippets of information here and there, rather than talking about his experiences at length. Over time, however, this trickle of information built up, offering a picture of Norman's ordeal at the hands of the Japanese and illustrating just how close to death he had come on more than one occasion. After spending two months at Changi, he was among those marched across Singapore to Adam Park, where he joined a workforce of thousands toiling on the construction of the shrine commemorating those Japanese who were lost in battle. The work was all to be undertaken by manual labour with only primitive hand tools and proved for many, including Norman, to be a foretaste of what was to come with another, larger building project in Thailand. Using the ingenuity which had been born of necessity during the previous months at Changi, and becoming increasingly adept at making the best of a bad situation, the prisoners managed to convert the bombed-out buildings of Adam Park into reasonable living accommodation. However, rations of food continued to be woefully inadequate. Sheila recalled:

my father would tell us about the lack of food, the small bowls of rice they had each day and how sometimes they had maggots and weevils in, which they ate…Father always joked that this was protein.

Such flashes of humour were essential in order to keep up morale, often masking the grim reality of what was, quite literally, the difference between life and death.

Work on the shrine was completed in September 1942, but worse was to come for Norman when, on 25 October 1942, he was among a party of 650 men, known as Letter Party 'X', selected for transportation to Thailand under the command of Lieutenant Colonel C. Morrison, Leicestershire Regiment. At the end of their four-day journey in covered metal goods trucks, a degrading experience which in itself spoke volumes about the way in which the prisoners were perceived by their captors, Norman and his comrades disembarked at Ban Pong and were marched to the nearby transit camp. With much of the camp underwater, the squalor of their new surroundings would have provided a stark comparison to what must, with hindsight, have seemed a comparatively civilised existence at Changi. After two days the group was marched to Kan'buri and then taken by barge to Chungkai, where Norman was one of many put to work on jungle clearing and embankment building. Their working days were long and exhausting. After drawing their tools in the morning, the prisoners were taken to the work site and given a quota of work to be achieved that day, regardless of difficult terrain, adverse weather conditions, or sickness. Norman later spoke of how he and one of his comrades had helped each other to cope. Said Sheila:

> I remember Father telling me about a sergeant – Mac – who looked after him. He would hide him in the bushes when he was ill and unable to work and, likewise, my father would hide the sergeant when he was ill. My father always said he would not have lived without the support from Mac.

After several months Norman was moved upcountry to Wang Pho, where the work was no less arduous, the ill-treatment from the guards no less severe, as he later told Sheila.

> I heard about men being buried up to their necks and left in the sun all day, of men being locked in cages without food or drink. I heard about the torture, the pulling of nails out, the pulling of teeth out. My father described the Japanese guards as being evil and sadistic. Beatings were a daily occurrence …. If you looked at a guard the wrong way or did not bow or kowtow, you were beaten.

Sheila recalled one incident in particular that her father had told her about, of which he would inevitably be reminded every year.

> It was my father's birthday. He had to watch three of his friends get beheaded with a sword. The Japanese had ordered the men to work seven days a week on the railroad and they had argued to work only six days. How he coped with that I do not know.

In June 1943, Norman was moved to Kan'buri hospital camp. In addition to having dysentery and malaria, which he contracted multiple times during his captivity, he was suffering from beri beri and had acquired tropical ulcers to both legs. 'He told me they used to use maggots to eat the rotting flesh,' said Sheila. Desperate times called for desperate measures; failure to remove the dead flesh invited the prospect of gangrene, which often left amputation as the only option. Norman remained at Kan'buri for some considerable time, too ill to be moved elsewhere. Once he had recovered sufficiently for him to be considered fit enough to resume work – albeit far from healthy – he was among a party of men transported back to River Valley Road camp in Singapore.

Though he had survived what later became known as the Death Railway, what followed was, perhaps, an even greater test of endurance. On 4 September 1944, Norman was one of 900 British prisoners forced into the holds of the *Kachidoki Maru*, bound for Japan. Conditions on board were horrendous, the prisoners tightly packed together with no access to sanitation and existing in pitch darkness once the Japanese had battened down the hatches. To make matters worse, they were forced to endure these conditions for thirty-six hours before the ship even sailed and, not surprisingly, Norman was one of many who acquired dysentery. Six days into the voyage, on 12 September, the *Kachidoki Maru* sank after being torpedoed by an American submarine. Norman was fortunate that he was not among the 400 prisoners who were lost. Many of the survivors were picked up by the Japanese, but he was among a group who were rescued by Chinese fishermen, who had no choice but to hand them over to the Japanese eventually. They were then transferred to another Japanese vessel, the *Hofuku Maru*, and joined the hundreds of prisoners already crammed below decks en route from Manila to Japan. They did not have to endure the appalling conditions on board for long before American planes attacked the convoy and brought the voyage to a tragic end. When the *Hofuku Maru* sank on 21 September, of the 1,289 British and Dutch prisoners of war on board 1,047 died. Having survived yet another brush with death, Norman later told his daughter that as he fought to stay afloat in the water he had felt what he assumed to be seaweed wrapping around his legs, only to discover that the 'seaweed' was, in fact, several sea snakes and that his friend, Mac, had pulled him onto some floating wood, yet again probably saving his life. Shortly afterwards the prisoners were picked up by the Japanese and taken to Bilibid prison camp in Manila, in the Philippines.

Weak and suffering from dysentery when he arrived at Bilibid, where most of the prisoners were American, Norman spoke little in later life about his time there. Medical records show that his health continued to deteriorate over the following months and he was held in the camp's hospital from November 1944 onwards. Medical provision was poor and the prisoners' rations of food hopelessly inadequate. A report later noted that at the time Norman arrived at Bilibid, the daily issue of food was no more than 170 grams, quite literally a starvation diet, and that on average between one and four men were being buried each day.

Graves at Bilibid Prison, the Philippines in early 1945. (Photo courtesy of www.militaryhistory.photos.com)

By the time the camp was liberated by American soldiers on 4 February 1945, Norman was acutely ill. He told Sheila that he and his comrades had woken up one morning to discover that the guards had gone. Weighing approximately half his normal body weight, Norman was by then unable to stand and could barely see.

> Father recalled American soldiers coming into the camp and weeping at the sight of the prisoners. He was gently lifted into a truck and a bar of chocolate was thrust into his hands. My father described the soldier who lifted him up as being a giant of a man, who could hardly speak for sobbing.

Norman was transported to hospital in Manila for treatment, where his hospital notes described him as suffering from malnutrition, beri beri, hyperaesthesia, weakness of extremities and diminished vision.

Norman was then flown to Leyte and, from there, put on board a hospital ship bound for the United States. Upon arrival at San Francisco he was admitted to the first of two hospitals where he received treatment over the next two months before finally being transported back to England, arriving at Southampton on 9 May 1945.

Despite the months of hospital care and a much improved diet, Norman's family were, nonetheless, shocked at his still skeletal appearance when he arrived home.

66 A Cruel Captivity

DISEASE INVESTIGATION CHECKLIST

Please ring round any ailments/diseases suffered during your capture or any subsequent health problems caused as a consequence of those diseases or conditions.

1. (Shrapnel) or bullet wounds.
2. Sensitive or vulnerable scar tissue.
3. (Torpedoed or sunk at sea.)
4. (Malnutrition & Privation with residual nervous symptoms.)
5. Surgical operations in POW camps.
6. (Malnutrition & Privation.)
7. (Malaria,) type & number of times.
8. Cholera.
9. Diphtheria.
10. Beri-Beri, wet.
11. (Beri-Beri, dry.) ✓
12. Sandfly Fever.
13. Denghie Fever.
14. Typhus.
15. Blackwater Fever.
16. Dysentery, amoebic.
17. (Dysentery, bacillary.) ✓
18. (Strongyloides.) ✓
19. Hook-worm.
20. Tape-worm.
21. Ring-worm. (Tenia).
22. Scabies.
23. Skin Disorders, including blisters or rash from Ringus or "Bleeding Tree", contact in Java/Sumatra.
24. Skin Cancer.
25. Rodent Ulcers.
26. Pellagra.
27. (Tropical Ulcers.)
28. (Depression.)
29. (Anxiety Neurosis.)
30. (Nervous Disorders.)
31. (Nightmares.)
32. (Bad Dreams.)
33. (Memory Loss.)
34. Agoraphobia.
35. Claustrophobia.
36. Hypertension.
37. (Teeth Loss.)
38. (Dental Problems.)
39. (Defective Vision.)
40. (Blindness, what degree) *Blurred Vis*
41. (Defective Hearing.) ✓
42. Tinnitus.
43. Gunfire Deafness.
44. Ear Inflamation.
45. Heart Conditions.
46. (Diabetis Mellitus.) ✓
47. (Respiratory problems.) ✓
48. (Asthma.) ✓
49. Tuberculosis.
50. Asbestosis.
51. Hepatitis.
52. Jaundice.
53. Sensitive Stomach.
54. (Dietary problems.) ✓
55. Hiatus Hernia.
56. Duodenal Ulcer.
57. Peptic Ulcer.
58. (Hernia.) ✓
59. Bladder problems.
60. Impotence.
61. (Piles.) ✓
62. (Happy Feet.)
63. (Foot Rot.)
64. (Results of beatings by Japs.)
65. Japanese Tortures.
66. Broken limbs, state which.
67. Limb loss, state which.
68. (Arthritis.)
69. Rheumatism.
70. (Calcium deficiency.)
71. Spinal problems.
72. (Skeletal or "bone" pains.)
73. Frost bite. (N.Japan).
74. Tetanus.
75. How near to atomic blasts if in Japan?
76. Journeyed through Hiroshima or Nagasaki after Atomic Bomb.
77. Schizophrenia.
78. Hodgkin's Disease.
79. Meniere's Disease.
80. Scrotum Dermatitis ✓

THIS LIST MAY FORM PART OF YOUR APPLICATION FOR A WAR DISABILITY PENSION IF SUBMITTED TO...

Part of Norman Finlay's medical notes compiled after his liberation from Bilibid camp, detailing the numerous physical ailments from which he suffered.

One of his sisters recalled that he was very disorientated for some time and that it was several months before he was able to eat properly as a consequence of his stomach being unaccustomed to normal sized meals. Still feeling the effects of beri beri, he was subsequently treated at Dunstan Hill Hospital, where he was also found to be suffering from an intestinal worm infection. Further hospital treatment was to come. Due to his ill health, it was over a year after his return home before Norman was able to find employment. Having finally secured a job as a colliery joiner, the physical exertion required soon proved too much for him, causing him to shake and sometimes lose consciousness, which led, in 1947, to his being diagnosed as having developed diabetes mellitus, which was eventually attributed to the prolonged malnutrition he had suffered as a prisoner of war. Norman continued to have difficulty holding down a job due to the instability of his condition but eventually found sympathetic employers at an engineering firm in Hebburn, where he worked as a progress chaser, staying there for over twenty-five years. Despite the catalogue of medical ailments acquired during his time in captivity and the impact of these upon his life, the pension he was granted in 1957 in recognition of his disabilities was minimal.

In 1949, a year after meeting Kathleen at a dance in Newcastle upon Tyne, they were married, settled in Gateshead and went on to have two children.

Sheila's memories of her childhood illustrate only too clearly the extent to which her father retained mental, as well as physical, scars of his captivity, something made very apparent by his diabetes.

> When I was young, I recall several occasions where mam would have to go to the neighbours to get help to hold my father down whilst he thrashed about on the floor shouting, whilst having a diabetic hypo. My father would shout and

Norman Finlay and his fiancée Kathleen in 1948.

curse the Japanese, sometimes shouting out in Japanese, and I have never ever forgotten the look of horror on his face as he relived his experiences. We had to hold him down whilst Mother poured sugared water into his mouth – there were no glucose injections then. On one occasion, Father thought he was trying to strangle a Japanese guard, he was fighting off a neighbour who had come to help hold him down …. As a young child witnessing this behaviour, it was very frightening. Here was our normally placid father shouting out and screaming. I was terrified. I can remember being afraid if I was left alone with him. I found it difficult to hug my father as I was always afraid he was going to go into one of his trances …. Often he had a blank stare in his eyes, which was very unnerving.

She added, 'When he was not suffering from his diabetic states he was the most gentle, kind man. He would open doors for people, doff his hat to women when greeting them, was polite and honest.' In addition to reliving his experiences of captivity during his diabetic attacks, those experiences also haunted him at night. Said Sheila:

he suffered many years of nightmares and torments, shouting out in his sleep, trying to strangle my mother on one occasion whilst in his sleep, and generally fighting during his sleep, kicking out and hitting my poor mother.

Norman's memories of his captivity also left him unable to cope with being confronted with Japanese people, for whom he retained a hatred for the rest of his life. Sheila recalled an incident when, during a family outing, they encountered a group of Japanese tourists, whereupon her father 'had become physically stiff, his eyes were blank and staring … . We took father home immediately, where it took several hours for him to come out of this frightened state. It was truly disturbing to witness'.

Norman died at the age of seventy-seven in 1996. Following his death, a representative of the British Legion suggested that his family appeal against the decision not to grant a full pension, on behalf of his widow. The appeal was successful, as the tribunal accepted that the conditions of Norman's captivity had contributed to his diabetes which, in turn, was a contributory factor in hastening his death. Towards the end of his life the nightmares, which had finally abated after many years, returned to haunt his sleep, causing him great distress. Sheila explained that in the absence of any attempt to offer men like her father counselling following their return from the Far East, she had repeatedly encouraged Norman to seek professional help to ease his mental turmoil, but that he had refused, saying he did

Private Norman McCandless Finlay 69

Norman and Kathleen Finlay at a FEPOW Reunion in 1982.

not want to 'dig it all up'. It seems clear, however, that memories of his experiences remained very close to the surface for the rest of his life.

> The effects of my father's time as a prisoner never left him. Many times when I asked my father to tell his story, his eyes would glaze over and he would look very sad and grey. I now understand how he *could* not talk to me, but feel sad that he was never able to offload the horror of that time.

Chapter 9

Able Seaman William Coates Nicholls

Royal Navy, Post Division

When Bill Nicholls started work in his father's business as an apprentice hairdresser, he could not have envisaged that his hairdressing skills would one day be of great use to him in a prisoner of war camp in the Far East. Bill's father had set up the business in the Somerset town of Bridgewater before the First World War had taken him away to fight in France, after which, despite being in poor health when he returned in 1918, he managed to get the business up and running again. Bill was born the following year and fourteen years later began working alongside his father, going on to become a fully trained men's hairdresser and an expert at cut-throat shaves. He was still working in the family business when war was declared in September 1939, and the following month enlisted in the Royal Navy at HMS *Royal Arthur*, a naval shore establishment in Skegness. After two months training he was transferred to another shore base, HMS *Drake* in Devonport, and it was from here that he joined the cruise liner SS *Andes* bound for Singapore, arriving in May 1940.

After Japan entered the war in December 1941, Bill was moved from his base at HMS *Sultan II*, a shore establishment in Singapore, to RAF Seletar. By the second week of February, with the Japanese having landed on the island and defeat seemingly inevitable, Bill was among a group who boarded an Admiralty tug, the *Ying Ping*, which was bound for Australia, carrying a number of key RAF personnel. Some years later, Bill recalled:

> we eventually left Singapore on Friday 13 and sailed for Australia, but were sunk in the Bangka Straits two days later. After sixteen hours in the sea clinging to the side of a small lifeboat, which only held fourteen men, we were picked up by an RAF aircraft rescue launch and taken to Bangka, where we became prisoners of war of the Japanese.

Bill Nicholls, around 1940.

Bill was fortunate to have survived the sinking of the *Ying Ping*. Of the seventy-five on board, fifty were lost. On 16 February, the day after the fall of Singapore, he and the other survivors were captured by the Japanese at Muntok on Bangka Island, where they were held for a week before being taken back to Singapore.

Unlike the vast majority of prisoners in Singapore who, for the duration of their captivity, were held in prison camps on the island or transported to camps elsewhere, Bill was among a group who were confined on board various ships which were anchored just off shore and spent the following two and a half years either sailing under the Japanese flag or working within the confines of the naval base. 'We were employed on various jobs around the naval base, such as road building, sawing timber for the Jap cookhouse, scraping the bottoms of ships, tending gardens, road sweeping.' He then spent a period as boat's crew, on board the *Rompin*, sailing to Java or Sumatra to bring back timber for use in the various building projects.

> We made two trips to Sumatra. The Japs pointed to a port in Sumatra and told us to take them there, so we had to work out the course and get them there. After one or two mishaps, such as running aground, we found the port and proceeded up the jungle river to a jetty, where we tied up and loaded large tree trunks. We took walks into the jungle along a light railway, which was bringing timber out to the jetty. On the second trip we were returning towing two barges alongside, plus very large tree trunks lashed on deck when we struck a very bad tropical storm which was very fierce and frightening. We lost both barges .... Eventually the storm blew itself out and we picked up one of the barges and returned to Singapore. On another occasion, we were returning to Singapore when we hit a ship which had been sunk and had no marker buoy. This put a small hole in the ship, but we got back alright and were taken into dry dock, where the ship was repaired. We were blamed for this accident and one morning they marched nine of us up to the Kempeitai headquarters and, taking six of us, one at a time, beat us with a stick like a baseball bat. They had two men hold our hands while one beat us. After taking twenty-six strokes I decided I'd had my lot and threw myself on the ground, where they left me. Eventually they threw a bucket of water over us and then locked us in a cell. An officer came out with a sword and made signs that he was going to chop our heads off. He then came back carrying six swords, still indicating he would chop off our heads, but after keeping us in the cell for another hour, they let us out and marched us back to the ship. One of our men had great difficulty making it as he had taken ninety-five strokes.

In September 1943, Bill was moved from the *Rompin*.

> They gathered together all the prisoners that were left and put us together on two old ships that were anchored about 200 yards off their headquarters in the naval base. At this time we were beginning to beat the Japs. You could see a big ship from the naval base and [they would] come back two days later limping in with a big hole in the side or stern, so we were sinking a lot of their ships. From then on our food supply got worse and worse and after another nine months our numbers had dwindled to around forty-five, because of illness, so they sent us to Changi jail.

The place at which Bill spent the remainder of his time in captivity remained etched very clearly upon his mind, as he was to recall over thirty years later.

> It had a twenty-two foot wall with watchtowers on each corner. Inside was a road around, then another wall eighteen feet high, inside which were built the cell blocks, three storeys high with a steel grid between the cells. In these blocks we lived, four men to a cell, and then the steel grid across the middle was packed with as many men as could be fitted in. Surrounding the jail were attap huts ... and thousands of men living outside.

It was during Bill's time at Changi that he found his skills as a hairdresser to be much in demand.

> I was employed as a hairdresser to the warrant officers, of whom there were approximately 150 living in a hut built in one of the courtyards in the jail. So I was transferred to a hut next door, which was much better than the cell block.

For this work Bill was paid twenty cents a day, as opposed to the daily rate of thirty cents for those who undertook heavy work.

> I had about six dollars a month to spend, which usually bought enough tobacco for one month, plus a sheet of newspaper to roll cigarettes. About the only other thing you could buy on the camp black market was some palm oil to put on your rice, which was supposed to contain some nutritional benefit.

There was certainly very little nutrition to be had in the ever-diminishing rations provided by the Japanese.

> From this time on, everything gradually got worse. We were receiving half a pint of plain, sloppy rice like porridge for breakfast, half a pint of plain cooked rice for lunch, plus a pint of rice in the evening with some vegetables which we had grown in the gardens surrounding the jail. With each meal we had a cup of tea without milk or sugar.

As an increasing number of prisoners succumbed to death and disease, the Japanese struggled to find enough fit men to form working parties. 'Men were going down more and more with malaria, dysentery, beri beri and all sorts of malnutrition problems.' From time to time Bill was assigned to a party working on an aerodrome that would become Changi airport.

> We were marched off in the morning to work and the airport was made by digging away a hill and filling a swamp. This work was all done by hand, digging and filling small baskets, which were passed along a line of men and then put into a cart and dumped where needed. While working there one day, three Flying Fort planes came over and dropped some bombs on the other end of the airfield, which the Japs were using. This was the first sign in three years of an assurance that our forces were fighting back.

Thanks to the bravery of those who took huge risks operating a secret radio, Bill and his fellow prisoners had been able to hear news about the progress of the war during their time in Changi jail. 'We eventually heard the news of a new type of bomb being dropped on Japan, then a few days later we heard Japan had surrendered.' Several days later came the official confirmation that the war had ended.

> So the great day for which we had waited for three and a half years dawned and most of the Japs disappeared. The few that remained, instead of being brutal guards, became very servile and instead of us bowing to them, they began bowing to us. A few days later some British officers and men dropped in by parachute and, in case they were in need of a haircut, I got in touch with them. I had my first taste of normal food, some eggs and bacon. What a marvellous treat after eating rice for three and a half years! A few days later the cruiser HMS *Sussex* came into Singapore town and the Admiral and some men came to visit us. A trip to visit the ship was arranged, so we set off from the jail to Singapore on a lorry. On the way to town we passed some Jap PoWs, about 100, being marched up the road by our soldiers, and we all cursed and shouted at them in Japanese and English. I think at that moment we felt exhilarated and really

free, but if looks coming from the Japs could kill, we would all have dropped dead on the spot.

Days later, as arrangements were being made to repatriate those fit enough to travel, Bill experienced what he later referred to as 'the saddest incident of the whole time of imprisonment,' when a friend and fellow prisoner died: 'It was very heartbreaking, and so sad, that after living through three and a half years of starvation and absolute hell, he should die just as we got free.' Bill was given a medical examination and the news that he would soon be on his way home, even though, he recalled 'you could count every bone down my body, they decided I was fit enough to travel'. Bill boarded the New Zealand troopship HMNZS *Monowai*, which sailed for England on 14 September. Having managed to get himself assigned to the mess, which happened to be next to the ship's galley, he later noted, 'we were offered the food that was left over and we never refused anything, and I arrived in England about one and a half stones heavier than when we left!' Recalling the reception he and his fellow ex-PoWs received when the ship called at Colombo, he noted, 'all the ships sounded their sirens. As we passed alongside a Navy warship they had the Marine band playing and although we had only been PoWs, we were treated like heroes.' After a brief stay in Colombo, the *Monowai* sailed for England and arrived at Liverpool docks on 8 October 1945.

After a perfunctory medical check, Bill returned home to Bridgwater and was one of many who had to deal with the fact that irrevocable changes had taken place whilst they had been away. Noticeably absent from those who met Bill at the railway station was his father, who had died in 1943. Physically, the most obvious sign of the damage caused to Bill's health as a consequence of prolonged vitamin deficiency was his poor eyesight. He later told his son Keith that, for months following his return home, his mother had fed him generous quantities of Marmite, renowned for its high content of Vitamin B, in an attempt to combat the problem, with some success, but his vision remained impaired for the rest of his life. It was during this period of recuperation whilst he was visiting his family that Bill met his future wife, Aileen.

They were married in June 1946 and their son was born the following year. Having been demobbed

Bill Nicholls and his wife Aileen when they married in 1946.

from the Royal Navy in early 1946, Bill returned to his father's hairdressing business, which he went on to run successfully until his retirement in 1984.

Although physically Bill had recovered sufficiently to enable him to move on with his life, his mental state took far longer to repair. Keith explained that his mother had discouraged Bill from talking about his time as a prisoner of war.

> She was trying to protect him from having nightmares after reliving his experiences. Of course, counselling had not been thought of in those days …. Talking in more detail about the terrible times he went through may have helped and may have reduced the number of horrific nightmares he had over many years. I think I was ten before he was completely free of them.

As the years passed, Bill began to talk a little about his time in captivity and then did so increasingly, eventually writing an account of his experiences in the 1980s.

> Had he got it all out of his system at an early stage it may not have been uppermost in his mind for the rest of his life. If you were with him anywhere socially, within ten minutes to quarter of an hour you would always overhear him saying to someone, 'when I was a prisoner of war…'. This continued right up to the end of his life.

In common with many who returned from captivity in the Far East having almost starved to death, Bill's experiences left him with a very firm appreciation of food, which, inevitably, spilled over into family life. According to Keith:

> I was never allowed to leave the table until I had completely cleared my plate, being told, 'You'll eat it all up. I don't care if it takes all night, you will finish it all before you leave the table.'

Bill's experiences also left him intolerant of those who complained about illness.

> He was a lovely man, but did not suffer anyone who was ill in any way, often telling them, 'there's nothing much wrong with you'. Unfortunately, this was usually directed at my mother, who suffered quite serious illnesses. The only response she ever got from Dad was, 'For God's sake, pull yourself together, woman. If you'd suffered like I suffered you would have something to be depressed about.' They were, however, devoted to each other.

For Keith, the evidence of his father having been a prisoner of war of the Japanese was all-encompassing from his childhood onwards.

For sixty years I was the son of a Japanese PoW. As a child I grew up with it – PoW Association meetings, British Legion meetings, two weeks out selling poppies in November, Dad always at the Bridgwater Memorial on Remembrance Sunday. It was our way of life. Dad never demanded it that way. It just happened.

Bill remained in reasonably good health until he reached his seventies, when he developed skin cancer, firstly on his head and face and then on his back. According to Keith, 'he always felt it had been caused by the fact that he was in just a pair of shorts in the hot Singapore sun, from dawn to dusk, for three and a half years.'

Though he underwent repeated surgery, cancerous growths continued to appear for the rest of his life. Despite all he suffered as a prisoner of war, Bill bore no bitterness towards the Japanese, having told his son that whilst he had certainly encountered many who had treated prisoners with brutality, there had also been a few who had shown a degree of humanity.

In 2005, sixty years after his liberation from Changi, Bill took the decision to return to Singapore with his son, an experience which bestowed upon Keith a deeper understanding of the emotional legacy borne by his father. Bill later said of the trip:

> The emotional part was going to Changi and the cemetery and seeing all the names of those that died. I looked at it and thought I could have been one of them and it was very upsetting. It brought it all back to me .... During the last nine months we were close to starving to death because the food rations were very poor.

The following year, while still receiving treatment for skin cancer, Bill was diagnosed with pancreatic cancer. Before his death in 2007, at the age of eighty-seven, it appears he had

Bill Nicholls in 2004, aged 84.

come to terms with all that he had suffered at the hands of the Japanese and the experiences which had dominated his thinking for much of his life ever since. Recording his thoughts following his return to Singapore, he said:

> It has been sixty years and I've just got to accept what happened and hope that the Japanese are more civilised than their fathers were. You can't live a life of hatred because it destroys you.

Chapter 10

AC2 Rosslyn Morris

Royal Air Force, No. 605 Squadron

Before the war intervened to irrevocably change his life, Ross Morris had been happy and carefree, remembered by one of his sisters as having been quiet and thoughtful, a gentle soul with a love of poetry. Born in 1922 in the village of Hawarden, Flintshire, he and his eight siblings had a very strict upbringing but it was, nevertheless, a happy childhood from which he emerged a confident and well balanced young man who, like many in the community, found employment at the local steelworks. He was still employed as a steelworker when, following the outbreak of war, he received his call up papers and, at the age of nineteen, enlisted in the Royal Air Force. Posted to 605 (County of Warwick) Squadron, which was based in the Midlands, Ross initially remained close to home during his training but, whilst at RAF Honiley in Warwickshire in the autumn of 1941, he learned that the squadron was soon to be sent overseas.

After travelling by train to Gourock on 7 December 1941, Ross and his comrades boarded the HMT *Warwick Castle*. Whatever anxiety they may have felt as they set sail for an unspecified destination will surely have increased when news reached them that Japan had launched almost simultaneous attacks on Pearl Harbor, Malaya and Hong Kong within hours of their voyage having begun. By the time they reached South Africa, the icy chill of the first part of their journey had been replaced by sweltering heat, leading to much speculation by those on board as to where they would be using the tropical kit with which they had been issued. For a time the ship circled in the Indian Ocean awaiting orders but, as a consequence of the escalating threat from the Japanese to the Dutch East Indies, the decision was taken to head for the port of Tandjong Priok in Java, rather than Singapore.

After disembarking from the *Warwick Castle* on 3 February 1942, the squadron moved into a barracks in Batavia which had previously been occupied by Dutch troops, and were then sent to the nearby airfield to prepare for the arrival of their planes. Three days later, with Singapore under siege from the Japanese and Sumatra perceived as being vulnerable to imminent attack, Ross was among those ordered to head for Palembang as reinforcements for the troops who were already there. Two days later they arrived by ferry at Oosthaven, and made their way to the airfield at Palembang, but the squadron's time there was brief as Japanese paratroopers had already landed on the island. With the Japanese now directing their attention towards Java and Sumatra following their capture of Singapore, Ross and his comrades headed back to Oosthaven, from where they managed to board a ship and return to Tandjong Priok. The speed of the Japanese advance was such that escape was all but impossible, however, but for a fortunate few and, after the Dutch bowed to the pressure to admit defeat on 8 March, Ross was one of the many RAF personnel still remaining on Java who became prisoners of war.

After being taken back to Batavia, Ross began his captivity in the confines of Boei Glodok, a civilian prison which had been emptied of its inmates to make way for military prisoners of war. The prisoners spent their first few days at Boie Glodok crammed into the cells, the only sanitary provision a hole in the floor. Allowed out only briefly once a day to wash themselves at a nearby well and fed upon meagre rations of rice and watery stew, some of the men were already suffering from dysentery. The overcrowded conditions and lack of hygiene soon caused more to follow suit, disease posing as much of a threat to the prisoners as did their captors. Ross was one of many to contract malaria but, despite the Japanese having a plentiful supply of quinine, they refused to provide it or indeed any other medical supplies. This initiation into life in Japanese hands was but a foretaste of what was to come in the following months and years. Four or five days after Ross's arrival at Boei Glodok, he and his fellow prisoners were allowed to organise latrines in the compound and to have some freedom from their cells, the presence of armed guards positioned upon the high walls of the prison enough to banish any thoughts of escape. The Japanese then began to make use of what they perceived as their readymade army of slave labour, and Ross was one of many who were assigned to work parties. Initially he was among those who were put to work breaking up cars in order that the metal from them could be sent back to Japan, after which he was sent to work at the airfield just outside Batavia, repairing runways damaged by Allied bombing.

Ross had been at Boei Glodok for about six months when he learned that he, along with most of 605 Squadron, was among a large party of prisoners to be moved elsewhere. On 11 October 1942, not having been told of their destination, the prisoners were taken to Tandjong Priok, where they boarded the *Dainichi Maru*. Descending into the bowels of the ship, the men were packed tightly onto and under the wooden platforms which had been installed around the sides of the hold for the purposes of transporting the maximum number of people in minimal space, ensuring the spread of dysentery. Allowed only limited access to the makeshift toilets rigged up over the side of the ship and with conditions below deck becoming increasingly unbearable, it was with some relief to those on board that the ship reached Singapore four days later. However, their stay in Singapore was brief. After leaving Selarang Barracks on 27 October, Ross and the rest of 605 Squadron were manhandled into the holds of the *Tofuku Maru*, bound for Japan. The men faced equally appalling conditions to those of their previous voyage, but this time for much longer, the spread of disease soon claiming lives. One of those on board with Ross was Alan Carter, also of 605 Squadron, who later noted that towards the end of the voyage 'our death toll had grown considerably since leaving Singapore and every day brought further deaths from dysentery .... Around thirty of our men had died during the four weeks we had been on the *Tofuku Maru*.'

Arriving at the port of Moji in Japan on 27 November, Ross and his comrades were ill-prepared in their tropical kit for the bitterly cold weather that awaited them. They were transported by train and then ferry to the island of Hokkaido, the northernmost of Japan's islands, and marched through the snow to Hakodate Main Camp.

The prisoners were issued with Japanese army clothing and housed in a collection of single-storey wooden huts where they slept on straw mattresses, the only form of heating that which was provided by a couple of stoves in each hut, around which the men huddled for warmth in the sub-zero temperatures. Ross and his fellow prisoners were assigned to parties working for the Hakodate Ship Building Company, doing various jobs such as welding and joinery. In ever-worsening weather conditions they were marched to and from work in heavy snow and rewarded for their efforts with a ration of rice and a mug of watery soup three times a day. However, a combination of malnutrition, bitterly cold weather and the refusal of the Japanese to provide any drugs with which to treat those suffering from disease, resulted in an increasing number of men becoming too ill to work. Since the policy of the Japanese at Hakodate, as

The huts in which the PoWs lived at Hakodate camp, Japan, photographed shortly after the war.

82   A Cruel Captivity

elsewhere, was one of 'no work, no eat' the rations which were issued had to be stretched even further in order to feed the sick, of whom there were many. Not all would go on to recover, as dysentery and colitis claimed more lives.

After several months work switched to the docks, where the men worked twelve-hour shifts, day and night, unloading ships. This at least offered the prisoners opportunities to steal much-needed food, though they risked severe punishment if caught.

Close-up of a photo of a group of prisoners at Hokodate camp, Japan in 1944. Ross Morris is in the centre, wearing a dark cap.

Ross was profoundly affected by the callousness and brutality of the guards. Any transgression of the rules, from talking after 'lights out' to failing to obey an order quickly enough, attracted severe beatings which fellow prisoner Alan Carter noted were best withstood without flinching.

> If you ducked or pulled your head back, then you received a double dose of punches. If you were knocked down and didn't immediately get up, then you

PoWs at Hakodate camp, Japan in 1944, including Ross Morris (bottom row, centre)

were really in trouble, for that was when the Japs showed their brutality by kicking you as hard as they could in the head and stomach until you had been rendered senseless.

Ross later told his brother that the Japanese did their best to chip away at the prisoners' morale, adding that on one occasion one of his friends had been blindfolded and made to stand before a firing squad for what must have seemed an eternity, for no reason other than to break his spirit.

Ross endured over two and a half years at Hakodate, the extra food he and his fellow prisoners were able to steal whilst working as stevedores helping them to survive the hardships of the freezing cold winters. All this was to change, however, when, in early June 1945, the camp was relocated to Bibai, to the north of Hakodate, which entailed a 200-mile journey by truck. After first building the huts in which they would live, the prisoners were assigned to work parties, all but the sickest being sent to the coal mines of the Mitsui Mining Company. Here they were made to work twelve-hour shifts – exhausting and often dangerous work for men no longer able to supplement their rations with contraband as they had done when working at the docks. As Alan Carter noted:

> morale in the camp was now at its lowest ebb as we could see that the hard work and lack of food were going to finish us off. The only news we were receiving was from the Japs, who kept telling us that we would never see England ever again, that we would work as slaves in Japan until we died.

By the time the camp was liberated, 114 prisoners at the camp had indeed died as a result of working as slaves of the Japanese.

The first indication Ross and his comrades had that their ordeal was at an end was when they woke up one morning in mid-August 1945 to discover that the guards had disappeared. Shortly afterwards, American aircraft dropped leaflets informing the men that the war was over, together with a walkie-talkie to enable contact with their liberators, and the following days brought air drops of food and cigarettes. Towards the middle of September the prisoners finally left Bibai, having been instructed to make their way to the nearby airfield, from where they were flown to Tokyo and then to the Philippines. After receiving medical treatment in Manila, Ross boarded HMS *Glory* on 3 October 1945 to begin the first stage of his long journey home, reaching Vancouver in late October. From there he travelled by train across the United States and boarded the RMS *Queen Mary* in New York, finally arriving in Southampton on 18 November 1945.

After Ross returned home to Flintshire he found it extremely difficult to come to terms with all that he had endured during the years of his captivity and to adjust

Liberated PoWs, including Ross Morris (centre, standing) on board HMS Glory in October 1945.

to civilian life. Although he had been discharged from the RAF in early 1946, he re-enlisted eighteen months later, only to be discharged soon afterwards for reasons of ill-health. The physical legacy of Ross's years in the Far East were very apparent from the repeated bouts of malaria from which he suffered and the bronchitis for which he was later awarded a pension. However, time would show that his problems went far beyond anything physical, the years of captivity having left an indelible mark upon his mind. Endeavouring to move on with his life, he eventually took a job as a welder at the nearby Shotton steelworks, around the same time that he met his wife-to-be, Blodwen, at a local dance hall. After marrying in November 1950 and settling down at Connah's Quay, Flintshire, Ross and Blodwen went on to have four sons and a daughter.

In an era when post-traumatic stress disorder had yet to be recognised, little consideration was given to the mental turmoil experienced by many of those who returned from the Far East struggling to deal with a range of emotions, from anger and bitterness towards their former captors to guilt at having survived when so many of their comrades had died appalling deaths. Although she was too young at the time to fully comprehend the reasons behind the difficulties her father was experiencing, Ross's daughter, Helen, has vivid childhood memories of how traumatised her father was by the years he spent in Japanese hands. Whilst he was vocal in his anger towards those who had held him captive, any attempt to articulate his memories of captivity caused him immense anguish and, in the absence of any professional help in coming to terms with his experiences, he turned instead to alcohol to numb the pain those memories caused him. According to Helen:

> he talked about the Japs, as he called them, and hated them. He cursed them every single day. I think I saw him at his worst. I do remember him talking to me about the war and what he had seen, and how he spent the days drinking and crying. The poor man was tormented. My dad had really bad nightmares most nights. He cried a lot, I think maybe survivor's guilt.

Ross Morris and his wife Blodwen when they married in 1950.

On a number of occasions Ross's inability to deal with his emotions reached a critical point and he was admitted to Denbigh Asylum, where Helen remembers being taken to visit him.

Inevitably, Ross's troubled mental state had consequences for those around him as his reliance upon alcohol increased and he directed his aggression towards those closest to him. Helen recalled:

> my mum was such a lovely woman and put up with so much from him. He didn't treat her the way she deserved but she stuck it out and never left him. I think many would have, but she was old school, for better or for worse. He was a very angry man who would use terrible language. I remember my dad throwing his dinner across the room and cursing my mum for giving him food he didn't want to eat a lot of the time. He would go to the pub and drink all day.

The impact upon Ross's family was huge. Heavy drinking took its toll on his already poor health, seriously affected his ability to hold down a job, and affected his children psychologically. Said Helen:

> because my dad didn't work much, it meant we didn't have much. We seemed to be the poorest in the street. Everyone in the street knew my dad as they had

seen him staggering up the road bumping into walls. I felt so ashamed, as my friends all had normal lives. Two of my brothers never left home. They tried to protect my mum from the mental abuse. They missed out on their own families and marriage. My eldest brother fought a lot with my dad …. I was scared to close my eyes at night dreading the arguments and fights. It broke my heart as my dad was physically small and weak. It was quite a traumatic upbringing and has stayed with me and with my other brothers.

Helen went on to add that occasionally there were glimpses of another side to her father, the memories of which she clearly holds very dear. 'I really loved him. He had such a kind side. When Dad was in a good place he would take me for long walks and tell me stories.' However, the anger and aggression he harboured were never far away and continued to fuel his heavy drinking with severe consequences for his health.

Thirty years after his release from captivity, Ross died at the age of only fifty-three. The official cause of his death was stated as chronic bronchitis and malnutrition. However, it is hard to avoid the conclusion that the psychological impact of all that he had endured as a prisoner of war and his inability to cope with it in the absence of any professional help was equally to blame. Explaining that she felt guilty for some of the things she had said about a much loved father, Helen added:

when dad passed away, calm fell upon the house. I missed him so much but the peace was so nice. He was a good man and I know he loved us all. I know it wasn't his fault that he ended up the way he did. The war took the best of him and left us with the angry, aggressive man I knew.

Chapter 11

Private Alfred Frederick Davey

4th Battalion Royal Norfolk Regiment

Alf Davey was a twenty-one year old soldier undergoing his military training in 1941 when he first met Elsie, the woman who would later become his wife. Some five years later, when Alf asked her father for his daughter's hand in marriage, he received a less than enthusiastic response. 'He said "No, I don't want you to marry my daughter." He knew what I'd gone through. He said to me, "you won't live that long."' Alf was to prove his future father-in-law wrong, going on to outlive his wife of over fifty-two years. However, such misgivings were entirely understandable, given all that Alf had experienced in the intervening years as a captive of the Japanese.

One of eight children, Alf was born and brought up in the small market town of Bungay, Suffolk. Agriculture provided much of the employment in the area and when Alf left school at the age of fourteen he took a job on a local farm. In 1938 he joined the Territorial Army and, when war was declared the following year, was serving in C Company of the 4th Battalion Royal Norfolk Regiment.

For several months Alf's training took place locally, with the battalion engaged in coast defence, guarding various locations against the risk of an invasion. However, in November 1940, the battalion was moved to Cambridge for more specialist training, then three months later to Hawick, and then to Blackburn in Lancashire. It was during his time here that he and Elsie met on a blind date, but within months the battalion moved again, to Ross on Wye, shortly after which Alf learned that he was to be sent overseas.

On 29 October 1941, Alf boarded the *Andes* at Liverpool and embarked upon the journey which would take him away from Elsie and from his native shores for nearly four years. After arriving at Halifax, the battalion transferred to the American vessel USS *Wakefield* and then sailed via Cape Town to Bombay, where they disembarked at the end of December 1941. Aware by now of the worsening situation in Malaya, the men spent the next three weeks encamped at Ahmednagar in India for further training and acclimatisation before re-embarking and learning of their final destination. The *Wakefield* arrived at Singapore on 29 January 1942, Alf and his comrades disembarking at Keppel Harbour amidst heavy aerial bombardment by the

88 A Cruel Captivity

Alf Davey around 1940.

Japanese. The battalion was initially charged with aiding the defence of the north coast of the island. Many years later, when Alf wrote an account of his experiences and also made a video recording, his recollections of the events which followed remained clear.

> One of the first things we had to do, we had to mine and barb wire the beaches. We didn't know what was going to happen, so it was just fear more than anything. You were wondering what was going to happen to you. Twenty-seven Japanese aircraft all came over at once and bombed. I recall we had five or six Brewster Buffaloes – the old fashioned type of plane.

Shortly afterwards, the Japanese landed on the north of the island and Alf and his comrades received further orders. Talking about this as recently as 2016, Alf recalled:

> we were told we were moving out, full battle order. We arrived at Bukit Timah, a rubber plantation, which we walked through without a shot being fired. We hadn't gone far on our way to our Company HQ when all hell broke loose. They came out from pop holes and were shooting from trees. Of course, we returned fire but several of our lads were killed. We eventually got to our Company headquarters and dug in. That night we posted all our machine guns so we could fire them from our trenches. Later that night a despatch rider came into our HQ. He asked where B Company was. Our Captain had a habit of swinging his revolver on his finger, just like John Wayne. He just shot him. He was a Jap. In the morning our front was piled high with Japanese.

Illustrating how clearly the events of 1942 remained etched upon his mind, despite the passage of over seventy years, Alf added 'our password that night was "Blackburn"'. Within days, Alf explained, the battle was over.

> Singapore had naval guns, which could fire out to sea, but they couldn't traverse and fire up the mainland, which was where the Japanese came down finally. They got to the causeway and cut the water supply off.

And so began Alf's three and a half years in captivity.
'We were marched to the barracks at Changi. After a few days we were off again. We went to River Valley camp.' Even at this early stage, the need to take advantage of any opportunity to acquire anything which would make life as prisoners of war more bearable had become apparent.

We went to clear the warehouses which had been bombed. We helped ourselves to much-needed clothes and boots. We went to work on the docks and had to go and load ships with iron ore and we used to scrounge as much as we could off the ships. We managed to get some Ovaltine tablets, which we crushed up and put in our rice to give it a little flavour. We used to scavenge as much as we could.

Such resourcefulness would later become not only a way of life but, as the months and years passed, often a life-saver.

On 22 October 1942 Alf was one of 650 prisoners transported to Thailand as part of Group 4. Alf later noted of the journey:

my lot went to the railway station and we were loaded into steel railway trucks, not knowing where we were going. Thirty men to a truck. You can imagine what it was like. I mean, some of these men had dysentery, some had malaria … and they were in a bad way. We had to open the doors of the trucks and hold them out in order for them to relieve themselves. It was red hot during the day and freezing cold at night. We had one meal a day for five days, five nights and that was rice. And then we got to a place called Ban Pong.

After spending the night at the transit camp, the prisoners were marched to Kan'buri, a journey of some fifty kilometres in conditions of intense heat and humidity. As Alf recalled, for some prisoners, suffering from a combination of exhaustion and disease, this was simply too much.

Some of the lads were too weak, they got so far and they couldn't walk any further. They just laid down. We went to help them, but we weren't allowed to. We had to leave them to die where they had fallen. So then we carried on to a place called Kan'buri. We stopped there a day and we managed to sort our feet out – blisters and what not.

After a day's rest, the party was on the move again. 'We were marched on again to another camp, Wang Pho, and we had to leave more lads by the wayside to die.' The march to Wang Pho took five days, and there Alf's party joined what was already a considerable workforce slaving on the railway.

At Wang Pho we worked hard on the railway, with tools which were absolutely useless. We had to dig one-metre squares of soil, put the soil on the embankment and put sleepers on it, which we had cut out of trees in the jungle. The work was hard and the rations were very poor. We bathed, swam and washed our clothes and blankets in the river, which was close to all the camps. We had one day off in ten. When you passed a Japanese, even a private, you saluted him. If you didn't, you would be beaten and kicked most mercilessly.

Alf was then assigned to a party of men working on the Wang Pho viaduct, a trestle bridge of some 100 metres in length being built around the cliff face above the river.

As the pressure to complete this feat of engineering intensified, with complete disregard for human life, the Japanese demanded that even those in hospital be brought out to work. Describing what became known as 'hammer and tap', a process by which the prisoners 'drilled' holes in the rock into which explosive charges were then placed, Alf recalled:

> at Wang Pho North we were building a bridge around a cliff. We had to drill through the rock, with your mate holding the drill and you striking with a fourteen-pound hammer. If he was weak, he would move and you would hit his wrist, sometimes breaking it. And then it was 'speedo!' The Japanese would bring the lads who were sick to hold the drills and the lads who couldn't move out of the way quickly enough would be blasted to death. The Japanese just laughed and pushed the dead over the side into the river below.

The Wang Pho viaduct, built around the cliff face by PoWs, photographed in the 1990s. (Photo courtesy of Shirley Barnes)

After several months at Wang Pho, Alf was moved to Tarsao hospital camp. 'Here I met quite a lot of my own battalion, the Royal Norfolks. Our own colonel was in charge and he was beaten nearly every day for disobeying orders and arguing with the Japanese.' Whilst at Tarsao, Alf was able to increase his chances of survival by getting a job which gave him the opportunity to acquire extra food.

> I managed to get a job in the hospital cookhouse, working twelve-hour shifts. All we wore was a piece of material like a loincloth, as we sweated all the time with the heat from the fires and the sun. The clogs we wore were what we had made out of bits of wood. The railway finished at Tarsao and we had to transport [Japanese] rations of chicken, duck, sweet potatoes and shallots up country to the next camp. We had to cross the river in a barge driven by Thais. The chickens and ducks were in bamboo cages, and we carried them by putting a bamboo pole through the cages and putting them on our shoulders. If a chicken or duck put its head through the cage it got a whack. We knew which ones we had killed and the Japanese would take all the dead out, saying '*presento*'. We would keep the ones we knew we had killed, which weren't diseased, and give away the rest. My mates and me would have a good meal that night.

Whilst at Tarsao Alf needed to have his appendix removed, an operation performed without anaesthetic due to the lack of medical supplies but of which he later recalled little, having mercifully lost consciousness. 'Some of the lads in my ward developed ulcers and died after having their legs amputated. Ten days later, I was back at work.' This was but one of several admissions to the camp hospital for Alf as he was repeatedly struck down by malaria. 'I got malaria and I was hospitalised for about ten days, then I'd go back to work and I'd get malaria again.' By this time, despite their best efforts, many of the camp doctors had very few drugs with which to treat malaria, dysentery, beri beri or tropical ulcers – all of which Alf succumbed to – resulting in countless unnecessary deaths.

Alf remained at Tarsao until May 1944, when he was moved to Tha Muang. On arrival he was assigned to a working party building huts for the Japanese. The bamboo used for hut building was always heavily infested with bed bugs, which fed on the men's bodies as they attempted to sleep and caused much misery, as well as disease. Alf recalled with a degree of satisfaction how he and his comrades had grasped the opportunity of exacting a fragment of revenge upon their captors. 'We collected all the bugs we could find and put them in their huts to give the Japanese sleepless nights, the bugs biting and sucking their blood!' At the end of 1944, Alf was moved farther north to work on a section of road which was being built between Wang Pho and Tavoy on the west coast, through the kind of terrain that would have been taxing for healthy workers. With the war no longer going Japan's way, the road was intended to provide them with a means of retreat. Ever poorer rations of food and non-existent medical supplies resulted in increasing numbers of prisoners succumbing to exhaustion, disease and death. As the seriously sick men were sent down the line to the hospital camps, many not surviving the journey, less sick men were sent up the line to replace them, the Japanese seemingly oblivious to the rationale that had they preserved the health of their workers rather than view them as expendable, they might have been more productive.

In June 1945, Alf was moved away from the railway to Nakhon Nayok, north of Bangkok, where he was among a party of men who were put to work digging large trenches around the camp. 'We had to dig gun emplacements in case our troops invaded,' recalled Alf, describing work that was being undertaken at many camps in Thailand and beyond at this time. This was not, however, the brutal workload of the 'speedo' period, an improvement in the guards' behaviour now matched by a welcome improvement in rations. Alf's first indication that the freedom of which he and his comrades had long dreamed was about to become a reality came during an encounter with someone from a nearby village.

> One morning we walked to the village and a naturalised Swedish man said to us, 'I hope to have some good news for you', and sang to the tune of, 'After the Ball is Over', 'I've heard the war is over'. We didn't dig any more that day. We went back to the camp and told the other lads what we had heard. Some didn't believe us. Many just cried. I had been a prisoner of war for three and a half years and now the war was over! Our own officers came from a camp nearby and told us not to retaliate against the Japanese. A couple of days later, American paratroopers who were spies and had been dropped into Kan'buri earlier came into our camp bringing medical supplies, rations and of course, cigarettes.

Two days later, Alf began his journey home.

> Twenty-five of us were to fly from Bangkok to Rangoon. The pilot took our names as we boarded. The engine on the Dakota wouldn't start so we boarded another Dakota aircraft and were taken to Rangoon hospital for check-ups. After the okay, we then boarded a ship and sailed for home. Stopping at Port Suez, one of my regiment said his family had received a telegram to say he was missing, presumed killed in an air crash. Leaving Port Suez, we gave the soldiers on the docks money to telegram home for us to say we were safe and not on the first Dakota, which had apparently gone down in the jungle.

94   A Cruel Captivity

Alf Davey and his wife Elsie when they married in 1946.

Alf Davey in 2013, aged 93.

Because the pilot had taken our names, we were presumed dead. It was ten days later when my family received a telegram from the Ministry to say I was alive!

Alf finally arrived in Southampton on the *Corfu* on 7 October 1945.

Once back on English soil, Alf travelled to see his family in Bungay and then returned to Blackburn to see Elsie. Regardless of her father's concerns about his future prospects, he and Elsie married in 1946 and went on to have two children together.

Despite all that he had been through in the previous three and a half years, Alf returned from captivity in reasonable physical health, the only obvious clues to his time in the Far East being the recurrent bouts of malaria from which he suffered from time to time and the fact that he was severely malnourished. Within six months of his return he was fit enough to look for work and took a job working on the roads for Blackburn Corporation, later finding work in the despatch department of the *Lancashire Evening Telegraph,* where he remained for over twenty years. There were, however, other reminders of his recent past – the nightmares from which he suffered since his return from the Far East and which, according to his daughter, Jennifer, never completely left him, so permanently were the memories of his experiences embedded in his mind. Talking about her father only months before he died, she explained, 'the bad dreams and flashbacks are something that can occur at any time – watching TV, reading a book, or not for any reason at all.'

Although for many years Alf seldom spoke about his experiences in the Far East, he began to do so at the age of eighty, after a friend who knew of his time as a prisoner of the Japanese asked if he would give a talk at a boys' school in Birkdale, Southport. The talk was so well received that Alf went on to speak to other groups, inspired as much by their willingness to listen as by his belief that future generations should be made more aware of what happened in a piece of history that receives too little attention. Asked about her father's feelings towards the Japanese, Jennifer said of Alf, then aged ninety-six, 'When people have asked him whether he would ever forgive and forget, he has always said, "never".' The horror of the ordeal which Alf endured in the Far East remained with him for the rest of his life, his memories an inescapable legacy of the captivity which caused untold misery and the deaths of thousands. It is a legacy he wished to pass on, in order that others are encouraged to learn and to keep alive the flame of remembrance, a sentiment echoed in the words he spoke after attending a Remembrance Sunday service two years before his death at the age of ninety-seven in 2017. 'It seems sometimes the conflict in the Far East is forgotten. I want more young people to know what happened. I will never forget.'

Chapter 12

Gunner William Henry Hall

135th Field Regiment, Royal Artillery (East Anglian)
(Hertfordshire Yeomanry) (TA)

Over forty years after he was liberated from a prisoner of war camp in Thailand, Henry Hall took the decision to return to the area where he had spent much of his three and a half years of captivity. He did so, he told his daughter, Christine, in order 'to bury a few ghosts'. Henry seldom spoke about his years as a prisoner of war, partly due to a need to spare himself the distress of mentally revisiting a part of his life with which he never really came to terms. 'He felt somewhat guilty about being a survivor,' said Christine. Henry was one of countless Far East prisoners of war for whom survival of an experience which killed so many of their comrades came at a price, for his memories of the manner in which so many men met their deaths remained with him for the rest of his life.

Prior to the outbreak of war, Henry had been working as a packer at a bed-manufacturing company in Croydon, not far from the village of Beddington in Surrey where he had been born in 1920. Home had been a cottage on the estate of the nearby manor house, where his mother had been in service and his father had worked as a farm labourer and, like many children of his generation, Henry's early life had been characterised by poverty and hardship. After receiving his call up papers, he was enlisted in the Royal Artillery in November 1940 and assigned to 135th Field Regiment after training.

Initially he was stationed at Catterick camp, where he became a driver, before further postings to Holt and Dumfries. It was following a further move to Macclesfield that command of the regiment passed to Lieutenant Colonel

Henry Hall, around 1939.

Philip Toosey, who, in the years which followed, went on to become a legendary figure for his ability to get the best out of the men under his command. Over the course of the following months, Henry underwent training on 25-pounder guns, and the regiment as a whole had their gunnery skills transformed and were deemed ready for the overseas posting which had been rumoured for some time.

On 29 October 1941, Henry boarded the *Sobieski* at Gourock, he and his comrades suspecting their destination to be the Middle East, given that their guns and vehicles had been painted a sand colour. It was only after they had crossed the Atlantic and transferred to the *Mount Vernon* that they discovered they were heading for Singapore. After disembarking on 13 January in the midst of a tropical storm, the men were ordered to head for Nee Soon, where they spent the next few days. Shortly afterwards, Henry found himself in Johore, the regiment having crossed the causeway to the Malayan peninsula in order to provide support for those troops already trying to halt the Japanese advance. Within days, however, it became apparent that they could do no more than slow down the enemy and they were forced to withdraw to the island. Due as much to the difficulties posed by the unfamiliar jungle conditions as to a breakdown in communications, Henry was listed as missing for a period but had rejoined his unit by the time the island fell to the Japanese on 15 February, and was captured together with the rest of his regiment. Two days later, Henry and his comrades marched to Changi, arriving at Roberts Barracks shortly before dusk. There they joined the multitude of troops already gathered, whose daily lives then became geared to restoring order out of the chaos into which they had been plunged in order to make their time as prisoners more bearable, from digging latrines to searching for firewood or scavenging for food, and much in between.

On 13 May, Henry was moved to River Valley Road camp, where he was to remain for ten months, assigned to working parties around the island. Most of the prisoners accepted the futility of any attempt to escape from Singapore; to the north lay the largely impenetrable jungles of the Malay peninsula, whilst Japan controlled the seas surrounding the island, added to which the chances of those who had been blessed with fair hair and colouring remaining hidden among the local population would have been remote. Nevertheless, attempts were made and, towards the end of August 1942, the Japanese demanded that all prisoners should sign an undertaking not to attempt escape, something which would have been in direct contravention of Army regulations. When the British commanding officer repeatedly refused to comply with this request, the Japanese response was brutal and uncompromising. All troops in the Changi area were ordered to assemble at Selarang Barracks with minimal provisions. Although Henry shared very little about his experiences in the Far East, he did record some of his recollections of captivity, albeit very briefly, some years later, having been asked to do so by another former prisoner. Of the events which later became known as the 'Selarang Incident', Henry noted:

> we were asked to sign a 'no escape' form. The officer in charge instructed us not to sign, so then the Japanese conscripted all the troops on a barracks square at Selarang, where normally about 900 troops used to billet. The Japs put all PoWs, about 16,000 there, where we had to sleep and feed. We also had to dig latrines.

Over the course of the following days, in the stifling heat and stench of the barracks square, dysentery cases increased. In the face of the continued refusal to sign, having already executed four men who had earlier attempted escape, the Japanese then threatened to fetch the sick and dying from the hospital to join the mass of prisoners already congregated, an act of barbarity which, for many, would have meant certain death. 'After four days, we signed', noted Henry, the British commanding officer having made it clear that they had done so only under duress. By the time this stand-off ended, Henry was one of many who had contracted dysentery, a disease which, in the appalling conditions of Selarang, was close to reaching epidemic proportions.

On 20 March 1943, Henry was among a party of over 500 prisoners who were transported to Thailand as part of D Force. A large contingent of Henry's regiment had already been sent to Thailand in October 1942 and, with news having trickled back to Singapore from various sources about the horrific treatment to which the prisoners were subjected, there were no longer any illusions about the move to the mainland being in any way beneficial to anyone but the Japanese. After arriving at Ban Pong, and disembarking from the metal trucks in which they had been entombed since leaving Singapore, the party was marched to Kan'buri. My father, Fred Cox, also arrived at Kan'buri in March 1943 as part of D Force and noted the overcrowding and poor sanitation which awaited them.

> We soon discovered that camp conditions were very basic, but by this time we had learned to expect nothing else from the Japanese. It quickly became obvious that there were not enough latrine trenches

The Selarang Incident, 1942. (Photo courtesy of Australian War Memorial)

to cope with such a large influx of men and that more would have to be dug. However, just as there were not enough huts for everyone to sleep in, such matters were not considered a priority by our captors.

Though many of the prisoners had had relatively little contact with the guards whilst at Changi, having been moved to Thailand they were under close scrutiny, and beatings as a result of some real or imagined slight to their honour became commonplace. 'When you passed a guard, you had to bow. If you didn't, the guard stood you to attention, then bashed you,' Henry later recalled. Already weak from malnutrition and vitamin deficiency before he left Singapore, Henry again became seriously ill. 'I had a bad attack of malaria at Kan'buri. There was only a small amount of quinine available,' he later noted. Few drugs were available to treat this and other diseases, save for those which could be illicitly obtained from the natives, or from the underground organisation which smuggled drugs, food and money to the prisoners at great personal risk.

At the beginning of April, Henry was moved upcountry to Wang Pho, where he joined the many prisoners already engaged in the construction of the Wang Pho viaduct. Despite the difficulties of taking the rail track around the side of the cliff and the perils of working some twenty to thirty feet above the river, the project was nearing completion when Henry's party arrived, but this was the height of the so-called 'speedo' period and no allowances were made for the increasingly poor state of health of the workforce, at immense cost to human life. Thus, although suffering from beri beri and struggling to walk, Henry was not only expected to work, but to work quickly, and later noted, 'while walking along, a guard walked behind me and every step he hit me with a bamboo stick'. Due to the prisoners' lack of resistance to infection as a result of their poor diet, the smallest scratch from bamboo frequently developed with alarming speed into a tropical ulcer, as Henry was to discover. In May 1943, Henry was moved upcountry to Kinsaiyok, where he was one of many tasked with excavating a path for the railway through extremely harsh terrain, working in pairs using 'hammer and tap', drilling holes to enable explosives to be placed in the solid rock face. The resulting piles of rocks would then be moved by hand by other groups of prisoners, many of whom no longer had any boots and worked barefooted upon unforgiving surfaces, the sharp rock adding to their injuries. In mid-1943 an outbreak of cholera swept down through the camps in the area in which Henry was based. This most feared of diseases was believed to have originated among some of the Tamil workers, whose lack of awareness regarding hygiene, coupled with the close proximity of the camps to the river, was all that was required for the disease to rapidly spread downstream. After three months at Kinsaiyok, Henry was moved farther north to Kroeng Krai, where there were many deaths from cholera, causing him to later record, 'my friend who slept next to me was sick. Later he went to the cholera hut.' Henry never saw his friend again. Many victims survived for no more than a few days; some died within hours of the first signs. Henry briefly noted of this time, 'when we got back from working we were detailed to go to the cholera hut to burn the dead on log fires,' a period of his captivity which was to remain a vivid memory.

As a result of Henry's deteriorating health, in early December 1943 he was among a party of approximately 300 prisoners at Kroeng Krai who were sent by train to Tarsao hospital camp, not all of whom survived the journey. He remained there until April 1944 when, suffering from beri beri and repeated bouts of malaria and dysentery, and with his leg ulcer still unhealed, he was moved to Nakhom Paton, a large hospital camp about thirty miles from Bangkok, which had been established at the beginning of 1944. The camp had been built to accommodate up to 10,000 sick men, but its much improved conditions came too late for the many thousands who had already died in the squalor of jungle camps farther upcountry. Henry remained at Nakhom Paton for the rest of his captivity. On 15 August, it was announced to the assembled troops that the Japanese had capitulated and that the war was over, and three days later the process of repatriating the many prisoners at Nakhom Paton began. Within the next few days Henry boarded a Dakota and was flown to a hospital in Rangoon, where he was given further medical treatment. Shortly afterwards, he boarded the *Corfu* to begin his voyage home, arriving at Southampton on 7 October 1945.

When he arrived back in England, Henry returned to his parents' home near Croydon and, after a period of recuperation, resumed work at the bed factory, where his employers, aware of his captivity in the Far East, had kept his job open for him. It was whilst working at the factory that he met the woman who later became his wife, Irene.

Henry Hall and his wife Irene when they married in 1947.

They married in September 1947 and went on to have two daughters and outwardly, at least, it appeared that Henry had come to terms with the events of the previous few years. Inwardly, however, he remained tormented by his experiences in captivity, as Christine explained.

> Dad used to have terrible nightmares, according to my mum, he would scream to 'leave him be', and Mum would hold him until he calmed down. This went on for the first two years of their marriage and gradually, with Mum's understanding and help, they were not so often.

The impact of having been so brutally treated by his captors in the preceding years also impinged upon Henry's working life and he was fortunate to have had sympathetic employers who made allowances for his past sufferings. According to Christine, her mother had told her that on one occasion Henry had punched a fellow employee who had sworn at him. 'Dad explained that for all the years he was sworn at and beaten by the Japs, no-one else was ever going to get away with it,' exhibiting behaviour that was, she said, completely out of character for her father who was, ordinarily, 'such a laid back, quiet, private man'. Henry's years as a prisoner of war also left him with a legacy of physical problems. In addition to suffering recurrent bouts of malaria following his return from the Far East, in 1963 he required treatment at the specialist FEPoW unit at Queen Mary's Hospital, Roehampton, where he was given a skin graft for the leg ulcer he had acquired some twenty years earlier at Wang Pho as a result of a tiny scratch from a bamboo pole wielded by a Japanese guard. He was also placed on a treatment programme for strongyloidiasis, which had, until then, remained undetected since his return from the Far East.

Whilst he rarely spoke about his experiences as a prisoner of war, at times Henry found it impossible to conceal the anger he still harboured towards his former captors, resulting in behaviour which caused distress to his young family. Christine recalled an occasion when, during a family holiday in Portsmouth when she had been about ten years old, her father had noticed the presence nearby of some oriental-looking naval officers, whom he assumed to be Japanese.

> Dad started shouting at them in a very angry manner which my sister and I had never witnessed before, shouting, 'I wish I had a spade to bash you with as you done to my friends'. My mum had to grab him to calm him down, as my sister and I were crying.

So vivid were Henry's memories of his experiences in captivity that the passage of time did little to heal his mental scars. When, at the age of sixty-eight, he was being brought out of an induced coma following surgery for a brain haemorrhage, the first face he saw was that of a Japanese anaesthetist. Christine recalled:

> I shall never forget the fear in my dad's eyes when he looked into this young man's face. He then started getting very agitated. I immediately knew the reason why and leant in to reassure my dad that he was not in a Japanese PoW camp, but in hospital, and then he calmed down. The doctor asked me whether Dad had suffered a head injury at all in his life, which I said yes to, as he told my mum that he used to be beaten by the Japanese soldiers about the head.

Against the odds, Henry made a full recovery and apparently could remember nothing of this incident later. Despite his unwillingness to talk to his family about his time in the Far East, Henry regularly attended FEPoW meetings, sometimes with his wife, apparently contributing little in the way of conversation about their shared past but seemingly deriving some comfort from simply being in the company of those who, like him, had experienced the horrors of captivity. Indeed, it was only at the suggestion of someone within the FEPoW group that he briefly, but somewhat reluctantly, put pen to paper to record a little about his experiences at the hands of the Japanese. 'The friends he met there were fellow FEPoWs from his regiment whom he stayed lifelong friends with,' said Christine.

In his late seventies Henry was diagnosed with terminal stomach cancer, suspected to have been linked to the malnutrition from which he suffered during his captivity. With only a short time to live, he spoke of some of the memories which still haunted him. According to Christine, 'he said that he would never forget to his dying day

Henry Hall in 1995, when he and his wife were invited to attend a Buckingham Palace Garden Party.

the horror of seeing the heads of PoWs impaled on bamboo poles along the camp's perimeter when walking to join the work parties.' Nor had he been able to banish the memory of having to dispose of the bodies of cholera victims. 'He said that as the bodies burned they would sit up and he then had to poke them down.' Henry died in February 2001, aged eighty. 'He wasn't afraid to die, he told us. He had already been to hell and back and survived.'

Chapter 13

Gunner William Harold George Pick

77th (Welsh) Heavy Anti-Aircraft Regiment, Royal Artillery (TA)

Until Bill Pick enlisted in the Royal Artillery in August 1940, his life had been lived almost solely within the confines of the small town of Cinderford in Gloucestershire, in what was then the heart of the coalmining area of the Forest of Dean. Born in 1915, he and his two siblings had grown up in Cinderford where their father worked in one of the many local mines. Although his was a happy childhood, the family's shortage of money meant that Bill had to forego the scholarship he had been offered to attend the local grammar school, a move which might, perhaps, have improved his prospects of employment and led him farther afield. As it was, after leaving school he had followed his father into the mines and his life had become embedded in this close-knit community; he joined the Cinderford Brass Band, through which he met his wife, Nell, and was employed as a colliery surface worker at one of the local mines by the time he received his call up papers. Just over four months after he and Nell married in April 1940, Bill enlisted and left the area for what was probably

Bill Pick and his wife Nell when they married in 1940.

Bill Pick in 1940.

the first time in his life to begin his military training, little knowing that within a few short years his horizons would be broadened in ways he could not possibly have imagined.

Initially based in South Wales, in August 1941, Bill's unit, 240 Battery, 77th (Welsh) HAA Regiment, Royal Artillery (TA), underwent further training at Blandford Forum and then moved to Headingley and Hawarden before travelling to Glasgow towards the end of November prior to going overseas.

On 7 December 1941, Bill boarded the *Warwick Castle* at Gourock, oblivious to where he was going or when he would return. Within hours of the voyage getting underway, as the familiarity of Cinderford and its inhabitants receded ever farther behind him, Singapore was coming under attack from the Japanese, ensuring that his fate, together with that of all of those on board, rested in the Far East. During his time at sea Bill wrote several letters to Nell, who at that time was working at the Royal Ordnance munitions factory in Hereford. On 27 January 1942, after the decision had been taken to divert the *Warwick Castle* to Java rather than sailing for Singapore, he wrote:

> I don't want you to worry about anything, as I shall be alright. You know me, I shall turn up like a bad penny some day and when I do, it will be to stay. You will never be able to get rid of me, even if you want to. Of course, we hear the news on the ship and I am very pleased with it lately. I don't think it will be long darling.

Clearly, he was trying to reassure his wife, and possibly himself, that all would be well, his note of optimism about the war suggesting that he and his comrades had no idea that they were experiencing their last few weeks of freedom.

The 77th HAA Regiment arrived in Tandjong Priok in Batavia on 3 February 1942, although much of their equipment and transport had been either damaged or mislaid in transit. After staying overnight in a Dutch army barracks, the regiment headed for Sourabaya, one group travelling by road, the other, including Bill, by rail. On 6 February their train collided with another which, although stationary at the time, was loaded with fuel and ammunition, with tragic consequences. Thirty members of 77th HAA Regiment died in the collision and almost a hundred others were left injured, many seriously. Though Bill walked away from the crash relatively unscathed, it left him with a lifelong aversion to rail travel. Three weeks after the fall of Singapore, after the Dutch also capitulated, on 8 March 1942 Bill was captured at Sourabaya. He was taken back to Batavia and held at Boei Glodok prison, where he spent the following week sharing the insanitary and overcrowded conditions of the cells. Bill was then among the many prisoners who were assigned to working parties, and put to work repairing bomb damage at the airfield until mid-April, when he was moved to Tandjong Priok, a large transit camp adjacent to the docks. He remained here for the following twelve months, existing on small rations of poor quality rice twice a day and very little else, hardly sufficient to sustain men who were employed repairing runways, picking up and loading unexploded bombs or unloading ships.

When Bill learned, in April 1943, that he was among those who were to be transported to the Spice Islands (also known as the Molucca Islands), he may have welcomed the prospect of leaving Tandjong Priok behind him. He was soon to discover, however, that he was entering a phase of his captivity which many of his fellow prisoners would not survive. After travelling by train to the docks at Sourabaya on 24 April 1943, Bill was one of a group of over 1,000 men who were transported to the island of Ambon in two ships, the *Mayahashi Maru* and the *Nishii Maru*. Although in later years Bill talked about his years as a prisoner of war, he said little about this particular experience, but one of those who accompanied him to Ambon was Aircraftsman William Mundy, who later recalled of the voyage:

> the holds had been converted with two tiers of bunks around the sides of the holds .... When we went aboard, the covers were over the holds and we only had a small trap door and steps to go down into the hold .... Food was passed down to us, as we were only allowed to go up singly to the deck, to the 'toilet' once a day, so you can imagine the conditions down in the hold.

After disembarking at Ambon, Bill and his fellow prisoners began their march to Liang, to the north of the island, where they were to be put to work on the construction of an airfield. After marching so far, the prisoners were allowed to stop for the night, after which, according to William Mundy:

> next morning, on the march again. You had to keep going, the Japanese would not tolerate any stopping for a rest .... In the evening of the second day we arrived at what was to be our 'camp'. The huts which were to accommodate us were still under construction, so we had to sleep on the ground in the open. The surface was rough coral.

Bill later briefly noted of Ambon:

> had a terrible time. No camp ready for us and in the wet season. Camp had to be made on top of a coral island. Great lumps of coral everywhere and very poor tools to break it away.

Elaborating upon this and recalling a typical day on Ambon, William Mundy noted:

> at about 8 am we were assembled in groups of fifty, we had to number off in Japanese and if we slipped up we received a kick, a punch or a blow to the head. Once the guard in charge of the group was satisfied that he had the correct number, we were marched off along the track for about two miles to a coconut plantation where some were allocated to chopping down the trees, others removing the roots. Fortunately, the roots of coconut trees are shallow in the ground. This left holes to be filled ... . The remaining groups were employed filling these holes. Some were provided with *chunkles*, like a wide Dutch hoe. The remainder were given a bamboo pole and a basket to hang on it. The task for those with the *chunkles* was to chip the coral surface where it was high and fill the baskets with the chipped material. When the basket was full it was carried on the pole between two prisoners. Woe betide you if the basket was not full, further blows to some part of the body.

Not only was work extremely difficult with only such basic tools, but many prisoners found their eyesight was badly affected by the glare from the sun shining upon the white coral. Nevertheless, over the course of the following months, existing on near starvation rations of a diet consisting almost exclusively of rice, Bill and his fellow prisoners slaved to build an airstrip. According to William Mundy, the camp doctors 'endeavoured to keep as many working as possible as the Japanese only allowed sufficient rice for those who were working and this had to be shared with those in the "hospital".' In order to supplement their poor diet, Bill's son, Alan, said his father 'told stories of killing and eating snakes, lizards and birds. Everything edible in the jungle was harvested despite the considerable risks of poisoning in this wholly unfamiliar environment.'

Having arrived on Ambon already weakened by vitamin deficiency and malnutrition, the following months saw the prisoners' health rapidly deteriorate even further, with death the outcome for many. 'Dysentery broke out immediately. Forty or fifty fellows died in the first few weeks,' wrote Bill, who later described to his son the grim reality of dealing with the deaths of fellow prisoners.

A particularly unpleasant story was of the repeated need to deal with the corpses of fellow prisoners who had died. There being no wood for coffins, the bodies were carried to their graves in palm leaves. In the hot conditions there was a need to bury the bodies quickly but there was little to prevent body fluids escaping onto those bearing the bodies on their shoulders.

Bill remained on Ambon for seventeen months, fortunate to have survived the experience when so many did not. 'Of the 1,000 men, 300 got back to Java,' he later wrote.

As horrific as the voyage from Java to Ambon had been, the return voyage in September 1944 was immeasurably worse. Due partly to the very real risk of the ship being torpedoed, the increasingly sick prisoners endured weeks at sea, battened down in the holds. Bill noted:

took us five days to get to Ambon and a month to get back. Skulking among the small islands for fear of American submarines. Dysentery on board. Many buried at sea. Eaten alive with lice. Killing lice took up a great part of the day. We lived in the hold and only came up for '*benjo*' (toilet). Always a queue.

After having returned to Java, Bill was then forced to endure another hellship voyage when, in January 1945, he was among a party of 1,000 prisoners who boarded an OSK Ferry bound for Singapore. Upon arrival, he was taken to Tanjong

The cemetery at Ambon, photographed by former Far East prisoner of war William Mundy.

Pagar camp near the docks where, towards the middle of 1945, Bill noticed a change of attitude in the guards, exemplified by the sudden issue of a stock of Red Cross parcels to the prisoners. Of this time Bill noted:

> except for the very limited food supply, it was the best time we had. And we stuck it to the end. Even had the first Red Cross parcels in three years. The Japs had kept them all that time and a lot of the food had got spoilt.

Given that by the time the camp was liberated in August 1945, Bill was severely emaciated it is, perhaps, not surprising that over forty years later, one of his most enduring memories of those first moments of freedom was that 'we got bread baked on the cruiser *Sussex*'.

On 15 September, Bill boarded the SS *Almanzora* to begin his journey home. Like thousands of others, he was returning to a world which had changed a great deal in his absence, and from a war which not all loved ones had survived. During the voyage home, which took nearly a month, he wrote two letters to Nell. In the first of these, postmarked 27 September 1945, he mentioned his brother, Sid, who had also enlisted in the army and had still been serving in the UK at the time Bill had been sent overseas. Unbeknown to Bill, Sid had followed him to the Far East and was serving in the 2nd Battalion Welch Regiment, in Burma, as part of the so-called 'Forgotten Army' when, on 18 May 1945, he received injuries from which he later died. In his letter to Nell, Bill also referred to his health, somewhat prophetically. 'I have been a little off colour since writing last. I caught a bad cold or something and I have been very chesty.' He was still clearly no better when he wrote the second letter nine days later. 'I can't seem to throw off this cold completely,' adding that despite the vast improvement in his diet, 'not very fat yet.' He concluded this letter to Nell with a PS. 'I am writing all this without having the least idea of my reception at home. You may intend to throw me out.' His words, in all likelihood, were intended to be jovial but, perhaps, also betray the kind of anxiety and apprehension many, including Bill, may have felt at the prospect of returning home to families with whom they had had little or no contact for three and a half years, and, moreover, returning as men irrevocably changed by all that they had experienced at the hands of their Japanese captors.

The *Almanzora* reached Southampton on 17 October 1945, at which point, no doubt, Bill's desire to return home as soon as possible is likely to have eclipsed any concern for his health. After the cursory medical check to which all those returning from the Far East were subjected, he made his way to Cinderford, where bunting had been hung in the street to welcome him. Anecdotal evidence from his family suggests that Bill weighed no more than six or seven stones when he arrived home and was, very clearly, not a well man. Shortly afterwards, he was admitted to Gloucestershire Royal Infirmary, where he was found to be suffering from tuberculosis, almost certainly as a result of the years he had spent in captivity, and for which he later received a pension. Although he was allowed home briefly towards the end of December 1945 to enable him to spend his first Christmas as a free man since 1941 with his family, he was then readmitted for extensive treatment at this hospital, after which he was admitted to Standish Hospital in Stroud, which specialised in the treatment of respiratory diseases.

When Bill's health finally permitted, he returned to work at the colliery near Cinderford where he was given a job in the workshop. Meanwhile, he and Nell settled down to family life and went on to have two sons. Over the course of the following years, although Bill's health improved considerably, he was required to attend hospital as an outpatient until the early 1950s, was registered as disabled and was to suffer respiratory problems for the rest of his life. In his later years Bill had also to contend with the trauma of losing both his hearing and his sight. Unlike many of his former comrades, Bill spoke readily of his time in the Far East but his experiences had, according to his son, affected not only his physical health but also his emotional wellbeing:

> Nell has told me that Bill suffered from loss of sleep, flashbacks and nightmares for many years after the war. Bill was more than happy to recount stories of his captivity to those interested. However, Nell was often concerned that these would bring on nightmares and she discouraged him.

Despite others trying to persuade him to do so, he showed no interest in joining FEPoW clubs or attending reunions. This was not, according to Alan, for any emotional reasons but because he simply wasn't sufficiently interested. He was, said Alan,

Bill and Nell Pick on their Golden Wedding Anniversary in 1990.

'a very quiet, almost introspective, kind and gentle person …. His war experiences would, I am sure, have given him a good sense of perspective and he demanded little.' As for his father's views about his former captors, said Alan, 'in the later years of his life he did not hold any animosity for the modern Japanese nation. Perhaps it would be going too far to say that he had forgiven the Japanese.'

The odds had been stacked against Bill surviving his captivity. In addition to the fact that many of those who sailed on Japanese hellships lost their lives, of the 4,110 servicemen who were sent to the Spice Islands, 2,827 of whom were British, fifty per cent never returned. Alan believes that a crucial factor in his father having survived captivity when so many perished was the fact that he had someone to come home to. 'He had something to live for, a young wife, a home, family and a future.' And, having survived, it seems clear that Bill's life centred firmly on his family life in Cinderford in the same way it had done before the war had torn him away. Despite the ill-health bequeathed to him by his time in captivity, Bill went on to live to the age of eighty-seven and died peacefully in his own bed on 11 November 2002, Armistice Day.

Chapter 14

Signalman Lewis Pope

Royal Corps of Signals

When Lewis Pope discovered a passion for music in his youth he had no inkling that it would one day prove to be his salvation. However, after returning from three and a half years of captivity as a prisoner of the Japanese, only by immersing himself in music did he find solace as he struggled to come to terms not only with his experiences in the Far East but also with a society which had little real comprehension of an episode of the war which had taken place half a world away.

Born in 1906 in Motherwell, Lanarkshire, Lewis's early life had been marked by tragedy and upheaval with the death of his mother soon after childbirth when he was two years old, followed by the arrival of two more brothers and another sister after his father's remarriage. Upon leaving school, although he took an apprenticeship as an armature winder, Lewis also took piano and organ lessons and eventually decided that his future lay in teaching music. After taking a job as an organist and choirmaster in Kirkcudbright, he began to give private piano lessons and to play at recitals and choral events, and it was at one of these that he met his wife, Grace. When they married in December 1939, although Britain was at war, there was no indication that little more than eighteen months later Lewis would be in the Far East and that Japan's subsequent intervention in the war would lead to the couple being separated for over four years.

Following his conscription into the Royal Corps of Signals, Lewis underwent his basic training in Yorkshire and although, for reasons of security, all correspondence was censored, he still managed to let Grace know wherever he was being posted by means of a series of code words which he used when writing postcards to her. By mid-1941 he had been sent to a holding battalion in Catterick but his subsequent posting in July was to take him farther afield than any other had done, when he was sent to the Far East. Having arrived in Singapore, Lewis took up his post at Southern Area Fortress Signals, which was responsible for internal communications within Singapore Island, based at Fort Canning. His daughter Felicity, with whom he shared very little of his experiences of captivity, recalled that 'he told me that they had been trained on the latest signals equipment but when they arrived in Singapore

Lewis Pope in 1941.

it was to find that what was there was not up to date'. As the Japanese worked their way down the Malayan peninsula at the end of January 1942 to launch their assault on the island, Lewis spent the following weeks frantically relaying and receiving information as various units tried to co-ordinate their efforts to shore up Singapore's defences but, on 15 February, he became one of the many who were taken prisoner. Shortly afterwards Grace was informed that he was missing, believed to be in Japanese hands, but it would be a further eighteen months before she received confirmation that he was still alive.

Whatever reluctance to talk about his ordeal Lewis showed in his later years, he had evidently felt very differently in October 1945. Within days of his return from the Far East, in direct contravention of the order given to all returning service personnel not to speak of their experiences at the hands of the Japanese, he gave an interview to a newspaper, determined to shed light upon the horrific treatment suffered by Far East prisoners of war. In his interview Lewis described how, after the capitulation of Allied forces, he had made the dispiriting march to Changi, where he spent the following six months, the reporter noting that the food had been 'of the worst possible description, an ordinary meal consisting of a tin of rice, and half a teaspoonful of sardines each, an ordinary tin of these having to be divided between fifteen men'. The report went on to say that Lewis had, however, described conditions generally at Changi as having been 'tolerable', owing to the fact that the camp had been under the administration of Allied forces, the prisoners having relatively little involvement with the Japanese. Compared to what followed, Changi would, indeed, have seemed tolerable. On 25 October 1942, Lewis was among a party of 650 prisoners, known as Letter Party X, who were sent to Thailand under the command of Lieutenant Colonel C.E. Morrison, 1st Battalion Leicestershire Regiment.

Detailing the journey Lewis had then taken to Thailand, the report went on:

> The prisoners were taken in cattle trucks, thirty-five in a truck, the journey lasting four days. Only eight meals were given in the four days, the normal ration being a little rice and some watery stew – 'more water than stew', as Mr Pope put it. No drinking water was supplied and when a train on the single track railway stopped at the prisoners' halting place the men, with one accord, made a concerted rush to the engine and greedily drank from the small trickle of water issuing from the escape pipe.

Two days after arriving at Ban Pong, Lewis and his fellow prisoners left the waterlogged conditions of the transit camp and were marched to Kan'buri, and then taken by barge to Chungkai, where they became part of the huge labour force toiling on the railway. The newspaper's account of Lewis's experiences continued:

> The prisoners were quickly given work to do, and particularly hard, arduous and, at times, dangerous toil it proved to be. Armed only with a *chunkle*, shaped something like a Dutch hoe, they were compelled to build embankments and bridges from dawn until dark every day, a continuous period of twelve hours.

Lewis spent over six months at Chungkai, before moving farther up the line to Tha Khanun in May 1943, where the problems presented by the terrain were exacerbated by the torrential rain of the monsoon. The report went on:

> Each man was given an allotted task in the morning and if that was not completed by the end of the day, the defaulters had to labour, sometimes until 2 am, until it was finished, or they had a heavier burden added to their next day's task.

Like many of the camps in the area, Tha Khanun was hit by cholera the following July. 'Although he was fortunate enough to escape this death dealing disease, Mr Pope suffered from malaria on several occasions and severe tropical ulcers,' it was noted. Lewis was then moved down the line to Kinsaiyok, heavy monsoon rain adding to the difficulties of shovelling and carrying earth from one place to another and inevitably slowing down each day's progress, to the fury of the guards who invariably reacted with violence. The report described Lewis's account of ill-treatment by one of the Japanese railway engineers who had, 'lashed him across the bare back with a bamboo cane. He was pelted until he fell unconscious to the ground, and when he recovered he was immediately put back to work.' Describing Japanese soldiers as 'sadistic', Lewis related that:

> violators of camp rules were immediately put into what the Japs called the 'No Good House' – a four feet bamboo cage – where they lived like beasts, hardly any food being given to them at all

adding that:

> even the smallest Nipponese soldiers apparently delighted in baiting, insulting and striking the tallest Allied prisoners. Nor was there the slightest thought of retaliation ... otherwise grim punishment for the entire camp, such as half rations for a week, would be inflicted. When a prisoner met a Japanese soldier

he had to bow meekly to him and smartly salute and woe betide the man who failed to do so.

Lewis remained at Kinsaiyok until February 1945, when he was among a party of men who were moved away from the Thai–Burma railway to Kachu Mountain Camp, Phetchaburi, to the south of Bangkok. He told the reporter that this entailed:

> a forced march into the jungle which lasted ten days …. The men marched a hundred and forty miles under a blazing sun. Many of the prisoners died on the road and those who survived were afflicted with huge ulcers on their feet and dangerous body sores, which severely sapped the small amount of energy they had left. They were given a little rice and salt fish for breakfast, with more rice and watery stew at night, after which they were forced to sleep outside, on many occasions in torrential rain. Arriving in Eastern Thailand, the prisoners constructed an aerodrome far up in the hills and thereafter assisted the Japanese to prepare defence positions to counter the expected Allied invasion …. The camp conditions were horrible in the extreme. Situated in paddy fields, which were often flooded, no sleep could be had for the bugs, lice and rats with which the place was infested.

Located in the shadow of the large mountain from which it got its name, the camp had no nearby river, the only source of water being a well which had been dug in the camp, and the shortage of water and poor sanitation gave rise to increasing sickness among the prisoners. As a result of the camp's remoteness, Lewis and his fellow prisoners, who had no secret radios, were isolated from the news that was passed up and down the camps on the railway, and therefore had no indication as to the status of the war. Lewis remained at Phetchaburi until the

A large cutting at Kinsaiyok, Thailand, showing the unforgiving terrain through which the prisoners had to build the Thai-Burma Railway. (Photo by kind permission of the Thai-Burma Railway Centre)

following July when he was moved to Nakhon Nayok, north of Bangkok, where he was among those put to work digging trenches, preparing tank traps and gun emplacements, apparently to counter the anticipated Allied invasion. Lewis told the newspaper that he and his fellow prisoners had been officially informed of the Japanese surrender on 17 August, and that 'a Union Jack was produced from some mysterious place and was at once hoisted to the flagpole while the Japanese guards gazed in wonderment at the strange scene.' On 8 September, Lewis left the camp for Bangkok, from where he was flown to Rangoon to undergo a medical examination. Finally, on 23 September, he boarded the SS *Indrapoera*, and arrived at Southampton on 18 October 1945.

After undergoing the routine medical check at which the majority of prisoners were reluctant to say anything which might delay their return home, Lewis, weighing just over seven stones, made his way back to Kirkcudbright. According to his daughter, a cousin who was present at her father's homecoming,

> remembered my dad coming off the train and walking home looking very thin and unshaven. Apparently he didn't want any fuss made and was a bit embarrassed about the bunting and things which had been hung up for his welcome home. He just wanted peace and quiet and to get back to as near normal as possible.

To this end, Lewis fell back on his love of music, became involved with the local church as choirmaster and organist and also trained as a teacher on a post-war scheme. He and Grace settled down to life in Kirkcudbright and their daughter arrived in 1947. However, the legacy of Lewis's years in captivity continued to be felt long after the bunting had been put away. For at least ten years after his return from the Far East he suffered recurrent bouts of the malaria which he had contracted in Thailand and was left with weakness in his legs from beri beri, something for which he was later granted a small disability pension. Lewis was also left with what was for him, perhaps, the cruellest of the physical reminders of his time in captivity as it affected his ability to play music. Felicity explained:

> I know he had several fingers broken in the camps. He could never achieve the final exams for the Royal College of Organists and he used to hum in frustration at a particularly difficult piece if his fingers were not as nimble as he hoped.

Felicity's childhood was littered with signs that her father's experiences in the Far East had remained with him.

Lewis Pope indulging his love of music in 1962.

I'm not sure when I realised my father had had a different sort of war. I think it just permeated. Obviously we never had rice in the house in any shape or form, even tapioca was a bit suspect. I know he ate every bit of food on his plate and I used to get into trouble if I left anything or got a bit fussy about food. My mum just gave me the things I liked to keep the peace. We went once on holiday and he was very upset when he discovered there was rice at the bottom of his plate of soup. Mum had to explain and ask for it to be taken away.

She added that her father hated waste.

We recycled just about everything and ended up with loads of screws, nails, etc. He always insisted we empty jam jars completely, scraped them out til they were almost clean and we used to have to get the very last bits out of ketchup and sauce bottles – 'add a wee bit of vinegar and shake'.

Felicity explained that there were other idiosyncrasies of her father's, which served to compound the feeling that his wartime experiences may not have been the same as those of the fathers of many of her contemporaries.

We used to go for picnics at the shore and he was frequently to be found wearing a towel as a sarong. You can imagine how he stood out from the other dads. He said he had got used to it in the war. As a young child before I went off to bed – and when he was growing elderly and had an afternoon nap – these were always prefaced by 'All men - *yasumi*!' (the Japanese term for 'rest').

Referring to one of the earliest published memoirs about Far East captivity, Felicity added, 'I also found myself reading bits of *The Naked Island* by Russell Braddon while others in my class were reading *Ann Frank's Diary*'.

For Lewis, as for many who had been exposed to the worst excesses of Japanese brutality and the death and disease of their prison camps, the adjustment to 'normal' life was also made immensely difficult due to others' failure to comprehend what they had been through. Felicity recalled her father having been asked by his brother, who had served as a major in the Army Catering Corps, 'why "none of your lot ever tried to escape"'.

I have never seen my father so angry and upset … . Eventually he said that they had been made to watch as two Australian lads who had been caught trying to escape were forced to dig their own graves and were then beheaded. I don't think my uncle had realised until then just how different life had been for those held by the Japanese in contrast with PoWs in Germany. Father had to explain that, for the Japs, you became a non-person once you surrendered and you were theirs to exploit as they wished.

As time passed, it became increasingly apparent that Lewis's mental health had been affected by his time in captivity. By the 1960s he had become head teacher in the music department of Kirkcudbright Academy. According to Felicity:

we went away every weekend to our caravan. It was not far from home and I think my dad liked to switch off from school. It didn't matter that I missed out on hockey matches etc. and all the other things my friends did at weekends. It was more important, I think, to keep Dad happy and this helped. All went well until we had a new rector in my last year at school. I was at university when my dad had a breakdown. He had come home in a terrible state. Something said or done by the rector had reminded him of one of the guards in the camp and he just broke …. He was on sedatives. Eventually his doctor decided that the best thing was for him to take early retirement, leave Kirkcudbright and get right away from any memories. So they uprooted themselves – quite a thought as my mother had never lived anywhere else but Kirkcudbright – and moved to the south coast of England.

Lewis Pope and his wife Grace on their Golden Wedding Anniversary in 1989.

In later life, Lewis did, to some extent, manage to come to terms with his experiences and find some sort of peace. He and Grace eventually joined a FEPoW group and, according to his daughter, he bore no animosity towards the present-day Japanese people, the love of music which had sustained him since he returned from the Far

East continuing to do so for the rest of his life. According to Felicity, 'music helped keep him calm. He frequently spent time listening to classics and withdrawing from the world.'

Lewis died in 1994 at the age of eighty-eight. It is a reflection of the extent to which his experiences as a prisoner of war remained with him that he was very specific about his funeral arrangements, as Felicity explained.

> I understood he had been quite ill in one camp. The doctors had put him on burial party duties until he was more recovered and could return to work. He used to shake his head at people travelling to see their loved ones' graves. He left instructions for a funeral with a Scottish minister and requested that no-one attend it. I think he felt that too many of his fellow companions had been denied proper burials.

Chapter 15

Corporal William Taylor

6th Battalion Royal Norfolk Regiment

During the three and a half years that Bill Taylor was a prisoner of war, the thought of going home to the wife he adored sustained him in a way that nothing else could have done. 'My darling, there has not been a day that I have not thought of you,' he wrote when his ordeal was finally over. In the bleakest moments of his captivity, when death, disease, starvation and ill treatment were part of the fabric of everyday life, the most powerful weapon that Bill possessed in his battle for survival was his desire to return home to his wife, Julia.

Finding strength in the face of adversity was nothing new to Bill, who was born in Ouseburn, Newcastle upon Tyne in 1915 to a single mother. Given the vast number of men who had lost their lives in the First World War, he was but one of countless children whose fathers were absent from their lives but, unlike many of them, he had never met his father. His mother's subsequent marriage and the acquisition of two half-brothers gave Bill's young life some stability for a time, which was then shattered by his mother's death from tuberculosis. Once he had completed his apprenticeship as a carpenter and joiner he decided to leave home to try his luck in London where the prospects for work seemed better. Soon after his arrival, not only did Bill manage to find work, but through his employment he met Julia. They married in September 1938, little knowing that within twelve months the world would be at war and that the intervention of the Japanese would cause them to be separated for nearly four years.

In June 1940, Bill enlisted in the Royal Norfolk Regiment and was assigned to the 6th (City of Norwich) Battalion. After spending the first few months of his training in Norfolk, where the battalion was engaged in coast defence, in January 1941 they were moved to Dumfries for more advanced training, and it was whilst he was

Bill Taylor and his wife Julia in 1939.

there that he learned that his first child had been born – a child who, tragically, lived only a matter of weeks. Over the next few months, training intensified, with the battalion moving first to Cheshire, and then to Lancashire, during which time Bill earned promotion to corporal. He then discovered that he was to be posted overseas and on 27 October travelled to Gourock, where he boarded the HMT *Duchess of Atholl*. After crossing the Atlantic to Canada, the battalion boarded the *Mount Vernon* at Halifax and sailed on to South Africa and then, finally, as a result of the deteriorating situation in the Far East, to Singapore, where they disembarked on 13 January after eleven weeks at sea.

With the Japanese pushing ever closer to the island, no time was spared in sending the battalion into the battle for Malaya. Bill later talked to his son, Peter, about the events which followed.

> As Dad told it, the regiment moved into action and ran into trouble very quickly, with the troops getting split up under heavy fire in the jungle area and communications breaking down. It was chaos. The patrol he was in was cut off from others and was treading lightly, avoiding the Japs where they could. Dad related crawling through a thicket to make an observation, only to be deafened by a Japanese mortar being fired only a few yards away. The next thing, his officer crested a ridge only to be immediately 'cut in half' by a Jap machine gunner; the Sergeant Major was also killed with the patrol's Bren-gun carrier. The reduced patrol withdrew into the jungle, cutting their way through at times. Dad was now the senior soldier of the patrol and he continued to try to link up with some other Brits. However, the jungle was relentless and finding a proper direction was very hard, not being able to properly observe the sun through the canopy .... As night approached they found themselves in a rubber plantation. They came upon an empty hut where the patrol gratefully took refuge and rest. Unfortunately, a native who informed the Japs of their location had observed the patrol. Subsequently, the hut was surrounded and Dad and his little patrol were now prisoners of the Japanese.

The hut where Bill and the other members of the patrol had been captured was located on the Pulai Rubber Estate in Johore and, on 7 February 1942, they were taken to Pudu Jail in Kuala Lumpur. Conditions inside the huge concrete and stone jail provided a brutal introduction to the treatment the men could expect as prisoners of the Japanese. Pudu had previously been a civilian prison and initially Bill and his comrades were held in what had been the women's quarters, which were overcrowded and insanitary. Conditions became even more difficult as the passing days brought a steady stream of new arrivals, men captured in battle or picked up shortly afterwards, many of whom were wounded and, like Bill, exhausted and starving, having been at the mercy of the jungle for days or weeks. Any hopes Bill may have had that he would not have to contend with these conditions for long were dashed a week after his arrival at the jail, with the news that Singapore had fallen. Several weeks later the Japanese opened up the main jail to the prisoners, which eased the overcrowding, by which time many of them were suffering from dysentery and a range of deficiency diseases, about which medical officers could do little given the Japanese refusal to provide any drugs, despite their ready availability.

Although a change of administration at Pudu in May 1942 saw the introduction of a canteen, allowing those who had money the chance to buy extra food and add desperately needed vitamins to their diet, this was of little help to those in most need of the extra vitamins, who were too sick to work and, therefore, received no pay. The prisoners had so little control over their lives that they no doubt derived enormous satisfaction from any acts of sabotage they were able to perform. On the questionnaire which liberated prisoners were later asked to complete by giving details of the camps at which they had been held, any incidences of ill treatment, and any acts of sabotage they had carried out, Bill noted that whilst at Pudu he had been engaged in 'destroying machine guns, British ammunition, mortars, cycles, lorries, busting up aero petrol and tampering with aircraft left unattended'. He later told Peter that he had at one time been assigned to a working party loading captured weapons onto lorries. 'He used to laugh about the fact that he would remove the firing pins from the guns and throw them away.'

Bill remained at Pudu Jail until 17 July 1942, when he was among a party of 109 British and Australian prisoners transported back to Singapore, where he rejoined his unit at Changi. The vast majority of the prisoners on the island who, unlike Bill, had not sampled life as a prisoner of war elsewhere, remained oblivious to the fact that whatever the shortcomings of Changi, conditions in a camp under British administration were immeasurably better than those which existed on the mainland, where the callous indifference of the Japanese to the prisoners' welfare became far more apparent. However, Bill's time in the comparatively civilised environment of Changi came to an end some eight months later when, on 19 March 1943, he was among a party of approximately 550 prisoners transported to Thailand under the command of Lieutenant Colonel G. Carpenter, 1st Cambridgeshire Regiment, as part of D Force. After arriving at Ban Pong, the party was marched to Kan'buri and, after two days' rest, moved on to Wang Pho, where the men joined the thousands of prisoners already being pushed to the limits of their endurance to complete work on the Wang Pho viaduct.

Bill remained at Wang Pho for the next two months, during which time he was assigned to a rail-laying party. Forced to work on a project aimed at enhancing the Japanese war effort, Bill later told his son that, like many prisoners, he did what he

The Wang Pho Viaduct, Thailand, photographed shortly after the war. (Photo by kind permission of the Thai-Burma Railway Centre)

could to undermine the ultimate success of the railway. 'He did say that they always put in very shoddy work when unobserved, leaving out bolts, etc.' The arrival of the monsoon season in April threatened to hamper progress, inciting the guards to ever greater brutality as 'speedo' took precedence over everything, regardless of the consequences. Constantly berated by their guards to work faster, inhuman treatment was commonplace.

> Dad said that he had been struck many times around the head with bamboo sticks; he thought that his poor hearing was due to these beatings. At one stage he thought he was going to die when made to kneel in front of a Jap officer brandishing his sword.

The following June, Bill was among a party of prisoners moved farther upcountry to Kinsaiyok, where they were put to work on jungle clearing and embankment building. Five months later Bill was moved down the line to Tarsao hospital camp. He later spoke of having suffered over a hundred bouts of malaria as well as having contracted dysentery a number of times. He remained at Tarsao until March 1944, when he was moved down the railway to Tha Muang, a larger hospital camp. By the following October, Bill's health had recovered sufficiently for him to be moved back up the line briefly to Tha Mayo before being returned two months later to Tha Muang.

Bill's days working on the Thai-Burma railway came to an end in mid-1945 when he was assigned to a large party of already exhausted, vitamin deficient and emaciated prisoners who were transported to Eastern Thailand for the purposes of building a road through the mountainous terrain between Pratchi and Mergui in Burma. Bill later told Peter that during his last few weeks at Pratchi, he and his comrades had noticed a change in attitude of some of the guards, the reasons for which they could only guess at. Awaking one morning in August to the realisation that the guards had disappeared, the prisoners then discovered the store of Red Cross parcels which the Japanese had stockpiled rather than distributing, the contents of which might well have saved the lives of those who would never enjoy the freedom which now beckoned.

Throughout their captivity, isolated from the rest of the world in a succession of camps, the value to the prisoners of any link with their loved ones at home was incalculable and Bill was more fortunate than many in that he received numerous letters from his wife. Knowing only that her husband had been taken prisoner as part of the 18th Division, Julia wrote to him regularly in the hope that the letters would somehow reach him and, in so doing, provided the kind of lifeline which prevented him from losing the will to live, often a vital element in the survival of the desperately sick. Now that he finally had the chance to do so, Bill wrote to Julia.

> My darling, I have waited so long for this moment when I could write down what I want to write. I am in a small camp ninety miles north of Bangkok waiting for a plane to fly us to India.

Employing typical British reserve, and clearly keen to downplay any concern for his health, he went on:

> I do hope, darling, that you are feeling well, as I am just now .... I received forty-three letters and cards since 1943 but never a photo, which I yearned for .... In a few more days we shall have been married seven years. I am going to have a party that day with my pals. I have always remembered that day, even though I have been miles in the jungle. I shall have some tea without milk or sugar, which has been a lucky man's drink all these years. The substitute for the cake will be something made from rice. Well, darling, I am using about the one and only pencil the Japs have not taken so I must close now as there is a queue for it. Your loving husband, Bill.

Bill was flown to Rangoon, where he received a medical check. He later told his son that he had asked the nurse who examined him if the years of malnutrition and disease would affect his chances of fathering children, voicing a fear which was shared by many of his comrades and which, sadly, for some was proved to have some basis. Declared fit to travel, Bill boarded the *Corfu* and began his journey home, via Colombo, from where he sent a telegram to his family. As the ship approached Southampton on 7 October, Bill later told his son that:

> a loud hailer message advised those on board that no firearms would be allowed into England and that anyone caught with one would face court martial. Dad said that all you could hear after that was the sound of splashes of weapons being thrown over the side.

Once home again, Bill and Julia resumed married life on the outskirts of London and in 1947 moved to Romford, Essex, where the birth of a son was followed by that of a daughter. Having been demobbed from the army, Bill relied on his carpentry and joinery skills to earn a living but found that his ability to do so over the next few years was hampered by extreme fatigue, coupled with pain and stiffness in his legs. Suspecting that his condition was in some way connected to his time in the Far East, Julia contacted the Red Cross, who arranged for him to be admitted to the specialist FEPoW unit at Queen Mary's Hospital, Roehampton, in 1950. Bill was diagnosed as having a parasitic worm infection, contracted during his time in Thailand, and as suffering the long-term effects of vitamin deficiency. After receiving treatment, he was subsequently awarded a disability pension in respect of infective hepatitis, dysentery, malaria, intestinal worm infection and residual nervous symptoms attributable to his time in captivity. Further medical investigation at hospital in Woolwich was necessary in 1982 due to a resurgence of the pain and stiffness in his legs, together with chronic bronchitis. In addition, the partial deafness from which Bill had suffered since his return from the Far East, which he had long believed to be a consequence of the numerous beatings around the head he had received from the Japanese, was also officially recognised in 1987 as attributable to his time as a prisoner of war.

Unlike many of those who returned from captivity in the Far East, Bill was not troubled by nightmares about his ordeal. This may have been partly due to his having ignored the instructions given to all returning prisoners not to talk about their experiences at the hands of the Japanese. His tendency to talk at some length about the things he had been through was, however, sometimes at the cost of marital harmony, as Peter explained.

> Dad always talked about his experiences, to the point that mum wanted to shut him up. But I am now aware that the fact that he talked of his experiences was therapeutic for him and probably stopped him from having nightmares.

Bill found an additional outlet for his need to talk in his occasional attendance of FEPoW reunions, sharing memories of past experiences with those able to empathise. According to Peter, his father tended to focus on the ways in which he

```
                    DEPARTMENT OF HEALTH AND SOCIAL SECURI
(DHSS)              NORTH FYLDE CENTRAL OFFICE (WAR PENSION
                                        Norcross, Blackpool, FY5 3

                                        Telephone: CLEVELEYS 856
In any reply please quote:                      STD Code 0253-856

      M2/560397                         18TH MARCH 1987


            MR W TAYLOR
```

Dear Sir/Madam,
The Department have decided to continue the present assessment of your disablement unaltered from   1.04.87   to   31.03.91
Your war pension is based on an interim assessment of the degree of disablement of 30   per c arising from   MALNUTRITION AND PRIVATION WITH HELMINTHIASIS
      (ANKYLOSTOMES) AND RESIDUAL NERVOUS SYMPTOMS, INFECTIVE
      HEPATITIS, DYSENTERY, MALARIA, BILATERAL SENSORI-NEURAL
      DEAFNESS

If you have any question about this assessment or you consider that it is not appropriate to your disablement, please write to me at the above address.

You have a right of appeal to an independent Tribunal if you are dissatisfied with the assessment. Details of this right for which there is a time limit are given overleaf.

May I remind you that the War Pensions Welfare Officer will be pleased to assist you on pension or other matters. Please do not hesitate to get in touch with him about any problems or difficulties on which you would like his help or advice. The War Pensions Welfare Service operates through the local offices of the Department. You can get the address of your nearest local office at the Post Office.

                                        Yours faithfully,

                                        L PARSONS

Form MPB 239C (M) (S)   FOR HEAD OF WAR PENSIONS BRANCH

Bill Taylor's pension assessment in 1987, showing the long-term effects of captivity upon his physical health.

and his comrades had managed to find humour in the darkest of times, rather than dwelling on the more horrific aspects of captivity. He described his father as a very gregarious man, and very much an optimist, aspects of his character, he believes, to which his father's survival of an ordeal which killed so many others may at least in part be attributed.

Whilst Bill may have found talking about his ordeal to be therapeutic, neither this, nor his positive outlook upon life did anything to dilute the bitterness he felt towards

Bill and Julia Taylor on their Golden Wedding Anniversary in 1988.

his former captors. 'For as long as I can remember, he would never eat rice, even the Ambrosia cream type. Nor would he knowingly buy anything that appeared to be made in Japan,' said Peter, adding that 'the main thing that stayed with dad was the inhuman treatment …. He had been scarred by the experiences he had endured and maintained a hate for the Japanese for the rest of his life.' Bill died in 1999, at the age of eighty-four, three years after the death of his wife, whose letters to him during the long years of his captivity had been so instrumental in keeping hope, and him, alive.

Chapter 16

Sergeant Robert John Rutherford

9th Battalion Royal Northumberland Fusiliers

Following the fall of Singapore on 15 February 1942, other than having been notified that he was missing, Bert Rutherford's mother received no further news of him at all until May 1943, when she learned that he was a prisoner of war. She had written to him every week without fail since he had been posted overseas and continued to do so throughout his captivity, just one of many mothers agonising about the fate of sons lost, in some cases forever, to a war on the other side of the world. However, her anxiety extended not solely to one son caught up in the chaos of war in a foreign land, but to two; she wrote not just one letter each week but two. Because not only had Bert been sent to the Far East, but so had his brother Tom.

Born in 1919, Bert was the youngest of three brothers brought up on a farm, near the village of Mindrum, Northumberland, where the boys' father worked in the stables as a groomsman. Shortage of money meant that Bert was unable to accept the offer of a scholarship to the grammar school, with the result that upon leaving school he instead served an apprenticeship as a stonemason and in 1936 joined the Territorial Army. Following the outbreak of war in 1939, Bert and Tom were called up to serve in the 9th Battalion of the Royal Northumberland Fusiliers. Assigned to Z Company of the 9th, a machine-gun battalion, they were based in Berwick. After undergoing six months basic training, in April 1940, appropriately, on St George's Day, the brothers left Southampton to

Bert Rutherford, around 1940.

join the British Expeditionary Force in northern France, where they saw action against German troops, and were evacuated from Dunkirk at the end of May.

The following month the battalion reassembled in Launceston, Cornwall, where, after further training, they were engaged in coast defence, before moving to the Scottish borders in January 1941 for intensive training. Following a further move to Cheshire in May, Bert, who had been promoted to sergeant, learned that he and his brother were soon to be sent overseas, their destination rumoured to be the Middle East. On 30 October 1941, Bert and Tom boarded the *Warwick Castle* at Liverpool, bound for Nova Scotia, where they transferred to the USS *Orizaba*, before continuing their voyage eastwards, via Cape Town and Mombasa, arriving at Bombay on 6 January, almost a month after Japan had entered the war. They were then transported to Deolali, north of Bombay, to undergo two weeks of intensive training and acclimatisation. Once back in Bombay, the battalion boarded the SS *Félix Roussel*, aware now that their destination was Singapore.

For Bert and his brother there was to be no gentle introduction to the conflict with Japan, as the ship came under attack by twenty-seven Japanese aircraft on the approach to Singapore, the two bombs which hit the *Félix Roussel* leaving two fusiliers dead and fourteen wounded. Later the same day, 5 February, 1942, the battalion disembarked at Keppel Harbour under cover of darkness. Almost immediately, others took their place as the ship filled with women and children, evacuees fleeing from the advancing Japanese, as well as RAF personnel who had been ordered to leave. Z Company was ordered to move to the naval base at the north of the island and for the following ten days Bert and his brother were heavily involved in the action. By the time the battle for Singapore ended, Z Company had lost several men and was located at Mount Pleasant. Bert spoke little in later life about the events which followed, but one of those who was at his side during the fighting later recalled how they had reacted with disbelief to the order to cease fire, until they discovered their company commander, Captain Henry McCreath, attaching a white mosquito net to a flagpole and were told of the surrender. With the battle over and a reluctant acceptance dawning upon Bert and his comrades, they watched as the Japanese approached, kicked their machine guns in rage, and enquired, by way of gestures, which of the men were machine-gunners, to which all, including Bert, responded that they were truck drivers. The men were assembled and ordered to undergo the humiliating march to Changi where they discovered that, due to the sheer volume of prisoners already amassed there, they were among those allocated an area in the open, only later acquiring tents which offered some shelter from the heat and the rain.

Bert and his brother had trained and served together since their enlistment in 1939 but the early days of their captivity saw them separated. By the end of February

Tom had been moved to a camp at Keppel Harbour, whilst Bert was assigned to a working party repairing damaged buildings elsewhere, the Japanese wasting no opportunity to exploit prisoners' building skills. Whilst the brothers were separated they did whatever they could to stay in touch by writing letters which were passed onto them by fellow prisoners, something which risked punishment for all concerned had they been discovered. It is clear from these brief notes, written in pencil on whatever paper could be found, that sickness, work and shortage of food were the dominant features of their day to day life. On 10 July 1942, Tom, whose letters were the only ones to survive, wrote from Keppel Harbour to his brother:

> Dear Bert, I am writing this on the chance of getting it to you somehow or other …. Most of the lads are doing dock work, except joiners, bricklayers and plasterers. They sent Ted and I out as brickies, but since then we have also been plastering and tiling as well. We built three baths at Jap HQ (more like sheep dippers but built to Jap plans) …. In between times we tiled four small roofs and went around all the rooms, patching up the plaster …. This firm doesn't pay big wages, ten cents a day, but Ted and I can always manage a small loaf and egg each at night. The grub here is a lot better than Changi but far behind my idea of a feed.

Another letter to Bert, written in August 1942, hinted at the uncertainty with which the prisoners were forced to live.

> A lot seem to be going away to Japan, a boat load went past today again. Some of the lads seen Beckwith-Smith[*] on the dockside and he said there would be no British troops left on the island in thirty days' time, so it looks as if we may all be going.

It is clear from Tom's letters that he was receiving replies from Bert, who had been back in Changi since July and was evidently in better health than his brother. Having succumbed to dysentery and suffering the effects of vitamin deficiency, Tom wrote, 'at last I am allowed up but I feel pretty weak on my legs, but it will just take a little time to get my strength back again.' There was, however, little to aid prisoners' recovery, a letter written shortly afterwards noting:

> I am back in bed again owing to weak legs. Both them and my hands are numbed, as you will see by the writing. The MO says it will just take time, and there isn't anything to hurry out for.

---

[*] Major General M.B. Beckwith-Smith, commander of the 18th Division. In August 1942, he and other senior officers were moved from Singapore to Formosa (now Taiwan).

In November 1942 many of the 9th Battalion were sent to Thailand, a fact which must have been a cause of anxiety to Tom, who wrote seeking reassurance that his brother was still on the island and was clearly too ill to have been included in the draft himself.

> I hear you are not away up the mainland, so I am hoping it is true and trust you get this OK … . I had dysentery for about a week. I lost a good bit of flesh through it …. The MO won't let me up yet. Hope to see you soon.

Bert was, indeed, still in Singapore, perhaps having requested to remain with his sick brother on the basis that the survival of one or other would be greatly increased by their being reunited and facing whatever ordeals lay ahead together.

Both Bert and his brother remained in Singapore until 15 May 1943, when they were among a group of 600 British, 300 Australians and fifty American prisoners, known as J Force, who boarded the *Wales Maru*, bound for Japan. By this time, fifteen months into their captivity, ill-health among the prisoners had become the norm, varying only by degrees. Many of the least sick among their huge pool of labour had already been relocated by the Japanese and, by the standards of any civilised nation, all of those remaining would have been judged to be hospital cases. Conditions on the *Wales Maru* did nothing to improve the health of those on board, with little food or water provided by the guards and with many of the men who were tightly packed into the holds suffering from dysentery and unable to reach the few *benjos* provided in time. The prisoners were allowed on deck for brief periods twice a day, when they took the opportunity to collect buckets of sea water to use for bathing, but the hatches were closed whenever it rained, giving them no relief from the overpowering stench in the holds. During the last days of the voyage the *Wales Maru* was attacked by the American submarine USS *Tinosa*, whose torpedoes apparently only narrowly missed their target. The ship, however, had sustained damage in the urgency to escape attack and began to let in water, to the understandable terror of those below decks. Finally, on 7 June, twenty-two days after leaving Singapore, the *Wales Maru* reached Moji, Japan.

Having disembarked, the prisoners were divided into groups, after which Bert and his brother found themselves boarding a train to an unknown destination. In marked contrast to the kind of journeys experienced by many of their fellow prisoners who had been sent to Thailand, this was a passenger train, one intended for human cargo, albeit one on which the blinds were kept drawn throughout the journey. Several hours later the prisoners arrived at Mizumaki in Fukuoka Prefecture, on the southern island of Kyushu. From there they were taken to Fukuoka Camp No. 15B*, where the vast majority of the other prisoners were Dutch, and where they were to be held

---

* The camp was renamed Fukuoka No. 9D in December 1943, then No. 6D in August 1945.

for the remainder of their captivity. Like many of the other camps to which prisoners transported to Japan were sent, Fukuoka 15B was located in a mining area. At the Takamatsu Coal Mining Company the prisoners worked in three continuous eight-hour shifts, often deep underground and in dangerous circumstances. In mid-1942, whilst still in Singapore, Tom had written to his brother, 'I don't think we will be prisoners for that long,' little knowing that it would be a further three years before he and his brother would taste freedom and that they would spend twenty-seven months of their captivity working as coalminers in Japan. Accommodation at the camp consisted of ramshackle two-storey wooden buildings, each shared by about eighty prisoners, the only concession to some kind of comfort being straw mattresses on the floor.

By the time the cold winter months arrived the prisoners had been issued with tunics and trousers to replace their tropical kit, but a combination of exhaustion, malnutrition and a lack of medical provision soon resulted in widespread sickness and many deaths, and ill-treatment by the guards was commonplace.

Despite the relatively close proximity of Nagasaki to Mizumaki, the prisoners at Fukuoka 15B were not aware of the dropping of the atomic bomb on 9 August 1945, nor that Japan had subsequently admitted defeat, until a change in the general demeanour of their captors allowed them to hope that their captivity was coming to an end. Within days of receiving official news of the surrender, United States forces dropped relief supplies by parachute to sustain the prisoners until such time as

Severely emaciated PoWs at Fukuoka camp, Japan in 1943/44, including Bert Rutherford (seated in centre) and his brother Tom (standing to Bert's right).

ALLIED PRISONERS

レンゴウグンホリョヘ

The JAPANESE Government has surrendered. You will be evacuated by ALLIED NATIONS forces as soon as possible.

Until that time your present supplies will be augmented by air-drop of U.S. food, clothing and medicines. The first drop of these items will arrive within one (1) or two (2) hours.

Clothing will be dropped in standard packs for units of 50 or 500 men. Bundle markings, contents and allowances per man are as follows:

BUNDLE MARKINGS

50 MAN PACK	500 MAN PACK	CONTENTS	ALLOWANCES PER MAN
A	3	Drawers	2
A	1-2	Undershirt	2
B	22	Socks (pr)	2
A	4-6	Shirt	1
A	7-9	Trousers	1
C	23-30	Jacket, field	1
A	10	Belt, web, waist	1
A		Capt, M.D.T.	1
B	12-21	Shoes (pr)	1
A	1-2	Handkerchiefs	3
C	32-34	Towel	1

BUNDLE MARKINGS

50 MAN PACK	500 MAN PACK	CONTENTS	ALLOWANCES PER MAN
B	10	Laces, shoe	1
A	11	Kit, sewing	1
C	31	Soap, toilet	1
C	4-6	Razor	1
C	4-6	Blades, razor	1
C	10	Brush, tooth	1
B	31	Paste, tooth	1
C	10	Comb	1
B	32	Shaving cream	1
C	12-21	Powder (insecticide)	1

There will be instructions with the food and medicine for their use and distribution.

C A U T I O N

DO NOT OVEREAT OR OVERMEDICATE   FOLLOW DIRECTIONS

INSTRUCTIONS FOR FEEDING 100 MEN

To feed 100 men for the first three (3) days, the following blocks (individual bundles dropped) will be assembled:

3 Blocks No. 1
(Each Contains)

2 Cases, Soup, Can
1 Cases Fruit Juice
1 Case Accessory Pack

1 Block No. 5
(Each Contains)

1 Case Soup, Dehd
1 Case Veg Puree
1 Case Bouillon
1 Case Hosp Supplies
1 Case Vitamin Tablets

1 Block No. 3
(Each Contains)

1 Case Candy
1 Case Gum
1 Case Cigarettes
1 Case Matches

3 Blocks No. 2
(Each Contains)

3 Cases "C" Rations
1 Case Hosp Supplies
2 Cases Fruit

1 Block No. 7
(Each Contains)

1 Case Nescafe
1 Sack Sugar
1 Case Milk
1 Case Cocoa

1 Block No. 10
(Each Contains)

3 Cases Fruit
2 Cases Juice

Notification received by the PoWs informing them of the Japanese surrender and air-drops of supplies.

they could be recovered. Hours before doing so, they dropped leaflets informing the prisoners that their incarceration was at an end. How sweet the following words must have seemed: 'The Japanese Government has surrendered. You will be freed by Allied Nations forces as soon as possible.' However, the accompanying instruction,

```
                    U.S.S. LUNGA POINT (CVE 94)

TO OUR PASSENGERS:

     I am certain that I speak the sentiments of all hands when I say to you that
the part we are playing in getting you home is by far the most satisfying operation
of our career. We have been on the way to you for over a year via Leyte, Lingayen
Gulf, Iwo Jima and Okinawa. Shooting down Kamikazes and demolishing enemy install-
ations brought us great personal satisfaction because it hastened the end of the war
and your release. Therefore, we want you to feel perfectly at home while on board.

     There are certain Ship's Regulations that I would like to call to your attention,
probably the most important being that smoking is not allowed on the hangar deck.
You may, however, smoke on the fantail or the flight deck. Butt Kits are provided
on the flight deck. Use them; do not throw butts over the side. Also, due to
interference with the operations and routine of the Ship it is requested that
passengers do not wander around the ship other than to the flight deck, fantail and
mess hall.

     The head (toilet) assigned to our passengers is on the deck below the hangar
deck opposite the lanudry. It may be reached by going down the ladder from the
fantail. Also there are temporary head and shower facilities on the fantail.

     Meal schedule for passengers is as fellows:

          Breakfast  0700
          Dinner     1200
          Supper     1730

     You will eat after the crew finishes - do not line up until word is passed.

     A Petty Officer has been assigned to each block of passengers to help you in
any way he can. Do not hesitate to call on him if he can assist in making you more
comfortable. Also an Officer will be on watch at all times on the hangar deck.

     In order to expedite repatriating you gentlemen it may become necessary to
billet two men to a bunk necessitating your sleeping in shifts. This will only be
for a short run, though, and will mean all of our ex-P.O.W.'s will be returned to
more comfortable surroundings faster, and we know thats what you want.

     On behalf of all hands I wish to extend you a warm welcome aboard and to ex-
press the hope that you will soon be re-united with your loved ones and enjoying
the privileges of citizenship which you so richly deserve.

                                                    W. R. HOLLINGSWORTH,
                                                    Captain, U.S. Navy,
                                                    Commanding
```

Letter to liberated PoWs on board the USS *Lunga Point* from the ship's Captain.

'do not overeat or overmedicate' must have seemed strangely alien to men who had had the opportunity to do neither for a very long time.

Some two weeks later, Bert and his brother were among the 117 British prisoners who had survived their captivity at a camp where seventy-four of their fellow prisoners had died, and for which three of the Japanese were later found guilty of war crimes and executed.

After travelling by train to Nagasaki, Bert and Tom boarded the USS *Haven*, an American hospital ship, where they received medical attention. Beginning their long journey home, on 20 September they then boarded the USS *Lunga Point* and sailed via Okinawa to Manila. In a letter welcoming the PoWs on board, the captain of the *Lunga Point* pointed out, in a somewhat apologetic tone, 'in order to expedite repatriating you gentlemen, it may become necessary to billet two men to a bunk, necessitating your sleeping in shifts,' something which is unlikely to have troubled men for whom the mere provision of a bunk would surely have seemed a luxury, having endured the horrific conditions of a Japanese prison camp for the previous three and a half years.

After reaching Manila, Bert and his brother boarded the USS *Marine Shark* on 10 October and sailed via Honolulu to San Francisco, disembarking on 1 November. They then travelled by train to New York where they boarded the RMS *Queen Mary*, finally sailing into Southampton docks on 18 November 1945.

When Bert and Tom arrived back home in Mindrum on 22 September, relatives recall that their own mother did not recognise them. At well over six feet tall, Bert still weighed only six stones upon his arrival home, despite the much improved diet of the previous few weeks. Not only was he emaciated but vitamin deficiency had left him with rotting teeth, and the leg ulcers which he had acquired had still not healed and required treatment. It also became clear as time passed that prolonged malnutrition had left him with enduring digestive problems, which necessitated treatment over a number of years at Queen Mary's Hospital, Roehampton. Meanwhile, it was at a dance which had been organised to welcome home the returning prisoners of war that Bert met his future wife, Hazel. They were married in 1949, settled down to life in Crookham, Northumberland, and their son was born the following year.

Having been discharged from the army, once Bert's health had recovered sufficiently he returned to stonemasonry and secured a job with a local building firm, work which he continued to do until he eventually retired.

According to his son, John, Bert spoke only fleetingly of his experiences in the Far East to his family, and cited as an example an instance during the 1970s when, prompted by his son having answered the door to a religious group, Bert had told him that during his captivity, he and others had resorted to using the pages of the Bible as smoking material, explaining that although doing so troubled their consciences:

> They eventually felt that it would be acceptable to smoke the fly leaf because there was nothing on it, then the dedication because that wasn't really a bible story, then the contents because they all knew where everything was,

Bert Rutherford and his wife Hazel when they married in 1949, together with Bert's brother Tom and Hazel's sister Rena.

> then Genesis because everybody knew that story, and so on, until they found a justification for smoking the whole of the Old and New Testaments.

The fact that Bert was a founder member of the local branch of the FEPoW association suggests that he perhaps tended to reserve discussions of his experiences in the Far East for the comradeship of FEPoW meetings. Similarly, his membership of the local part-time fire brigade perhaps offers clues as to how he learned to cope with memories of the more distressing aspects of his captivity. John explained:

> he was clearly moved by some of the tragedies he witnessed but he never crumbled in the way many people, understandably, would have done. I am sure that he learned, in a way that most of us without his experiences in Japan

cannot, how to compartmentalise such horrific events and prevent them from leaking out and impinging on the rest of his life. 'Ay well, you just have to get on with it' was a frequent refrain.

By and large, it appeared that outwardly, at least, Bert did 'get on with it'. Neither he nor his brother received any form of pension in recognition of the damage to their health whilst serving in the army, with the result that, 'in the rare times he mentioned his wartime experiences, he was as bitter about the British Government as he was about the Imperial Japanese Army,' said John. Tellingly, towards the end of Bert's life, when he was admitted to hospital with terminal cancer, a time when he needed peace, the family were told that the events of some fifty years earlier were evidently preying on his mind and causing nightmares. 'The horrendous experiences of Japan were still haunting him at that stage of his life,' said John. Bert died at the age of seventy-two, on 5 February, 1992, fifty years to the day since he had arrived in Singapore.

Chapter 17

Private Eric Gordon Barnes

2nd Battalion Argyll & Sutherland Highlanders (Princess Louise's)

When Eric Barnes decided to enlist in the army in March 1936 he was very clear about which regiment he wanted to join, even though, as a Londoner, the Argylls would not have seemed the most obvious choice. They were, he said, his 'top regiment' and he would do whatever was necessary in order to join them, even if this entailed re-inventing himself. Employing the kind of singlemindedness and determination that would serve him well in years to come, twenty-year-old Eric, known to everyone as 'Barney', left London behind him and headed for Scotland where, having lied about where and when he was born and claiming to have no next of kin, he enlisted in the 2nd Battalion of the Argyll and Sutherland Highlanders.

Born in 1916, the youngest of four brothers, Barney was brought up in Tottenham, North London. After a somewhat unsettled childhood, Barney left school at the age of fourteen and took a job as a bricklayer's labourer. Within a few years, with little to keep him at home and keen to escape an impoverished lifestyle, he set his sights upon joining the army, specifically, the much-respected Argylls, with their motto 'Sans Peur' – without fear. After undergoing basic training at Stirling in Scotland, Barney was posted overseas in March 1937 to India. The following year he was sent to Waziristan on the North West Frontier of India and remained there until September 1939, when the battalion was moved to Singapore. Unlike many of the men who would soon find themselves transported to the Far East to defend British interests against the growing threat posed by Japan, the 2nd Battalion of the Argylls were well prepared for what was to come. Prior to Japan's invasion of Malaya in 1941, Barney and his comrades had received months of intensive training in jungle warfare in Malaya, earning them the nickname, the 'Jungle Beasts'. Nevertheless,

Eric 'Barney' Barnes in 1941.

in January 1942, having fought a courageous rearguard action and inflicted heavy casualties upon the Japanese, the battalion incurred substantial losses following the Battle of Slim River. Many of those who survived the battle returned to Singapore, but Barney was not among them and, having disappeared into the jungle to evade capture, was listed as missing. He remained at liberty until 15 April, when he was finally captured in Negeri Sembilan on the western coast of the Malayan peninsula south of Kuala Lumpur and, after initially being held in police barracks, was then taken to the city's Pudu jail.

The vast building, constructed in the shape of a Saint Andrew's cross had, over the course of the previous weeks and months, become home to several hundred British and Australian prisoners. Having had to exist for weeks upon only what the jungle had been able to provide, many, like Barney, were starving and exhausted by the time they found themselves in Japanese hands, the manner of their capture having left some with little more than the clothes they stood up in. Life inside Pudu certainly provided no comforts and Barney joined a prison population suffering the effects of untreated tropical diseases and vitamin deficiency and among whom there had been many deaths, thanks in no small part to a diet almost exclusively of rice and the continued refusal of the Japanese to provide any drugs. He was at least spared having to endure the gross overcrowding which had existed in earlier months prior to the Japanese opening up the main wings of the prison to accommodate the continuing influx of men. Fuelled only by a meagre amount of food, Barney was one of those who were assigned to working parties repairing the bridges which had been damaged during the conflict. Those who did not work were denied even these pitiful rations but, aside from a selfish few, here, as at many camps, the kinship born of the collective struggle for survival made it unthinkable for those who had food not to share it with those who had none.

Tha Makhan camp, Thailand. (Photo by kind permission of the Thai-Burma Railway Centre)

On 14 October 1942, some six months after his arrival at the jail, Barney was among a group of 150 Argylls who were crammed into metal goods trucks and transported to Thailand to join the workforce being amassed for the construction of the Thai-Burma railway. Four days later Barney and his fellow prisoners arrived at Tha Makhan.

The camp was under the command of Colonel Philip Toosey, upon whom the fictional character at the heart of the film, *Bridge on the River Kwai* was somewhat erroneously based. Colonel Toosey had been instructed by the Japanese that the prisoners were to build two bridges over the River Mae Klong, firstly a wooden bridge, and then, a hundred metres or so upstream, a more permanent structure of concrete and steel capable of withstanding the swell of the river in the monsoon season. Barney was among the many increasingly weak and disease-ridden men who, over the following months, built the wooden bridge entirely by hand, using only the most primitive of tools, with pile-driving achieved by sheer manpower rather than machinery, and all under the unforgiving glare of the sun. Before its construction was complete, work had already begun upon the more complex operation of building the steel bridge. Although heavy machinery was brought in for this project, it required no less of a labour force, with thousands of men scrambling over bamboo scaffolding, constantly berated by the guards if they weren't seen to be working hard enough. Although Barney seldom spoke in any detail to his family about this time, he later told his daughter, Janice, 'if you were caught slacking, you would pay for it. He said you did as you were told if you knew what was good for you, and sometimes that wasn't good enough'. Construction of the steel bridge was completed in April 1943, both bridges later becoming the focus of many a raid by Allied aircraft. Barney remained at Tha Makhan until late 1943 when he was sent first to Chungkai and then, in early 1944, to Nong Pladuc at the southern end of the railway where he was put to work in the marshalling yards.

Barney remained at Nong Pladuc until May 1944, when he became one of the many prisoners who, following completion of construction of the railway, were transported back to Singapore prior to being sent to Japan, often to be employed in heavy industry or mining. After a brief stay at River Valley Road camp, Barney was among a party of 500 prisoners who were taken to the docks and put on board the *Teia Maru*, bound for Moji, Japan. The prisoners remained confined below decks for much of the fourteen-day voyage, sustained by nothing more than two mugs of rice each day and, occasionally, a mug of watery soup, conditions in the airlessness and heat of the ship's hold, appalling. On 19 June the *Teia Maru* arrived at Moji, from where Barney was then taken to Funatsu Branch Camp, later renamed Nagoya No.3, in Gifu Prefecture. Here, in place of the bamboo and attap huts of the Thai jungle, the prisoners were accommodated in single-storey buildings which, as Barney was to discover, offered little protection from the cold in the freezing temperatures of the Japanese winter. Prisoners at the camp were used by the Mitsui Mining Company, concerned with the mining and refining of lead and zinc. For the remaining fifteen months of his captivity Barney worked long hours in often dangerous conditions, for which he and his fellow prisoners were rewarded with a diet consisting of little other than watery soup and paltry rations of rice, at great cost to their health. Cruelty and the neglect of basic human needs were commonplace, and medical treatment all but non-existent. A fellow Argyll who later testified to the ill treatment of prisoners at the camp for the War Crimes trial stated that one of the guards repeatedly made sick prisoners work in the foundry and that almost all of the camp's prisoners suffered from poor health, malnutrition and deficiency-related diseases.

Standing at six feet three inches tall, Barney was never likely to have been able to blend into the background during his years in captivity and, confronted daily with the short in stature Japanese, it was, perhaps, inevitable that he would be singled out for punishment. So it proved, on more than one occasion. Though he withheld much about his time in the Far East from his family, he did relate details of how he had been punished for perceived misdemeanours on a number of occasions. The Japanese winter of 1944-45 had been the coldest since records began, in itself a punishment for those who had the misfortune to be singled out by the guards at Nagoya. Barney later told his daughter that he had been:

> stripped naked and made to kneel in the snow overnight as a punishment. A guard who was said to be 'a bit decent', gave him a pin to stick in himself and said, 'don't sleep if you want to live'.

Unfortunately, like-minded guards, prepared to show a little humanity to their captives, were, by all accounts, very much in the minority. Barney also disclosed to his family that he had been tortured. Janice explained, 'Dad was held against fire until he blistered. This was to extract information, but he didn't give them what they wanted.' (Such was the impact of the experience upon him that, for the rest of his life, he would never again sit close to a fire.) Barney also said that on another occasion, guards at Nagoya had deliberately broken the toes on one of his feet as a punishment. According to Janice, he said that 'they clamped his foot in something and did the damage breaking each toe slowly', injuries which were still very apparent when the American liberating forces arrived on 6 September 1945, by which time thirteen prisoners had died at the camp. Weighing only six stones, Barney was taken to a holding camp in the Philippines, where he received medical attention before being transported to Canada, finally arriving at Southampton on board the RMS *Queen Elizabeth* on 5 November 1945.

For the entire duration of Barney's captivity his family had had no idea of his whereabouts. The Japanese had periodically provided the prisoners with pre-printed postcards to send home, a chance to let their loved ones know they were alive, even if the statements they were encouraged to mark with a tick, such as 'I am in good health', bore no relation to the truth. Possibly because Barney had claimed to have no next of kin when he enlisted in the Argylls, he chose not to take advantage of this opportunity, lest his deception be discovered. It was, therefore, only by chance that shortly after the war had ended his family learned of his survival. According to Janice, 'his mother went to the cinema just after the war and saw a piece of news film with her son in it. She went to the projectionist and demanded it be replayed for her.' The footage, shown as part of a Movietone news film, had been taken in Japan and showed a severely emaciated but still recognisable Barney, clad only in a 'jap happy' or loin cloth, and a pair of wooden clogs, hobbling towards the camera. Footage from the film is believed to have been used as evidence of Japanese brutality in the subsequent War Crimes trial.

Once back on English soil, Barney soon encountered the kind of general disinterest with which many returning Far East prisoners of war were viewed upon their return to a society which had celebrated the end of the war months earlier. According to Janice, Barney said that after arriving at Southampton and travelling back to North London a street vendor refused to sell him a newspaper on the grounds that they were for his regular customers only. 'Dad said he'd been a prisoner after fighting in the Far East. He was told it didn't matter where he'd been, regulars only.' Demoralising as this must have been, Janice explained that her father seldom exhibited anything other than a very positive outlook, as epitomised by his oft-repeated remarks such as 'something's better than nothing', and, 'we must never give up, we find a way,' suggesting that the hardships endured during his captivity had honed his attitude towards life thereafter. As he set about the task of adjusting to life after captivity, Barney settled in Enfield, North London, and found work as a bricklayer, unaware at that time of the extent to which the years spent in the hands of the Japanese had affected his health in the long term. Like many of his fellow prisoners, he had suffered from malnutrition and contracted dysentery, malaria and beri beri, and had lost most of his teeth as a result of prolonged vitamin deficiency. Following his return from the Far East, as well as experiencing nightmares, he suffered from recurrent malaria and repeated bouts of dysentery, for which he required hospital treatment until the early-1960s. Meanwhile, in the spring of 1948, Barney met Lilian, a Red Cross worker who had been visiting his mother, and within six months they married, their daughter arriving three years later.

Janice grew up with an awareness of her father having been a prisoner of war. In addition to admonishments about wasting food, the lasting impact of Barney's captivity upon him had become only too apparent. 'Nightmares, bouts of malaria, attacks of dysentery – they were accepted parts of family life.' Gradually, however, it became apparent that his health problems went beyond the recurrence of diseases he had suffered during his time in the Far East. Barney not only began to suffer from extreme fatigue and to sleepwalk, but also developed stiffness to the left side of his body. In the mid-1950s, after numerous visits to the doctor, followed by a barrage of tests in hospital, he was diagnosed with early-onset Parkinson's disease. Recent research suggests the origins of the disease to be in the gut, rather than the brain and, though the link has yet to be proven beyond doubt, it invites the possibility that

Eric 'Barney' Barnes with his wife Lilian when they married in 1948.

the malnutrition Barney suffered as a prisoner of war was at the root of the disease which went on to severely lessen the quality of his life and, ultimately, to shorten it. Over the following years his condition became progressively worse but, showing the same strength of spirit which had helped him survive in captivity, Barney remained determined to do his best to live a normal life. Unable to continue working as a bricklayer, he instead took a job as a postman, working nights outside in the parcels section at the sorting office. (Barney had spoken of having been made to 'live in a cage' during his captivity and, as a consequence of being so confined, would not take any job which required him to work indoors.) Janice explained:

> he still carried on going to work in all weathers outside. He said he'd worked in monsoon rain so downpours here were not a worry. But his health was failing badly. He was still having his dysentery attacks, but now he couldn't undress himself easily. Dad never complained, but he became more and more disabled. He shuffled, knees bent, dragged his feet, his left side wouldn't do as he told it, and he was having numerous falls. The Works doctor would try to persuade him to retire. A very resolute 'no' was his answer.

By the early-1970s, Parkinson's disease had tightened its grip upon Barney, his falls becoming more frequent and their consequences more distressing. On one occasion, having broken his ankle, a plaster cast was applied, and then re-applied several more times after he kept removing it, to the bafflement of all concerned until a doctor glancing at his medical history noticed that he had been a captive of the Japanese and realised the source of the problem. It emerged that Barney associated the application of a plaster cast to his ankle with the occasion nearly thirty years earlier when his toes had been broken by his Japanese captors, causing him immense anguish. Another more serious fall was to have tragic consequences when, in 1974, Barney tumbled down an escalator. Though he was in excruciating pain, medical professionals repeatedly misdiagnosed the damage to his neck as no more than a strain. It was more than a fortnight before it was realised that, with a tenacity which had no doubt been at the heart of his endurance of a brutal captivity, Barney had managed to survive thus far with an undetected broken neck. Tragically, by the time he was admitted to hospital, it was too late.

Despite all that he had suffered during his captivity, to the end of his life Barney felt extremely proud to have served his country as an Argyll and to have been part of a battalion which had fought so valiantly in Malaya. His battle against ill-health was fought with equal courage but, ultimately, it was a battle he was unable to win and he died at the age of only fifty-eight, his life almost certainly having been cut short by the long-term effects of years of malnutrition as a prisoner of the Japanese.

Eric 'Barney' Barnes with his wife Lilian at their daughter Janice's wedding in 1968.

Chapter 18

Detective Crown Sergeant William Gordon Wilson

Royal Naval Dockyard Police, Hong Kong

Christmas Day 1941 was a Christmas like no other Willie Wilson had experienced in his thirty-one years, and one which he would certainly never forget. It was a day that would be forever remembered as 'Black Christmas' by those who, like Willie, had been caught up in the carnage that had followed Japan's vicious attack upon Hong Kong on 8 December. And it was the day upon which Willie became a prisoner of war and witnessed the Colony's surrender to the Japanese.

Born in 1910, Willie was brought up on the family farm at Curley, Rathfriland, in Northern Ireland, together with his sister and four brothers. Unable to envisage a future for himself in the local farming community, in 1931 he left life in the Irish countryside behind him and enlisted in the Royal Ulster Rifles, being posted to B Company of the 1st Battalion. Following tours of duty in Egypt and Palestine, he was posted to Hong Kong, something which was to completely alter the course of his life. In March 1937, after almost six years' service, Willie was, at his own request, discharged from the Rifles and enlisted in the Royal Naval Dockyard Police (RNYP) based in Hong Kong. Over the course of the next four years he was promoted to detective sergeant and went on to become a fingerprint expert.

By late 1941, with international tensions rising as a result of the increasing threat posed to British interests by Japan, the vulnerability of Hong Kong to invasion had been recognised, but despite two battalions of Canadian troops having been sent to bolster the numbers of those ready to defend the colony, this proved

Willie Wilson, around 1937.

no deterrent. On the same morning that the Japanese attacked Pearl Harbor and Malaya, they also launched a fierce assault upon Hong Kong and, as a member of the RNYP, Willie was among those mobilised to defend the dockyards. The 14,000-strong Hong Kong garrison, many of whom had no combat experience, fought hard to defend the Colony against the battle-hardened Japanese troops, but were heavily outnumbered. The battle for Hong Kong raged on until 25 December, a day notable for the savagery of the Japanese against troops and civilians alike; the murder of staff and patients at a field hospital which had been set up to treat British soldiers was an atrocity that was to be mirrored two months later in Singapore, when the Japanese stormed the Alexandra Military Hospital with similar consequences. So it was that on Christmas Day 1941 Willie was one of eighty-four members of the RNYP who were taken prisoner. By the time the Governor of Hong Kong surrendered the Colony to the Japanese, 1,550 of those defending the garrison had been killed.

With Hong Kong in Japanese hands, it was the beginning of forty-four months of captivity for Willie, during which time his family received no news as to whether or not he was still alive. Together with his colleagues in the RNYP he was marched to North Point, a former refugee camp near the harbour. He was later to talk of the sight which met his eyes upon his arrival at the camp, where evidence of the bloodshed of the battle and the brutality of his captors was all around. Willie's daughter, Florence, remembers as a child overhearing her father talk 'about how cruel the Japanese were to the Chinese. I remember him saying about the dead bodies of men, women and children floating in the sea around the prison camp'. Conditions at North Point were overcrowded and insanitary. At the outbreak of hostilities the Chinese had looted the camp of everything that could be moved and the wooden huts in which the men lived were mere empty shells of buildings, with neither windows nor doors and many also without roofs. The Japanese provided a few basic tools for the prisoners to do what they could to rebuild the huts and make them more habitable, but there was no sanitation, no running water and, for the majority of prisoners, nothing on which to sleep but a concrete floor. Neither were there any cooking facilities, the poor quality rice which constituted the prisoners' rations having to be cooked in old oil drums over open fires.

Early in 1942 Willie was moved to Shamshuipo camp, in the Kowloon district. The largest of the camps in Hong Kong, Shamshuipo had been a British army barracks and now held most of the prisoners from the British army and the Hong Kong Volunteer Defence Corps as well as those from the RNYP, and it was there that Willie was to remain for over three years. Those buildings, too, had been stripped of most of their contents and it was left to the prisoners to pool their ingenuity and scavenge the area around the camp for anything that could be improvised to make their surroundings more habitable and aid their survival, the Japanese from time to time supplying items that had been looted from stocks on the island. After some weeks, food rations began to include some vegetables and, occasionally, small quantities of fish, but far below that which was needed to prevent vitamin deficiency and malnutrition on a large scale. For most, the only way of supplementing the poor diet was by bartering with the Chinese traders at the camp fence, which carried the risk of punishment.

In mid-1942, Willie was assigned to a working party of over 500 prisoners who were required to make the daily trek to Kai Tak Airport, which had been badly bomb-damaged during the invasion but which the Japanese sought to expand for their own use. Equipped with nothing more sophisticated than picks and shovels, the men were tasked with building a second runway, but first had to level a large hill which stood in the way of its construction, something which Willie later described to his daughter.

> I can remember him talking about having to move tons of earth by hand in wheelbarrows, while being sick and undernourished, in the baking hot sun and having no protection or proper clothing or footwear.

With their working day sometimes beginning as early as 4.00am, the prisoners faced a walk of some three miles to the airport before beginning a twelve hour shift, for which they were paid ten cents each day, after which they still had to contend with the three-mile walk back to the camp. As the number of sick increased, it became

Shamshuipo camp, Hong Kong, photographed shortly after the camp was liberated.

increasingly difficult to find enough 'fit' men to work, with the result that some of the sick were carried to work on stretchers in order to make up the numbers, adding to the tally of men who died from the neglect of their most basic needs. As the months passed, those on the work parties did, at least, benefit from the opportunity this presented of picking up news of the progress of the war, sometimes even managing to smuggle newspapers back to the camp, often a huge boost to morale. This was not, however, without its risks, the guards needing little or no excuse to hand out beatings and abuse the power they had over their captives. If they suspected that items had been smuggled into camp, protracted searches were carried out, often followed by the interrogation and beating of any alleged culprits. According to Florence, the name of one guard in particular was mentioned by her father in the conversations she overheard as a child, and it was a name which lodged in her memory, arousing great curiosity. Only when she was older did she learn that a guard who was known to all those at Shamshuipo as the Kamloops Kid, a Japanese-Canadian who had been born in Kamloops, British Columbia, had meted out brutal treatment to her father and many others and was later prosecuted for war crimes and executed.

As time went on, the poor diet and the complete lack of medical provision at Shamshuipo resulted in widespread disease, from which many did not recover. The death toll resulting from dysentery and a variety of deficiency diseases, for which the doctors could do little without drugs, was compounded by the outbreak of diphtheria, which lasted several months. Only belatedly did the Japanese provide a small quantity of serum to treat some of the diphtheria sufferers but it did little to stem the number of deaths which, according to one of those who kept a diary during his time in Shamshuipo, was in the region of 200 men between May and December 1942. With so many men severely emaciated and close to death, had the Japanese not allowed the distribution of some of the Red Cross supplies that had been received towards the end of 1942, more deaths would surely have occurred. The effect upon the prisoners' health, and upon their morale, was immense and the death toll slowed, suggesting how easily the Japanese could have prevented so many men from dying completely unnecessary deaths had they simply provided them with a little nutritious food.

It was due only to the courage and initiative shown by some of Willie's friends that he did not add to the death toll himself when, in addition to repeated bouts of malaria, he contracted tuberculosis. One of those who had saved his life, fellow member of the RNYP, Andy McAleese, later explained to Florence that:

> in the camp they had a so-called 'hospital hut' for ill patients and another hut where the Japanese put men whom they thought were dead or dying. Dad's friend told us Daddy had been thrown into this second building, the 'death house', on three occasions and he rescued him, knowing he was still alive, albeit only just.

Willie remained gravely ill for the duration of his time at Shamshuipo and, although he was spared from being among the twenty per cent of Hong Kong's defenders who died in captivity, his life was irrevocably changed, and shortened, by tuberculosis. Had he not been so ill, it is probable that he would have been among the large number of prisoners, including some of those from the RNYP, who, from September 1942 onwards, were transported to Japan to be employed in their war economy. Some welcomed the move, in the mistaken assumption that in the Japanese homeland they would receive better treatment, but it was a move which proved to be a death sentence for many. Those prisoners who formed the second draft to leave Shamshuipo for Japan in September 1942 were on board the *Lisbon Maru* when she was torpedoed by an American submarine, with the loss of over 900 lives.

By mid-1945, in much the same way that many of the prisoners at other camps in South East Asia were assigned to work parties digging deep trenches around the camps, ostensibly for the purposes of countering any Allied invasion, so parties of prisoners from Shamshuipo were put to work digging tunnels into the hillside, supposedly to be used as defensive positions. However, since the Japanese High Command had issued an order to the effect that in the event of an American invasion of homeland Japan, all prisoners of war were to be killed, the tunnels appear to have been ordered with a more sinister purpose in mind, a purpose which may well have been fulfilled had the bombing of Hiroshima and Nagasaki not brought the war to an end.

On 11 August, the shouts of the Chinese from outside the camp fence fuelled rumours that the war had ended, but it was another four days before the prisoners received confirmation that their ordeal was over and several weeks before the camp was liberated. American aircraft dropped supplies into the camp and foraging parties were allowed outside to search for desperately needed food. For Willie, who, prior

Hong Kong harbour under attack from US forces in 1945. (Photo courtesy of Australian War Memorial)

to his capture by the Japanese, had weighed around ten and a half stone, freedom came not a moment too soon. Upon his liberation from Shamshuipo, this once fit and healthy man weighed four and a half stone and was in dire need of medical treatment. He was among those who were taken by a hospital ship to a holding camp in the Philippines from where, on 25 September, he left Manila on board HMS *Implacable* bound for Vancouver. After then travelling across Canada by train, Willie boarded the SS *Île de France* bound for England, arriving at Southampton on 31 October 1945.

Although Willie's captivity was now behind him, it had bequeathed to him a legacy of illness which would affect him for the rest of his life. From Southampton he was taken to the Royal Naval Hospital in Gosport, Hampshire, suffering from tuberculosis and malaria, and remained there for the next two months before being transferred to Musgrave Park Military Hospital in Belfast, in order to be nearer his family. During his time there, so ill did Willie become that surgeons were forced to remove large sections of his lungs in order to save his life, and he remained in hospital for a considerable length of time. 'The medical profession called him the "miracle patient", as they did not think he would survive,' said Florence. Finally, two years and four months after the war had ended, and just days before Christmas 1947, Willie was declared fit enough to return home, almost six years to the day since the nightmare of his captivity had begun. The close-knit community of Rathfriland, who

Willie Wilson and his wife Jeannie when they married in 1952.

had supported his family throughout the years when his fate had remained unknown, gave Willie a warm welcome upon his return. Few would have been more pleased to see him home again than Jeannie, the childhood sweetheart who, like his family, had heard nothing from him during his captivity, but their plans to marry met with a degree of opposition from Jeannie's family amid concerns that he would not live very long. In addition to having been left with dental problems and reduced vision as a consequence of vitamin deficiency, Florence recalls, 'I remember him suffering from huge boils on his neck and his doctor saying they were due to his treatment in captivity.' Willie's health continued to deteriorate and in 1950 he had further surgery to remove the remaining part of his right lung due to TB. Nevertheless, he and Jeannie were eventually married in 1952 and went on to have two sons and two daughters.

Willie's years in the Far East had also left their imprint upon his mind, as evidenced by the nightmares from which he was still suffering over a decade after his return from Hong Kong. Florence recalled that, 'as a small child, I remember Daddy shouting during the night and Mummy would tell us he had had a very bad time in the war and was having bad dreams.' There were also other pointers to the deprivations he had suffered. Although he never again ate boiled rice, Florence said:

> Daddy did not like us to waste food. I can remember him saying to (us) that if we had to survive for almost four years on two small bowls a day of dirty rice with maggots and other nasties in it, we would be cleaning our plates at every meal.

According to Florence, Willie remained very bitter towards his former captors. 'Daddy told us we were never to buy anything made in Japan or Korea. He was very bitter towards the Japanese.' Although Willie shared relatively little of his experiences in the Far East with his family, he did, however, remain in contact with the friends responsible for his survival and was, for many years, secretary of his local branch of the British Legion.

Meanwhile, Willie's health problems severely affected his job prospects. Having found employment in the office of an engineering firm, the subsequent long periods of absence he was forced to take due to illness meant that he was unable to hold onto it, and further attempts to earn a living were similarly compromised by his ill-health. Florence explained:

> Daddy suffered from chronic illness for the remainder of his days. He had a huge vegetable garden at our home and used to sell his produce to the local shops. He would work in the garden for a while, then would have to come in to the house and go to bed for a rest.

Despite requiring repeated hospital treatment in the years following his return from the Far East, according to Florence it was only after a struggle that her father was awarded a pension in recognition of the fact that his medical problems were attributable to his time as a prisoner of war.

Over thirty years after having been rescued from the so-called 'death house' at Shamshuipo and having lived far longer than his doctors had predicted, Willie died in May 1975 at the age of sixty-four. According to Florence, Willie's doctors stated that had it not been for the fact that the tuberculosis he contracted during his captivity had left him with only part of one lung, he may well have survived the coronary which killed him.

Chapter 19

Gunner George John Gagen

148th Field Regiment, Royal Artillery (Bedfordshire Yeomanry) (TA)

Though he had an impoverished start in life, George Gagen's upbringing at the heart of a friendly community, together with his naturally sunny disposition, equipped him with something far more precious than money; they gave him a gift for communicating with people – something which in later years was to become central to his survival as a prisoner of the Japanese. An only child, born in Wandsworth, London, in 1920, George and his parents lived in rented rooms, moving from place to place as necessity dictated. His father had been left in poor health following his service in the First World War and, with few job prospects, made a living from selling goods door-to-door. Though in later years George joined his father as a salesman, upon leaving school he took a job as a brewer's labourer. However, following the declaration of war in 1939, rather than waiting for his call-up papers to arrive, he volunteered to serve his country, enlisting in the Royal Artillery and being assigned to 148th Field Regiment.

After beginning his training in East Anglia, in January 1941 George was moved to Hawick, where the regiment remained until the following April, their training schedule hampered by heavy snow. Possibly as a result of the disruption caused by the severe weather of the Scottish winter, during the four

George Gagen around 1945.

months he spent at Hawick George found the time to become engaged to a local girl, little knowing that before long they would be separated for a considerable time. In May George's training continued with a move to the Rochdale area, followed by a further move in August to Monmouth for final intensive training at firing camps before going overseas. Two months later George and his comrades entrained for Liverpool and, on 29 October 1941, boarded the *Andes*, transferring to the *Wakefield* after their arrival in Nova Scotia before continuing their voyage eastward. Like many of the troops who sailed to the Far East, George had no previous combat experience, and the three weeks' intensive training he and many others subsequently received when they reached India went only so far in preparing them to face the kind of savagery they were to encounter from the Japanese in Singapore.

With the island under heavy attack from Japanese planes as the *Wakefield* arrived at Keppel Harbour on 29 January, the regiment disembarked and was ordered to move to the north-east side of the island, an area which would become only too familiar to many, including George, before long. Within days of their arrival, the causeway linking Singapore to the mainland was blown up but this did little to stall the speed of the Japanese advance. George was among a party of men who were ordered to move to the east of the Bukit Timah Road to support troops near the golf course, shelling with 25-pounder guns, but their efforts were in vain. Like many of their comrades, the regiment had arrived too late to make any real difference to the outcome of the battle, and a little over two weeks after disembarking from the *Wakefield*, George became a prisoner of war. Two days later, on 17 February, having marched to the Changi barracks complex, he found himself among the thousands who, during the weeks which followed, discovered for the first time in their lives what it was to be desperately hungry. He later told his family that he realised during the early days of his captivity that survival depended upon a willingness to eat whatever was necessary, however unpalatable.

At the end of April 1942, George was moved to River Valley Road camp where he was assigned to a working party repairing buildings which had been damaged in the battle of the previous weeks. This was a welcome opportunity to acquire extra food from local traders whenever possible, something at which George became very accomplished, learning the basics of the Malay language in the process. Six months after his arrival at the camp, George discovered that his negotiating skills were to be put to a greater test when, on 30 October 1942, he was one of 650 prisoners, known as Letter Party S, transported to Thailand under the command of Lieutenant Colonel C.E. Mackellar, Royal Artillery. Emptying out of the goods trucks after arriving at Ban Pong, George and his comrades were marched to the transit camp, the squalid conditions which confronted them doing nothing to restore their flagging spirits after the discomfort of their journey. The following day they were told they were to march upcountry and, like many of those who had gone before them, were advised to leave behind any belongings which could not easily be carried as these would be transported by the Japanese, unaware at this relatively early stage of their captivity of the hollowness of such promises. The party marched to Kan'buri, where they were allowed a brief rest, after which, with several of the prisoners suffering from dysentery, they were marched on to Tonchan, some 130 kilometres north of Ban Pong.

Joining the army of dispirited men slaving on the railway at Tonchan, the party was initially put to work on jungle clearing, and then on embankment building. Much of the work involved the moving of earth from one place to another – exhausting work in extreme heat and all under the watchful eyes of guards only too ready to deliver encouragement in the form of a beating. A combination of the gruelling work schedule and a diet consisting almost exclusively of low-grade rice and poor quality vegetables resulted in an increasing number of men falling sick and a number of deaths at the camp. For George, as for many others, the search for food became something of an obsession, as he later told his family. His daughter, Susan, said that from what he had told her:

Dad used to spend his time looking for food. He was a good communicator and managed to talk in some way to the local people to find out what plants and fruits in the jungle could be eaten. In the camps it was mostly rice but sometimes animals would be killed and he ate almost anything, including snake.

In addition to supplementing his diet with whatever could be caught and killed, George bartered for food from the native Thai traders with what little money was available and, for the duration of his captivity, made food and its acquisition his priority. It was, no doubt, to his advantage that he did not smoke. 'Dad always said that those who smoked didn't last as long as the others as they were always trading things for fags, which was more important to them than food.' Trading personal possessions for food was widespread and often, quite literally, meant the difference between life and death. However, there was one item that George refused to part with – a ring. According to George's youngest daughter, Beverley:

he was very proud of a ring given to him by his parents for his twenty-first birthday, as he managed to keep it throughout his time as a prisoner. He told me how he sewed it into his pillow case so it was never found and taken by anyone.

Added Susan, 'it was probably not worth a lot but it meant everything to him and he cherished it until the day he died.' As much as for reasons of sentimentality, his determination to keep the ring may have been an attempt to retain a piece of his identity in a situation where, as a prisoner of war of the Japanese, he had lost almost everything.

George remained in the Tonchan area for over twelve months, first at Tonchan Central, then moving to nearby Tonchan South. By June 1943, the torrential rain of the monsoon had turned the camp into a quagmire, the prisoners wading ankle deep in mud and the tents with which they had been issued leaking badly so that, even when they slept, there was no respite from the continual downpour. Along with the mud, the monsoon also delivered disease with frightening speed as the lack of any concept of hygiene in the neighbouring camp of Tamil workers just upstream sparked an outbreak of cholera which quickly washed downstream to Tonchan and beyond. Although a severe lack of medical supplies meant that doctors were often unable to save cholera victims among the prisoners, they were, at least, treated with compassion. For the natives there was no treatment, nor any hope, and many simply crawled into the jungle to die. In November 1943, George was moved to Tarsao hospital camp suffering from malaria and dysentery and remained there until early 1944, when he was moved farther down the line to the hospital camp at Tha Muang. Despite his determination to eat virtually anything in his attempts to combat the deficiency-related diseases which had so many in their grip, he also acquired beri beri.

Although the Japanese had begun to send large parties of prisoners to other locations following the completion of the railway, George was among those who remained behind, and was held in camps along the track for the duration of his captivity. He later told his family that he had, by feigning illness, managed to avoid being included in one of the parties destined for onward shipment to Japan and, upon learning some time later that the ship on which that party was travelling had been bombed, felt that he had cheated death. In August 1944, he was moved to Chungkai for two months before being sent farther upcountry to Tha Khanun, where he was put to work wood cutting. The following December he was sent back down the track to Tha Makhan, by which time the two bridges there had become the target for repeated bombing by Allied aircraft.

It was whilst working on bridge repairs at Tha Makhan that George became friends with a fellow prisoner, Ralph, from the Royal Norfolk Regiment, forming what was to become a lifelong friendship which sprang from their support for each other in the battle to survive captivity. Said Susan of her father's friend, 'he was a country man from Norfolk, and I like to think they made a good team, with my dad's cockney charm and Ralph's country skills.' They remained together for the rest of their captivity, moving camp several more times as a combination of Allied bombing, monsoon damage and the fruits of prisoners' attempts at sabotage necessitated

The bridge at Tha Makhan, Thailand after Allied bombing, photographed shortly after the war. (Photo by kind permission of the Thai-Burma Railway Centre)

maintenance work on the railway. In January 1945, a move up the line to Chungkai was followed two months later by a move farther north to Arrow Hill, then another briefly back down to Tha Muang in July and, finally, back up the line to Ban Khao in August 1945.

In the final twelve months of captivity there was an increasing number of air raids targeting the track, sometimes unwittingly causing casualties among the prisoners. According to Susan, 'Dad told a story of when a train was bombed and the prisoners were ordered to remove the bodies. It was a horrible task as the bodies were in bits.' George was left with an awareness of the random nature of death and how luck played its part, telling his family that on one occasion when a bomb had landed nearby, an elderly Thai man standing next to him had been hit by shrapnel and was killed instantly; he also told them that on another occasion he had visited the camp doctor for what he knew to be a minor illness, only for the doctor to tell him he had malaria, which George knew not to be the case, the doctor having apparently been reluctant to pass men as 'fit' in order to try to prevent them from being moved to a camp where many prisoners were dying.

Following the surrender of the Japanese in August 1945 and the liberation of the camp, George was flown to Rangoon and, after a medical check, boarded the MS *Boissevain*, arriving at Liverpool docks on 12 October 1945. After making his way back home to Wandsworth, George discovered that his parents had been forced to look for somewhere else to live as their earlier home had been bombed, a stark reminder of a different sort of war which had been played out whilst he had been thousands of miles away. Aside from learning that their son was a prisoner in Japanese hands, George's parents had received no news of him until he had been liberated and, as he was an only child, his capture had taken a particularly heavy toll on his mother, whose health spiralled into severe depression from which she never fully recovered. George was later to comment that he truly regretted having volunteered his services to the army because of what it had led to, not least because of the way his parents had suffered on his behalf. Not only had they received no news as to whether he was alive or dead, but neither had his fiancée who, in the meantime, had chosen not to wait for him and married someone else. Whatever George's feelings were upon learning about this on his return home, he eventually went on to meet the woman who would become his wife, Barbara, in 1947, whilst both of them were queuing for the cinema. They were married in 1949 and eventually settled in Tooting, where they raised three daughters and a son.

George Gagen and his wife Barbara when they married in 1949.

Meanwhile, George began working as a salesman with his father and remained self-employed for the rest of his life, capitalising on the resourcefulness he had learned in his battle to survive, eventually becoming a scrap-metal dealer.

George had returned from the Far East carrying a number of physical reminders of his captivity. Years of existing upon a grossly inadequate diet left him with a legacy of digestive problems and, like many of his former comrades, he lost a number of teeth as a result of prolonged vitamin deficiency. However, his application for a pension in respect of the various physical ailments from which he suffered was refused. He also suffered from breathing problems as a consequence of a beating he had received from a Korean guard which had dislodged a piece of cartilage in his nose, something for which he eventually required surgery. George also bore deep psychological scars as a result of his ordeal. According to Susan:

> because of his experiences, after the war he had a 'short straw' and, sadly, used to blow his top quite easily, often taking it out on our mum. He had a very short fuse and used to get very angry over little things, for example, if his dinner wasn't ready or if my mum went out and left him on his own. He didn't like being left alone. I witnessed him flying into rages and he could be quite scary. He was, nonetheless, a very loving person.

It was not until the 1970s that it was officially recognised that George's mental health had been deeply affected by his years in captivity and that he continued to harbour a great deal of anger towards his former captors. Said Susan, 'it was only when he was in his fifties that he had an assessment and they decided he had suffered psychological damage. He went to a hospital in Woolwich for this.' George was subsequently awarded a very small pension but, as Susan went on to explain, 'he put in for an increase in pension from the MoD but it was not accepted'. Sadly, although this decision was eventually reversed, it was too late to be of any benefit to George.

Because George talked quite openly about his time as a prisoner of war, some aspects of the legacy of his captivity became part of the fabric of his children's lives. Susan explained:

> he used to use Japanese words at home quite a lot and taught us to count in Japanese. We were brought up by our dad never to waste food and if we left any on our plates he would refer to his experiences as a PoW and eat it himself. Our dad used to speak quite a lot about his experiences, mostly about the camaraderie and how they survived. He did also mention some of the grimmer aspects.

George Gagen and his wife Barbara attending a FEPOW Reunion in 1978.

George also frequently attended FEPoW reunions but, unlike many of those held captive in the Far East, he showed no bitterness towards the Japanese generally. According to Susan, 'he never bore a grudge against the Japanese and used to love meeting Japanese people and practising the bit of Japanese he picked up while a prisoner of war.'

Over fifty years after being liberated from a prisoner of war camp, it became apparent that George remained profoundly affected by his experiences in captivity when he suffered a number of strokes, which were judged to have been triggered by the anger he still harboured regarding those years. Following a further assessment at Hammersmith Hospital, an appeal against the decision not to increase George's pension was successful. Susan explained:

> it was accepted that his series of strokes was caused by bursts of high blood pressure, caused by rage relating to his experiences. The case went to appeal and my mum won with the help of the Royal British Legion, and largely due to a judgement made by a senior doctor at Hammersmith Hospital.

George suffered another stroke at the age of eighty and died shortly after his eighty-first birthday in 2001. His funeral was paid for by the Ministry of Defence, in recognition of the fact that his condition had been attributable to his experiences as a prisoner of war. Sadly for George, the battle for a decent pension had simply taken too long.

Chapter 20

Fusilier James Swordy

9th Battalion Royal Northumberland Fusiliers

When Jim Swordy was ten years old his father refused to attend the village Armistice Day parade, as had been his habit for many years, having served in the First World War. When Jim asked him why, his father apparently replied, 'they told us that there would never be another war, but there *is* going to be another war and you and your brother are going to be in it.' The words lodged in Jim's memory and would prove horribly prophetic, although his father could never have envisaged that the war in which Jim would be caught up would be not so much a war against bombs and bullets as one against disease and starvation at the hands of the Japanese.

Born in 1921 in the village of Shilbottle in Northumberland, home for Jim and his three siblings was a cottage in the tight-knit community of Bilton Banks, where all the menfolk worked at the local mine. Jim might never have found himself in a Japanese prisoner of war camp but for an early twist of fate when, after leaving school, he joined the Royal Navy as a boy sailor, only to be discharged a year later as a result of a perforated eardrum. After finding work as a labourer, he also joined the Territorial Army and when war was declared in 1939, was enlisted in the 9th Battalion of the Royal Northumberland Fusiliers. Two years later, along with the rest of the battalion, twenty-year-old Jim found himself heading for the Far East, unsure of what the future might hold.

Jim's recollections of Singapore, from the moment he stepped off the *Felix Roussel* on 5 February 1942 to the end of the battle for Singapore ten days later, he neatly summed up some fifty years afterwards with the words, 'in action 5 February 1942 to 15 February 1942 – bombed, shelled, mortared and machine-gunned'. He chronicled the events of the following three and a half years with varying levels of detail and also made a video recording. His comments about the earliest days of his captivity in Changi were brief: 'Issued with limed rice to eat. This resulted in constant hunger and blackouts after a short time.' At the end of March, Jim was assigned to a party sent to Farrer Park, tasked with clearing up the debris of battle in and around the town, returning to Changi in mid-April. The following month he was moved to Keppel Harbour, about which he recalled, 'made to work on docks loading and unloading ships. Occasionally forced to work twenty-four hour shifts. It was at this time that severe beatings were arbitrarily

Jim Swordy in 1940.

PoWs in the hospital hut at Wang Pho camp, Thailand. (Photo courtesy of Australian War Memorial)

meted out.' He also noted the savagery with which the civilian Chinese population were treated. 'Whilst working on the docks at Singapore, six Chinese men were beheaded and their heads displayed on poles in prominent parts of the city.' After several months of having to exist on a diet predominantly of poor quality rice, Jim also recorded the effects of vitamin deficiency. 'I began to suffer from scrotum dermatitis and dengue fever. We stole food from the ships and warehouses to supplement our diet.' Jim was among many who suffered these conditions, the former caused by a chronic lack of vitamin B, causing agonizing swelling and skin irritation which was both painful and humiliating and had the potential to prove fatal.

On 7 November 1942, Jim was among a party of prisoners transported to Thailand under the command of Lieutenant Colonel Flower of the Royal Northumberland Fusiliers as part of Group 1. 'We were packed into cattle trucks, thirty-three men to a truck, and taken to Thailand.' After arriving at Ban Pong, Jim and his comrades were taken to Kan'buri, from where they crossed the river by barges to reach Chungkai. After a brief stay at this camp they were marched on, reaching Wang Lan on 5 December, where they joined the throng of prisoners engaged in the construction of the railway. Jim was initially allocated to a party clearing the jungle for the railway's path, cutting down undergrowth and felling trees, after which he was put to work on embankment building, moving farther upcountry as each section of embankment was completed and a new one begun. In March 1943, Jim was among a group moved back down the line to Nong Pladuc, the base camp for the railway, where he was put to work in the marshalling yards. This was followed by another move several weeks later back upcountry to Wang Pho, where he was assigned to a party working on sleeper and rail laying along the railway track; after the men had laid a certain length of line, they were moved farther along from camp to camp, the amount of work demanded of the prisoners every day increasing in the determination of the Japanese to see the railway completed as soon as possible, irrespective of the cost in human lives.

By June 1943, the sleeper and rail-laying party had reached Tonchan, an area which had been badly hit by cholera. Jim recalled:

> we were forced to work under terrible conditions. The worst period was from May to October 1943. We were moved into the cholera area and the Japanese began a 'speedo' in order to get the railway completed. This was also the monsoon period, which lasted five months. Men were dying in hundreds. There was no medicine. The doctors tried to keep the sick men in the camp. However, the Japanese allowed no-one any mercy .... At Tonchan Spring camp there was an acute cholera problem. The camp had previously housed Australian troops, many of whom had died and been buried in shallow graves. It was common to come across bones sticking up out of the ground. A number of men from our unit died there. Across the line from us there was a camp full of natives who were dying .... We were made to bury them in a mass grave. I saw a man crawl from the mass grave barely alive.

Remembering the brutality shown by the guards, Jim noted:

> I was beaten on a number of occasions. One such beating was administered by a Japanese soldier who was known as the Bandmaster. He was executed at the end of the war for atrocities. I was tortured by being made to stand in the sun with a heavy box of bolts above my head. I was hit with sticks if I put them down. I was also made to stand with a stretcher of earth held up between two of us.

Increasing ill health was to prove no barrier to the guards' continued brutality. 'I suffered recurring malaria and was kicked and beaten whenever I collapsed to the ground. I suffered from dysentery, tropical ulcers, beri beri, foot rot, ringworm, earache and starvation.' He also noted the lack of mercy shown by the Japanese to those who attempted to escape. 'Whilst up the jungle, four men from my troop escaped and were recaptured. They were executed.' As tracklaying progressed, the party was moved farther upcountry and reached Tampi in July. With the monsoon in full flow, torrential rain hampered progress, the men were forced to work longer shifts and the number of sick increased. In October 1943, construction on the railway was completed but Jim's time at camps along the track was not yet over. 'After joining up with the Burma party at the 263 km mark, we were forced to cut trees for firewood for the engines. We were employed for quite a long while doing that.'

In April 1944, Jim and his fellow members of the 9th Northumberlands were told that they were being sent down to Nong Pladuc. However, during the march Jim became severely ill with dysentery and, though his comrades carried him for some distance, they were forced to leave him at Chungkai hospital camp. Jim recalled:

> Chungkai was a base camp where the sick were sent. We were all hospital cases. They were burying so many every day. I went to the river for a bath, and I met this chap from Gateshead. About three days running we met by the river and went on talking, and then the next day, he didn't come. I went to his hut and enquired and they said he'd died in the night. I said, 'Jim, you're getting out of here.' I knew that the rest of the battalion had got onto a train. I was there about a week and I went to see this doctor and I said, 'I want to join my battalion at Nong Pladuc.'

A week later, Jim was able to do so.

On 27 May 1944, the battalion was sent back to River Valley Road camp in Singapore, having been selected for transportation to Japan, about which Jim later noted, 'On 3 June, 300 of us were put on a ship. We were battened down in the holds to proceed to Japan.' The *Shonan Maru* was part of a large convoy which attracted the attention of the US Navy, who would have been unaware of the presence on board of Allied prisoners of war.

> We were hounded all the way by American submarines. Conditions were terrible and six out of our ships were sunk. We were down in the holds, terrified that ours would be the next ship to be torpedoed.

Such fear was justified during a voyage which saw heavy loss of life from another of the ships in the convoy, the *Tamahoku Maru*, all but 212 of the 772 of those on board having perished.

Upon arrival at Moji in Japan, the prisoners were taken to Osaka No. 16 Branch camp near the town of Iruka in the Mie Prefecture. Jim later recalled, 'we went by train to a small village called Iruka, up in the mountains. We were forced to work in a copper mine.' Jim recalled how, in some respects, captivity at Iruka was very different to that in Thailand. 'The first impression of Iruka was a proper camp, which we hadn't had before, a cookhouse, beds, blankets, a suit of clothes to wear.' Jim and his fellow prisoners were put to work in the mines of Ishihara Industries, often working alongside Japanese miners. 'We found that the miners were friendly, they weren't abusive, and we came to have a good relationship with them.' There was, however, little difference in the appalling way the prisoners were treated by the guards, the total neglect of their medical needs and the provision of meagre rations. By the following February, sixteen of the party of British prisoners who had arrived with Jim were dead; three had been killed in accidents in the mine, the remainder having died from largely preventable, treatable diseases. According to Jim, the first indication that he and his comrades had of the end of the war was from something they heard shouted from a neighbouring camp but, when asked, their guards told them nothing:

> They kept us from going to work, so that indicated there was something. And eventually somebody fetched a wireless into camp from the mine, and they listened in and heard the message from MacArthur that the war was finished. We could hear that supplies were being dropped at different camps.

Whilst waiting for supplies to arrive, the prisoners investigated a stock of Red Cross parcels and provisions which had been withheld from them.

> They had these clothes that had been sent through the Red Cross, these lovely brown boots, and when we realised that the war was finished we said, 'right, we'll have them', and we opened the stores and we got them. It was the 9th September that we were liberated by American and Australian marines. We resembled walking skeletons. They came in and piled us up on these wagons and we had to go about thirty miles to a railway station.

Jim and his fellow prisoners were taken to the docks, where they boarded an American ship and were given medical checks, during which Jim was found to weigh just six stones.

> They examined me and wrote down what was the matter with me, and it finished up that they put this card around my neck with all these various things about vitamin deficiency and what not.

On 11 September 1945, Jim wrote a letter to his parents from onboard an American ship, telling them:

> American Naval personnel took us aboard a ship, stripped us of all clothing, gave us a good bath and supplied us with clean clothes and then gave us a meal. From there we came to Yokohama and transferred to another American ship and we are now waiting to sail for Manila. We are having a real good time,

plenty of everything. And I don't think it will take very long to get home. Will certainly be home for Christmas.

And so began Jim's journey home, via the Philippines and the United States. His daughter Barbara recalls him telling her about the journey.

> They took them right through America and Canada on a train on the way home. They were lauded and treated like heroes at every stop. One American man gave dad a silver dollar, which he cherished.

Jim sailed from Nova Scotia on the *Île de France* for the last leg of his journey home. 'Our only interest was to get home,' he later said.

The ship docked at Southampton on 31 October 1945 and Jim later told his daughter that the first thing he did once back on English soil was to bend down and kiss the ground. After spending the night in a transit camp, he made his way back home to Bilton Banks, where at first his family did not recognise him. Although the village of Shilbottle had lost several men to the war, the family were fortunate in that

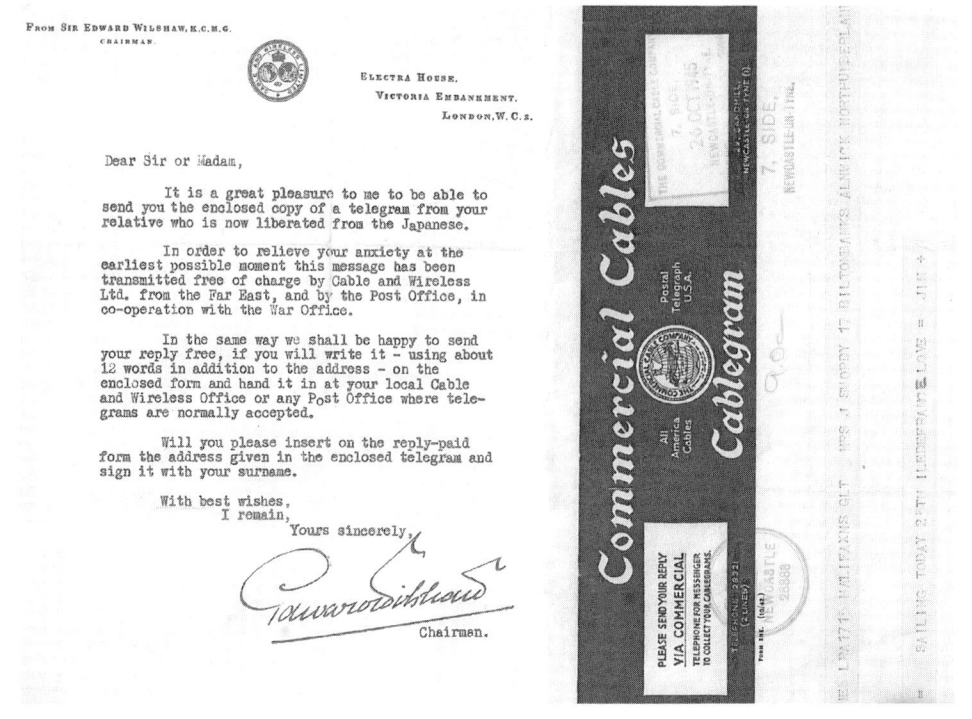

Telegram sent by Jim Swordy to his family in October 1945 informing them that he was sailing home on the *Île de France*.

Jim Swordy and his wife Jenny when they married in 1946.

not only did Jim return, but so also did his brother, whose future his father had also feared for.

After his return from the Far East, Jim remained deeply affected both physically and mentally by the experiences of the previous three and a half years. 'After a long leave I was given a very simple medical and discharged with a small pension for malaria and ear trouble. This was stopped after eighteen months.' Initially, Jim took work in the local mines but malnutrition and prolonged vitamin deficiency had taken their toll on his body. He suffered chronic digestive problems and was admitted to Dunstan Hospital for tests, after which he was advised to leave the mines and take a lighter job, so he took work as a bus conductor and, in the course of that job, met his wife, Jenny. They were married in 1946, Jim adopted her son and together they went on to have another three sons and a daughter.

Jim's ill health continued, however, and over the following years he sought treatment for a range of ailments, including a skin disorder, digestive problems, loss of bladder control, painful feet and increasingly poor hearing, all of which were linked to his time in captivity, and for which he was later awarded a pension. As time passed, Jenny was to discover the extent to which her husband had been affected by the time he spent in captivity, and continued to be affected some fifty years later. 'Counselling was unheard of at the time of my return from Japan. Over the years I have suffered from nightmares, which have induced me to fight and cry out in my sleep.' With searing honesty he added:

> I have often punched and kicked my wife during these nightmares, and on one occasion even bit her. I still suffer from the nightmares even after all these years. I have also been subject to bouts of bad temper, which my family have had to endure over the years. I still have mood swings and suffer acute emotional distress if I happen to view any sort of atrocity on television or in a film.

Jim often spoke about his time in captivity and had done so ever since his return from the Far East and, although emotionally scarred by his experiences, Barbara pointed out that her father harboured no bitterness or hatred.

> His experience did define his life but he was not bitter like most of his comrades. My dad taught us to be compassionate. He explained the Japanese behaviour in the war as a cultural thing and he instilled in us that war is futile.

It was with this attitude of mind that Jim, together with a group of his former comrades, returned to Japan in 1992. They did so in response to an appeal made in the spirit of reconciliation by a Japanese woman who wished to find the survivors of the camp at which sixteen British prisoners had lost their lives during captivity, to whom a memorial had been erected by the villagers of Iruka many years earlier. Returning to the site of their former prisoner of war camp, the group discovered that the villagers had tended the memorial to their fallen comrades ever since.

Jim found the experience of revisiting the place which, for so long, had held such painful memories for him quite overwhelming. 'After forty-seven years, it was very, very moving,' he said. Jim died in 2002, at the age of eighty-one. Since his return visit to Iruka he had corresponded regularly with some of those he had met, perhaps at last finding some sort of peace with the past which had caused him so much distress for so many years.

Chapter 21

AC1 John Stuart Robertson

Royal Air Force, No. 211 Squadron

When Stuart Robertson was photographed in 1942 by his Japanese captors, he was just twenty-one years old, in what should have been the prime of his life. Shaven-headed and wearing Japanese-issue prison clothing, his eyes stare straight into the camera lens, his gaunt face expressionless, a blank canvas which, nevertheless, manages to convey the sense of foreboding that doubtless filled many of the days, weeks and months that followed during his time as a prisoner of war. Whatever thoughts lay behind that blank stare as he faced the photographer he chose largely to keep to himself, only rarely talking in later years about his experiences in captivity.

Stuart was born and brought up in Motherwell, Scotland, where his father and grandfather ran the family business, a printers and stationery shop. He joined the business after leaving school but, in August 1940, following the outbreak of war, he was called up and at the age of nineteen joined the Royal Air Force. After reporting for active service at RAF Padgate, Stuart was then posted to West Kirby for basic training. This was followed by a move to Blackpool to undertake a rigger's course, after which he was sent to Cosford to train as a fitter in March 1941. Two months later he was posted to 30 MU (Maintenance Unit), RAF Sealand in Flintshire, his final posting before being sent overseas. On 31 July 1941, Stuart boarded the HMT *Orcades* at Gourock for the first leg of the journey which would take him to join No. 211 Squadron, operating as 72 OTU (Operational Training Unit) in the Sudan.

In mid-January 1942, following Japan's entry into the war and the escalation of hostilities in the Far East, Stuart found himself heading for

Stuart Robertson as a PoW at Mitsushima camp, Japan in 1943/44.

Singapore aboard the SS *Yoma*. However, as a result of the speed with which events unfolded, the island was on the verge of surrender before the *Yoma* could get there, so she instead sailed on to Oosthaven, Sumatra, arriving on 14 February. The squadron's time on Sumatra was brief, however, the Japanese having already landed on the island, forcing the men to retreat to Java, where many of the squadron gathered at a tobacco plantation in Purwokerto. Some of them were fortunate enough to make their escape by boarding the very last boats leaving Tjilitjap, to the south of the island, but Stuart was not among them and was captured at Tasikmalaya, beginning three and a half years of captivity. From Tasikmalaya, Stuart was taken to Malang, in eastern Java, and held at what had previously been a Dutch army barracks, where he and other prisoners were put to work on the construction of a runway at the aerodrome. Any doubts they may have had about the ruthlessness of their captors were put to rest a matter of weeks later when four of their comrades, who had attempted to escape, were recaptured. Two days later Stuart was among those forced to assemble at the aerodrome to witness the botched execution of the four men by firing squad. The men's deaths were anything but quick, the entire exercise a lesson in the capacity of the Japanese to take swift and cruel retribution against those who dared to defy them.

Stuart Robertson in 1940.

Six months after arriving at Malang, Stuart's time in Java came to an end when he was assigned to a party of over 2,000 men, known as Java Party 5C, who were selected for relocation elsewhere as the Japanese continued to redistribute their vast pool of labour to wherever its members could most productively be used. On 21 October 1942, he was among those herded on board the *Kunitama Maru* which, like the other vessels used for transporting prisoners from one location to another, carried no Red Cross markings to indicate the presence on board of prisoners of war, giving rise to the ever-present risk of attack by Allied aircraft or submarines. Any relief that Stuart may have felt upon reaching Singapore days later would have been short-lived, for his stay there was brief. On 30 October, he was one of 1,200 prisoners who were packed into the holds of the *Dainichi Maru*, bound for Japan. The voyage, via Saigon and Formosa, was infinitely worse than the one which had taken him from Java to Singapore. The first death occurred, rather poignantly, on 11 November, Armistice Day, but it was far from the last. Given very little food or water during the weeks at sea and rarely allowed any fresh air, disease rapidly took hold among the increasingly weak prisoners. As the weeks passed, it became a desperate battle to survive which not everybody won, and by the time the voyage ended, after twenty-six days at sea, eighty of those on board had died and many more were so seriously ill that they would not recover. It is difficult to imagine that anyone could emerge from such an experience psychologically unaffected.

On 25 November, the *Dainichi Maru* reached Moji in Japan and the prisoners were finally able to escape from the stench of the holds. The men were split into groups and Stuart was among those who now faced a two-day journey by train to Tokyo No. 3B camp, Mitsushima, in Nagano Prefecture. Having left the heat of Singapore behind them, they were plunged into the bitter cold of the Japanese winter and, upon arrival at the camp, were paraded outside and stripped naked prior to being weighed and measured. Neither the Japanese prison clothing with which they were issued to replace their tropical kit nor the wooden huts which became their accommodation offered much protection against the often freezing conditions. The huts had little or no heating and only dirt and sand as their base, becoming waterlogged in the rainy season, and frozen in the depths of winter. Such conditions proved lethal for some, as pneumonia began to add to the death toll. With water pipes and tanks frozen much of the time, there were occasions when the men could wash neither themselves nor their eating utensils, thereby issuing a further invitation to disease, of which there was already plenty. Despite the fact that dysentery, beri beri and scurvy was rife within the camp, the Japanese showed little interest in providing any drugs and it took the first death from diphtheria to prompt them to issue the prisoners with potassium permanganate to gargle with, but, with so much untreated disease, the deaths continued.

The British, American and Canadian prisoners at Mitsushima were used by the Kumagai-gum Construction Company and worked on the construction of a hydro-electric dam. For the following ten months or so, Stuart was among those put to work breaking rocks in the quarry and pushing them down onto tracks ready for loading onto buggies, or loading sand onto trucks. From information given on the questionnaire Stuart completed after his eventual liberation from the camp, it is clear that he was among many who took every opportunity to subvert efforts by the Japanese to use them as an efficient workforce. In response to the question as to whether he had undertaken any sabotage, he wrote, 'yes, all men did, whenever possible,' citing as an example, 'derailing trucks, refusing to work at high speed when Japs required'. The penalty for such acts of defiance would have been severe at any camp, but none more so than Mitsushima, which is generally acknowledged to have been one of the most brutal camps in Japan. Prisoners were regularly beaten for infractions of rules which did not officially exist. In addition to the random beatings and total indifference to welfare which was part of the fabric of Far East captivity, prisoners at Mitsushima were sometimes forced out of their barracks at night and made to stand to attention in freezing conditions for no other reason than to amuse the guards. For men whose health was already in such a perilous state, such treatment was sometimes a death sentence.

During Stuart's time at the camp, he and fellow prisoner, Malaysian-born Paul Loong, RAF, became friends, and remained in contact after the war. Like Stuart, Paul had for many years remained silent about his time as a prisoner of war, only in his seventies deciding to talk about his experiences and revealing a diary which he had secretly kept. Paul observed that during the first winter at Mitsushima, twenty per cent of the prisoners at the camp had died and that those who survived had been little more than 'walking skeletons', subject to frequent beatings by guards who never imagined that Japan would lose the war and that they would be answerable for their actions. The prisoners were required to work, regardless of the state of their health, which was not improved by the poor diet. Rarely would meals consist of anything more than a mixture of barley and rice with, occasionally, some vegetables but seldom any meat, and there were few medical supplies to treat the inevitable diseases to which the increasingly emaciated men succumbed as a result. Somewhat perversely, considering the total lack of concern for the wellbeing of their captives, the Japanese did allow the distribution of several issues of Red Cross parcels during the period of captivity, the food content of which no doubt went some way in preventing even greater loss of life. On 6 September 1943, Stuart was moved to Shinagawa Hospital in Tokyo, which dealt with all seriously ill prisoners from the camps in the Tokyo area. Records show that he remained there for more than a year, the reasons for which remain unclear, as it was something which he never spoke of. When asked about this by Stuart's son, Ian, Paul Loong's recollection was that Stuart had walked out of the camp with a soldier holding a rifle to his back and that, whilst he had certainly been ill, his health had not been any worse than the rest of the prisoners, all of whom had existed on a near-starvation diet for months and were suffering from a range of ailments. Stuart returned to Mitsushima on 28 November 1944, by which time Paul had been moved to a different camp and they were not in contact again until after the war.

For the first two years of their time at Mitsushima, Paul commented that the prisoners were continually told by the guards that Japan was winning the war and that they would spend the rest of their lives as their slaves. However, by the end of 1944 they were able to learn from discarded Japanese newspapers that the tide of the war was turning, giving them desperately needed hope for their future and providing a welcome boost to morale. By the time American forces liberated the camp, Stuart was one of 215 British prisoners to have survived, some fifty-nine prisoners having died during captivity. The ill-treatment at the camp was so severe that, following the War Crimes trial, six of the camp guards were executed and a further six given terms of imprisonment. Whether it was to Stuart's advantage to have been held at Shinagawa hospital for so long rather than at Mitshushima is questionable,

Stuart Robertson and his wife Margaret when they married in 1946.

however, as the medical officer and director of the hospital was prosecuted for having performed human experiments upon prisoners of war and sentenced to life imprisonment with hard labour. Following his liberation from the camp, Stuart boarded the American vessel USS *Rescue* on 4 September to begin his journey home. From Okinawa he was flown to Manila where, after undergoing a medical check, he boarded *Implacable* on 25 September, bound for Canada, and eventually arrived in Southampton on board the *Île de France* on 31 October 1945.

After returning home to Motherwell, Stuart resumed work in the family printing business and made a concerted effort to leave the horror of his years in captivity behind him. He became a special constable and also became involved socially with a local amateur dramatic group, the Manse Road Players. Shortly afterwards he married Margaret, who had served in the ATS on the searchlights in the South of England during the war together with his sister, and they went on to have two sons and a daughter over the next few years.

The past, it seems, had been neatly bottled up and was rarely mentioned. However, it became apparent over time that the years which Stuart had spent in captivity had left their mark upon his mental health. Ian explained, 'my mother has told us that he suffered from nightmares and would cry out in his sleep. He told her to make sure that she woke him up when that happened.'

Although as a child Ian had been unaware of the nightmares Stuart suffered, he was aware that all was not right with his father.

It was during my early school years that I realised that something was wrong. My dad came out of the police and withdrew from the Manse Road Players and became increasingly withdrawn. I seem to remember someone saying that one of the Manse Road Players had given him a hard time about something.

Ian went on to explain that from then on his father did not attend any of the school events in which he was involved, nor those in which he participated as a member of the Life Boys and Boys Brigade.

> My dad never attended any event that I was involved in. He never came to Life Boys or Boys Brigade annual parent night displays. I played football every Saturday for the Boys Brigade Company that I was in and I ran in the relay team in my last year at primary school, but my father was always absent. All the other boys' dads were there and it soon became very hurtful to me that he did not attend. I didn't understand it and there was never any explanation offered.

Neither was Ian able to comprehend what he perceived as his father's odd behaviour at times.

> He would never put the lights on in rooms at home when it got dark at night until the curtains were closed and he would shout at anybody who did. He said he didn't want to be seen from outside the house. He would also get under the kitchen table if there was thunder and lightning. He never bared his arms, even in the height of summer and never explained why. I came to the conclusion that there were marks, possibly prisoner numbers or maybe something else which he didn't want us to see. He also had painfully thin legs throughout his life. I never saw them either as they too were always covered. My dad never went out socially. He immersed himself in the printing business and only took two weeks each year to go on holiday, usually to somewhere on the west coast of Scotland, where none of us kids actually wanted to go.

Illustrating the way in which, for some families of former captives of the Japanese, relationships unravelled in the wake of so many unanswered questions and so much unexplained behaviour, Ian explained:

> over my teenage years, not understanding what the situation was, I became increasingly distant with him, lost communication with him and we didn't speak to each other for a number of years before I left home.

Ian had grown up with only a vague awareness of his father having been a prisoner of war, largely limited to knowing of the existence of a number of items which Stuart had brought back from his years in the Far East.

> There were two Samurai swords in a cupboard in my bedroom, there was a section of parachute that was significant – American air drop into the camp at liberation – and I also saw a photo, not sure when, that showed him walking out of camp in a loincloth and he was nothing but skin and bones.

Stuart had, at one time, kept another item from his days as a prisoner of war.

> I was told that he had a diary, but my grandfather had made him destroy it before he married my mother because there were things in it that she wasn't to see. It is a great pity that this didn't survive.

Had the diary survived and been allowed to disclose its secrets, Stuart's continuing silence about his experiences in captivity might not have had such profound consequences as, sadly, father and son were unable to repair their fractured relationship.

> Unfortunately, the damage had been done and I just couldn't connect with him. I have to say that he was not a bad man. He was very talented. He was interested in photography and converted a lot of the photos he took of the Scottish scenery into oil and water colour paintings and I still have many of them.

Stuart continued to run the printing business until he retired but became increasingly introverted. A lifelong smoker, he was diagnosed with emphysema in his sixties and spent the last year of his life bedridden, dying at the age of seventy in 1991. A post mortem revealed evidence of scarring on his lungs which the coroner attributed to illnesses he had contracted during his time as a prisoner of war. The scarring of his mind by the unspoken horrors of three and half years of captivity and the corrosive effect of his persistent silence appears to have been equally damaging. Said Ian:

> Who knows what would have been different if he had not been in Mitsushima, but it certainly has had a huge impact on my life, some of which I still don't understand, probably because I don't know the truth of what happened to my dad.

Chapter 22

Private Raymond William Charles Wyatt

5th Battalion Bedfordshire & Hertfordshire Regiment

When twelve-year-old Ray Wyatt's interest in wildlife led him to become the youngest member in the history of the Aylesbury Cage and Aviary Bird Club, little did he realise that it was an interest which would give him comfort during the darkest time of his life and help him to survive an experience that claimed the lives of thousands. Born in 1918, Ray and his younger brother were brought up in Aylesbury in Buckinghamshire and his interest in nature, particularly birds, began at an early age. As an asthma sufferer during an era when such children were discouraged from taking part in sporting activities, this was a pastime he was safely allowed to indulge and one that held his interest for the rest of his life. When war was declared on 3 September 1939, twenty-one-year-old Ray was working as a coach painter but within two weeks had left that job behind him, having enlisted in the Bedfordshire and Hertfordshire Regiment and been assigned to the 5th Battalion.

For the first eight months of his army service Ray was based in Bedfordshire, guard duties at airports, bridges and various other locations taking precedence over training. In May 1940, Ray and his comrades were moved to North Walsham on the Norfolk coast in an anti-invasion role. They remained there until January 1941, when they were posted to Galashiels and it was whilst Ray was here that he and another member of the battalion, Cyril, began a friendship which would last for the rest of their lives. As the likelihood of invasion lessened, so training intensified and the battalion moved to the Midlands, firstly to Uttoxeter in April 1941 and then to Atherstone a month later, followed by another

Ray Wyatt, around 1940.

move to Lichfield in September, where the men received the news that they were to be posted overseas. After travelling to Liverpool, the battalion boarded the HMT *Reina del Pacifico* and on 30 October 1941 sailed for Halifax, where they were transferred to the *West Point*. The men believed at the time that they were on their way to Egypt but, after sailing via Cape Town to Bombay, they discovered that their ultimate destination was to be Singapore. After undergoing a period of training in jungle warfare at Ahmednagar, the men re-embarked on the *West Point* and reached Singapore on 29 January 1942, whereupon Ray and his comrades were ordered to Birdwood Camp, to the north-east of the island. A little over a week later, when the Japanese landed on Singapore, the battalion was among the front-line troops based to the north-west of the city, with Ray attached to HQ 1 Platoon (Signals). However, by the end of the following week, barely a fortnight after having arrived in Singapore, Ray had become a prisoner of war.

After marching to Changi, owing to the sheer force of numbers assembled at the barracks complex, Ray was one of many who had to camp out in the open in tents as they tried to come to terms with their status as prisoners of war. He remained at Changi until the middle of April, when he was among a party of men marched over twenty miles across the island to Bukit Timah where they became part of the considerable labour force working on the construction of a Shinto shrine. There, Ray was put to work on road construction, for which he received ten cents per day, a meagre sum but enough to make a difference in an existence where the ability to earn money to buy extra food played such a large part in staving off disease. For the duration of their time working on the shrine, Ray and his comrades were accommodated in the battle-scarred buildings of a former RAF camp, where they remained until construction was completed in September.

A larger construction project now awaited Ray. On 22 October, he was assigned to a party of 650 men who were assembled at Singapore station to be packed into the goods trucks which would transport them to Thailand as part of Group 2. Arriving at Ban Pong four days later, the party were marched to Kan'buri, where they stayed overnight. The following day, after crossing the river by barge, they marched to Chungkai, where they were absorbed into the mass of prisoners working on the construction of the railway and put to work clearing swathes of jungle. Although Ray later said little about his time in the Far East, archive material relating to others in the battalion who were held alongside him provides an insight into his experiences. Within days of his arrival at Chungkai, Ray witnessed the deaths of some of his comrades as disease took hold of their vitamin-starved bodies, adding new depths of sadness to an already sombre occasion when, on 11 November, he and his fellow prisoners held two minutes' silence in memory of the fallen. The party was then assigned to embankment building and work on the cutting and told that if they completed a set quota of work in six days, they would be given a day off. The emptiness of such promises was soon revealed. Showing they were capable of working faster merely increased the amount of pressure placed upon the prisoners to maintain the pace, irrespective of any difficulties presented by the terrain, the weather, or sickness; if the day's quota of work had not been completed, work continued until it had been, with the result that the men often worked until dusk, and sometimes beyond. The asthma from which Ray had suffered in childhood had not left him and presented particular problems in an environment where no allowances were made for health problems; the guards regarded any failure to keep up with the pace as laziness rather than the consequence of illness and responded with brutality rather than sympathy.

In February 1943, the party was moved upcountry to Wang Takhain and put to work on embankment building. They remained there until the end of March when they were moved up to Wang Pho North, where work on the Wang Pho viaduct was nearing completion. Being forced to work twelve-hour shifts at a quarry, sometimes in torrential rain, would have endangered the health of the fittest of men but, as an asthma sufferer, the effect upon Ray's health was severe. When the party was moved back down the track towards the end of April, he remained at Tarsao hospital camp, separated from his unit for several weeks before rejoining them at Tha Makhan in June. Conditions at Tha Makhan, just fifty-six kilometres from the southern base of the railway, were an improvement on those in the camps farther upcountry, although there too, there was a desperate shortage of drugs with which to combat disease. Ray remained at Tha Makhan for several months, working in the shadow of the huge concrete-and-steel bridge the prisoners had recently finished building, a period of his captivity which left an indelible mark upon his mind.

It is clear from one of the few episodes of his captivity that Ray chose to talk about in later life that, given his love of nature and wildlife, the creatures with whom he shared his jungle surroundings served as a mild antidote to the horrors around him, thereby supplying a small slice of comfort in an otherwise hellish existence. For amidst the uncertainty of what lay ahead, with death a daily reality and disease waiting to strike at any moment, Ray collected butterflies. Whenever able to, he would take out his carefully preserved collection and quietly study them on his bamboo bed space. He later told his daughter, Jane, that on one particular occasion he was looking at his collection,

> when a guard stormed in the hut looking for a hidden radio. This guard went down the length of the hut, rifle butting as he went. Dad said that he thought,

'This is it, we are all in very serious trouble here'. However, when he reached where Dad was, he saw the butterflies and stopped. In pidgin English, he and Dad 'talked' about the butterflies. At the end, he and Dad bowed to each other and the guard left the hut causing no-one else any injury.

Thus, butterflies, among the few living creatures sharing the prisoners' jungle habitat which were not viewed as a potential source of food, nonetheless had their value.

After leaving Tha Makhan in October 1943, Ray was moved to Chungkai hospital camp, where the combined effects of malaria and tropical ulcers kept him away from his unit for several months. He was joined at the camp by trainloads of sick men who had been brought down from the camps farther upcountry, many of whom did not survive. That more men did not die was due in no small measure to the heroic efforts of hard-pressed doctors, who performed near miracles under the most difficult of circumstances, none more so than the renowned Australian surgeon Edward 'Weary' Dunlop, for whom Ray worked as a medical orderly once his health had recovered sufficiently. Though Ray had no formal training, he was one of many medical orderlies recruited from those who were convalescing, a strong stomach the only qualification needed in order to assist with the more gruesome aspects of treatment, compassion the only requirement for offering comfort to the desperately sick and dying. Jane knew nothing of her father's work as a medical orderly until the last years of his life, when a television programme featuring the surgeon was shown, prompting Ray to talk about the man whose work he had witnessed over sixty years earlier and allowing her to glimpse another dimension of her father's years in captivity. Ray remained at Chungkai until May 1944, after which he was moved away from the camps on the Thai-Burma railway to Lang Suan, east of Bangkok. There he was put to work on repairs to the Singapore to Bangkok railway line as a result of Allied aircraft carrying out an increasing number of raids. Following the liberation of the camp at the end of August 1945, Ray was transported to Rangoon, where he received a medical check and then joined the many impatient for their repatriation to England. Ray had less time to wait than many and boarded the *Corfu*, which arrived at Southampton docks on 7 October 1945.

Several months after having returned home to Aylesbury, it was whilst Ray was on a period of weekend leave that he met his future wife, May, whose family ran a shop sympathetic to the needs of returning servicemen and, at a time of great shortages, kept a stock of cigarettes under the counter for them. Ray and May were married in 1948, settled in Aylesbury and went on to have a son and a daughter.

Following his discharge from the army, Ray worked as a painter and decorator and, after moving to a bungalow which was to remain the family home for over forty years, built aviaries in order to indulge his passion for caged birds, the same love of nature which had helped to sustain him during his captivity now providing solace in a sometimes turbulent life. However, like many of those who returned from the Far East, Ray struggled with the massive adjustment required to live a 'normal' life after having endured the wretched existence of a prisoner of war for the previous three and a half years. With no help to cope with what would, in these more enlightened times, probably have been diagnosed as post-traumatic stress disorder, Ray struggled on alone, placing an enormous strain upon those closest to him. Jane said that her mother had told her that:

> It took Dad two months to be able to sleep in a bed. Up until then he was sleeping on the floor, as a bed was too soft. When home at weekends, he and Mum would sit up all night as he wouldn't dare to go to sleep for the nightmares he would experience. I often think how deeply Mum must have loved him to be willing to take on this man so tortured.

The extent of Ray's torment as a consequence of his years as a prisoner of the Japanese is evident in Jane's childhood memories. Wrestling with feelings of disloyalty towards a much-loved father, she explained that whilst her childhood had

Ray Wyatt and his wife May when they married in 1948.

been happy, the mental scars which captivity had inflicted upon her father had also had an impact on her own life.

> Dad had a temper. It was occasionally uncontrolled. I often had to walk on eggshells in case I said the wrong thing and he would end up shouting at me. Subsequently I cannot cope with confrontation face to face at all .... I also witnessed violence in the home. Dad, not often, thankfully, would, again, be unable to control his temper and it would result in him lashing out at Mum. As a child it was frightening to see him hit mum and the effect it would have on her. According to Mum, it was often around the time of VJ Day or Remembrance Sunday. I can only assume it was triggered by memories. I now cannot witness domestic violence portrayed on the television without feeling physically sick as I did as a child. I feel so disloyal to Dad ... . I have tried to understand why he did what he did, and to some extent I do. I am desperate to reiterate that I consider that I had a happy childhood and that I adored my Dad.

Jane went on to add that in addition to his experiences in captivity having left her father with an inability to ever leave food on his plate, they also left him with an intense dislike of enclosed spaces. 'He was always happier outdoors than in. Mum told me that he had seen friends and comrades driven mad by being in cages in the full sun, so perhaps that was it.' Ray's physical health also suffered long-term damage as a result of his time as a prisoner of war deeply affecting not only him but those around him.

> The fact that Dad had asthma before he joined up, coupled with the effects of captivity, caused him to suffer most winters from bronchitis. Most Christmases when I was a child, Dad had a period of illness that confined him to bed. It was very difficult as a small child not being allowed to be noisily excited over Christmas.

Until the 1970s, Ray also suffered from repeated bouts of the malaria which he had contracted during his time in Thailand and, unbeknown to him, for many years carried an even more tenacious reminder of his years in captivity in the form of an intestinal worm infection. He eventually received treatment for this condition at the Queen Elizabeth Military Hospital at Woolwich and was, somewhat belatedly, awarded a disability pension. His treatment continued until the 1990s, over forty years after he had left the jungle camps of Thailand.

Ray's reluctance to talk about his experiences lasted the rest of his life.

> He was in hospital well into his eighties with yet another chest infection, when one of the doctors asked him if he had ever been abroad. Dad answered that he

had been 'out East' many years ago, almost brushing it off. I then told the doctor where and when! I think that sums up just how little he wanted to talk about it.

In his later years Jane noticed a subtle change in her father's attitude towards the Japanese.

Up until the fiftieth anniversary of the end of the Second World War, Dad hated the Japanese. Nothing made by them would have had a place in our home. However, I am sure he softened after the commemorations. He was, at that time, fit enough to go up to London and finally march with his comrades. Although he still didn't talk about his experiences, I am sure he became reconciled to what had happened during those years. A lot of the anger had gone.

Jane said that it had once been suggested to her father, during a rare discussion of his time as a prisoner of war, that he had been too stubborn to die, to which he had apparently responded, after a lengthy pause, 'you're right ... otherwise they would have won!' Ray went on to live to the age of ninety-three, a stubborn streak, perhaps, partly responsible for a determination to continue to deny 'them' such a victory. However, although Ray survived long after his return from captivity, it is, perhaps, a measure of how much those years continued to prey on his mind in the last years of his life that he told Jane that, had he been in better health, he would have liked to have gone back to Thailand, in particular to see again the bridge at Tha Makhan.

Although over 600 bridges were built along the length of the Thai-Burma railway, the iconic steel structure spanning

Ray Wyatt in 2011, aged 93.

The bridge at Tha Makhan, photographed in 2017. (Photo courtesy of Eric Skilton)

the River Mae Klong – which has since been renamed the River Kwai Yai – has, for many people, come to symbolise the brutality of Japanese captivity and the suffering of thousands. Perhaps echoing the sentiments of many whose lives, like his, had been changed forever by those who had ordered its construction, Ray said that the bridge 'wouldn't let him go', so powerful were the memories it continued to evoke over sixty years later.

Chapter 23

Lance Corporal John Dunlop Petrie

3rd Battalion Singapore Straits Volunteer Force (SSVF)

By 1933, John Petrie had been living in Malaya for five years, had mastered the local languages, felt settled in his chosen career and was happy with the path his life was leading. He then took a decision which was to have a dramatic effect on the rest of his life when, amid a period of heightened concern for the future of the region, he became one of many local civilians who joined the Malayan Volunteer Forces. Since Singapore had long been widely regarded as an impregnable fortress, John could not have foreseen that in years to come the island would fall into enemy hands and that he would pay a heavy price for playing his part in the defence of the land which had become his home.

Born in Edinburgh in 1902, John was the youngest of three children and grew up in Alloa, where his father worked as a clerk. After leaving school he followed in his father's footsteps as an office worker and trained as an accountant but then, at the age of twenty-six, took a post as a British Crown Agent in Singapore. Though initially based on the island when he arrived in 1928, John was subsequently moved to Penang, where he worked in the Municipal Engineering Department. It was three years before John was able to return home to Scotland but during his first period of six months' leave in 1932 he met Catherine, who later became his wife. It was upon his return to Penang that John enlisted in the 3rd Battalion of the Singapore Straits Volunteer Force. During his next period of leave in Scotland in 1936, he and Catherine married and then returned to Penang together.

At the time of Japan's invasion of Malaya in December 1941 and the subsequent attack on Penang, John was on leave with his wife and young son in Australia, having decided against risking a wartime voyage to Scotland. After the news reached them, John and two other members of the SSVF

John Petrie, his wife Catherine and their son Graham in 1940.

who were also on leave in Australia cabled Malaya Command and were instructed to return to Singapore as soon as possible. Leaving his wife and son behind in Perth, on 10 January 1942 John, together with the other volunteers and almost 3,500 troops, boarded the RMS *Aquitania* and sailed for Singapore, transferring to smaller ships at Ratai Bay in the Sunda Strait. On 24 January, as they approached Singapore to aid in the defence of the island, they were passed by ships carrying those who were hastily making their escape. Unable to influence the outcome of events, three weeks after having returned to help defend the island against the Japanese, John was one of many members of the volunteer forces who faced being their captives, and for the following three and a half years was treated as a military prisoner of war.

After spending the first three months of his captivity at Changi, John was moved to River Valley Road camp in May 1942, the island with which he had become so familiar over the years now overrun by Japanese. Once the prisoners were assigned to working parties and allowed beyond the confines of the camps, John's local knowledge and his familiarity with the people, together with his ability to speak Chinese and Malay, were a distinct advantage when it came to bartering with local traders for extra food or desperately needed medical supplies. However, there was an extra dimension to his use of such skills because John was one of a number of Freemasons at River Valley Road and Changi who continued to practise their craft during captivity, notably performing charitable works aimed at helping those most in need, despite the obvious constraints placed upon them by their status as prisoners of war. John had become a member of the Freemasons in 1933, little knowing that within a decade he would be undertaking Masonic activities, already, by their nature, bathed in secrecy, with an even greater degree of covertness. Though the practice of Freemasonry in the camps on Singapore had been approved by the GOC, Lieutenant General Percival, as a 'means of preventing the deterioration of character and morale', it was vital that they conduct their business undetected by the Japanese, who forbade group activities of any kind. Two months after arriving at the camp, John played an integral part in the founding of the River Valley Road PoW Masonic Club, his name appearing with those of twenty-four others on the Roll of Founder Members, a handwritten scroll carefully crafted on rice paper which members of the club somehow managed to keep hidden. (Another of the founding members named on the roll was Major Cyril Wild, who had previously carried the white flag when the Allied Forces had surrendered to the Japanese, and who was later to head the War Crimes Tribunal.)

The club met once a week, often in the camp bakery, on the pretext of using the ovens to de-bug items of clothing or, alternatively, in the cobbler's shop. The fact that its members were able to engage at all in Masonic activity whilst in captivity owes much to the fact that on the occasions when the Japanese did detect their gatherings they appear to have viewed them as having a religious rather than secular basis. It was to their advantage that, as fellow prisoner and Army chaplain Eric Cordingly later reflected, the Japanese appeared wary of banning religion. Given the fact that in the eyes of the Japanese, because the sick did not work they were undeserving of even the pitifully small rations of food given to those who did, there was no shortage of those needing the help of others in order to survive; and for those whose lives were ebbing away to disease and could not be saved, a cigarette and kind words in their last hours were often a greater comfort than food. The club's activities were curtailed for a while at the end of July 1942, when John and some of the other founding members were moved back to Changi. However, one of them later recorded that their Masonic meetings resumed after a month, despite an increasing number of searches being carried out by the Japanese and the grave risks attached to being involved in Masonic activity.

The River Valley Road PoW Masonic Club Roll of Foundation Members. (John Petrie's name is tenth from the bottom)

John's participation in the activities of the club were halted on 13 May 1943, when he and a number of other volunteers were among a party of 545 prisoners transported to Thailand under the command of Lieutenant Colonel H.R. Humphries, Royal Artillery, as part of H Force. By this time, many thousands of men had been sent to Thailand to work on the construction of the railway but although earlier contingents had been half-starved and vitamin deficient when they left Singapore, they had been considerably fitter than those who now made up H Force. Many of the men who made up this party had been prevented from leaving with earlier work parties due to their

194   A Cruel Captivity

PoW Des Bettany's sketch of H Force leaving Selarang for the Thai-Burma Railway in 1943, the spectre of death looming over them. (Photo by kind permission of Keith Bettany, www.changipowart.com)

ill health. However, having worked scores of prisoners to the point of exhaustion and, in denying essential medical supplies, allowed disease to rage unchecked through the camps, the Japanese now sought to supplement their labour force by drawing upon the least fit among their captives. So it was that John, who, at the age of forty-one, was several years older than many of those in captivity, found himself among those crammed into metal goods trucks to endure the four-day journey to Thailand. With the Japanese having, from the outset, viewed their captives as entirely dispensable, the men of H Force were, in effect, replacements for those who had already been worked to death or had died from disease. Many would not return.

It was not simply the age and comparative ill-health of this, the last party of prisoners to be sent to work on the railway, which hampered their chances of surviving. Like the party of prisoners comprising F Force, who had been sent to Thailand the previous month, H Force remained under the control of Malaya PoW Command. The consequences of this were grave, since it meant that there was no infrastructure there for them – crucially, no supplies – since, there having been no transfer of authority, Thailand PoW Command felt no responsibility to provide any. When John and his fellow prisoners arrived at Ban Pong, they were forced to march over 130 kilometres up to Tonchan South, with little food to sustain them other than that which they had managed to bring with them. Though at times their guards marched the prisoners at night in order to avoid the extreme heat of the day, by the time they reached Tonchan they were exhausted and starving, and whilst some had money or valuables with which to barter for food from the natives, many did not, making what was already a dire problem of insufficient rations very much worse.

As work on the railway had fallen behind schedule, John was one of many men, who, however ill-suited to hammering at a rock face or shovelling piles of rubble, were given heavy manual labour, including a party of officers who had also travelled as part of H Force. With no quarter given for the men's increasing ill-health, punishment was brutal for those who showed signs of slacking, and Lieutenant Colonel Humphries was later to write a report on the treatment of the men under his command, citing the 'vindictiveness and sadism' of the Japanese guards. Given that so many of the younger and comparatively fitter men in the workforce succumbed to death and disease, it was perhaps inevitable that within three months of their arrival at Tonchan South, the men of H Force, including John, proved easy targets for various tropical diseases which the camp doctors, with few drugs at their disposal, could do little to treat. In addition to dysentery, malaria and deficiency-related diseases, which were already rife, cholera arrived in the camp in June 1943 to add to the death toll.

In August 1943, John was among a group of the most seriously ill prisoners who were moved to Kan'buri hospital camp, where he remained until the following December. Once he was considered fit enough to be moved, he was transported back to Singapore, to Sime Road camp on the outskirts of the town, where he was held for the remainder of his time in captivity. The camp had previously been used by the RAF and, although somewhat dilapidated, the wooden huts in which the prisoners were accommodated were a marked improvement upon the conditions John had endured in Thailand. However, an urgent need for food prevailed and, with the prisoners assigned to working parties according to age and fitness, much effort was put into digging vegetable gardens and growing sweet potatoes and other food crops with which to supplement their shrinking rations of rice. So desperate was the need for food that snails were also cultivated for their protein content. As 1944 progressed, there were further cuts in rations and, though a lucrative black market was in operation, by that time most prisoners had already sold most of their belongings in exchange for food. Only in the final months of their captivity were any Red Cross parcels distributed by guards who, sensing that the war was not going in their favour, suddenly became more accommodating. At the same time, prisoners were put to work digging tunnels within the perimeter of the camp, with no explanation offered as to their intended purpose. However, in the light of Japan's intention to 'annihilate them all and not to leave any traces'* of their prisoners in the event of an Allied invasion, the same guards who were showing the first spark of humanity in over three years were also overseeing the prisoners dig what promised to be their own graves.

Though many of the other founding members of the River Valley Road Masonic Club had also been conscripted to work on the railway, few apart from John survived the experience. Nonetheless, by the middle of 1945 there still remained among the prisoners held at various camps in Singapore at least 180 Freemasons, and although circumstances conspired against them finding the necessary privacy to hold meetings, the evidence suggests that John and his fellow Masons continued their charitable works for the duration of their captivity, their Masonic activity concluding after the surrender of the Japanese with a memorial service at Saint David's Church, Sime Road, on 2 September 1945.

Following John's return to Singapore from Australia in January 1942, his wife and son had remained in Perth until October 1943 when they embarked on a precarious voyage to Britain and settled once more in Scotland where John finally joined them towards the end of 1945. Of John's return home, his son, Graham, recalled 'I was too young to know or remember him until after the war, when he returned as a complete stranger to me.' The years of captivity had clearly taken their toll on John's health and he suffered recurrent bouts of malaria for many years. According to his granddaughter, Alison, her grandmother:

> often spoke of how ill my grandfather was when he came home and how thin he was also. She felt, too, that he remained in poor health because of his experience as a prisoner of war.

Less than a year after his return from the Far East, unable to adjust to life in his native Scotland, he took the decision to return to Penang and resume his career and was joined the following year by his wife and son. Though they endeavoured to resume the lives they had lived before the Japanese invasion, the intervening years had caused irrevocable changes. John's relationship with his son remained distant, not helped by Graham being placed in a series of boarding schools upon the family's return to Malaya, while John and Catherine went on to have another son. The family did not all live together again until they returned permanently to Scotland in

---

* In August 1944, Japan issued orders to all camp commanders for the 'final disposition' of all PoWs!

1956, following Malaya's independence, after which John found an office job which he held until his retirement a few years later.

John remained largely silent about all that he had witnessed and endured in captivity for the rest of his life. According to Graham:

> he rarely spoke about his experiences, to me or my younger brother, apart from occasionally making such comments as that the cricket commentator E.W. Swanton had been in one of the same camps as he was.

As a Freemason, John had already grown accustomed to drawing a veil of silence over one particular aspect of his life before his internment as a prisoner of war, and it would appear that he heeded the government directive of the time instructing former prisoners to 'take pains to spare the feelings of others' by not talking about their experiences. Said Alison, 'I think my granddad just wanted to forget if he could because he was told to,' one of many who, accustomed to obeying orders, felt compelled to say little or nothing about a part of their lives which was, inevitably, infused with horrific memories, irrespective of the emotional cost both to themselves and their families. Graham explained that whilst his relationship with his father 'was always a cordial and affectionate one, it was rarely intimate and he spoke seldom about his past'. Said Alison, 'my grandfather was a quiet man and perhaps he was not able to express his affection after what he had been through.' Though, for the rest of his life, John retained a loathing of rice and an abhorrence of food being wasted, according to Alison, he showed no sign of having harboured any bitterness towards his former captors, though Alison's grandmother was more forthcoming.

> She was very bitter towards the Japanese. She often spoke of losing everything. She felt that my granddad and the men he fought with and were imprisoned with were very much let down by the British government. She felt he may have lived longer if he had not been a PoW.

So little of his experiences as a prisoner of war did John share with his family that it wasn't until after his death that they discovered that he had been awarded medals in recognition of his service to his country, members of the volunteer forces having been perceived as no less entitled than those who had enlisted in the military. Whilst

John Petrie in the late 1940s.

John's silence about so much of this period of his life inevitably has left his family with unanswered questions, it in no way diminishes their pride in his not only having survived captivity, but also in the quiet way he went about helping others to do so.

John died in 1971 at the age of sixty-eight from bone cancer, the deprivations he suffered as a prisoner of war, particularly as a member of the ill-fated H Force, having done his long-term health no favours. Though no great age when he died, he was, however, more fortunate than many. Given that the death rate among the prisoners of H Force was over twenty-seven per cent, John's life could easily have ended over twenty-five years earlier, like those of so many of his comrades, beside the railway they were forced to help build.

Chapter 24

In the Shadow of Captivity

'I suppose you can imagine what it feels like to be free, and not have to work every day under the Nips, or can you?', wrote Bob Hall on 3 September 1945, shortly after his liberation from a camp in Thailand. Perhaps, even then, he suspected that it would be difficult for those who had not shared the experiences of the previous three and a half years to comprehend what he and others had been through.

When it came, the prospect of imminent freedom from their captors must have seemed quite surreal to men who had lived with uncertainty for so long and had witnessed so much death and suffering. Harold Prechner no doubt echoed the sentiments of many others when, just months after his return home, he recalled the moment of his liberation from Changi jail, Singapore:

> I cannot possibly describe, with words, my feelings when I first walked through the prison gates, a free man. I remember that I walked and walked alone, oblivious of the hot tropical sun beating down upon me. I felt I wanted to go on and on until I reached that paradise, that place which I had almost forgotten, except in my dreams, my home in London ... . Soon afterwards, I embarked for home, in a dream, wondering whether it could possibly be real.

Harold's elation at his release from the bonds of captivity was matched by that of Jim Swordy, writing to his parents on 11 September 1945 from Yokohama, following his liberation from a camp in mainland Japan: 'At last the long awaited day has arrived. I am a free man again and I just can't tell you how happy I am.'

It seems safe to assume that all of those whose stories feature in this book would have experienced similar emotions as they emerged from captivity to a freedom they feared they would not live to see. Their ordeal over, the joy and relief springing from the words of these men is evident, with no hint of the difficulties to come, no suggestion that the years of their captivity would cast a long shadow over the remainder of their lives. However, it seems clear that although individual circumstances differed and the depth to which the men had been affected by their years as prisoners of war varied, the kind of problems my father faced in putting the past behind him were mirrored in the lives of these twenty-two men and, doubtless, in those of many others.

As Julie Summers observed in *Stranger in the House*, of all the British servicemen who returned home at the end of the Second World War, those who had been held captive in the Far East faced the greatest problems in re-adjusting to civilian life. Not only had many of them had little or no contact with their families for the previous three and a half years, or more in some cases but, as a result of the appalling conditions in which they had been held, many returned as changed men; bodies irreparably damaged by the long-term effects of malnutrition and vitamin deficiency and, in some cases, still carrying the remnants of tropical diseases which would recur for many years; and minds forever haunted by sights once witnessed, never to be forgotten. Far from their ordeal being over when they were repatriated, for many a different kind of ordeal was just beginning. In an era when counselling had yet to be recognised as an appropriate response to those who had suffered trauma, men struggled to manage emotions which, for the duration of their captivity they had been forced to keep in check, but which now sought release in the midst of families who were ill-equipped to cope.

Some of those who contributed information to this book did so only after overcoming crippling feelings of disloyalty towards fathers whom they had loved deeply but whose behaviour had at times caused them great distress and sometimes made them difficult to be around. Some told me that they had not spoken before of how much their childhoods had been affected and how, as children, they had witnessed behaviour in their fathers which seemed at best, idiosyncratic and at worst, terrifying; behaviour which they only later came to understand was a product of their fathers having been unable to leave the horror of their experiences in captivity behind them. The stories of these men help to illustrate the extent to which families shared the cruel legacy of Far East captivity as they witnessed the torment of loved ones whose minds refused to let go of the unforgettable.

The plight of those who returned from the Far East in such poor physical condition, harbouring tropical diseases and having experienced so much brutality, was quite unprecedented at the time and the system in place to deal with them fell hopelessly short of meeting their needs. Not only was no attention given to monitoring their physical health in the months that followed, but neither was any consideration given to the often fragile mental health of men who had survived such a harrowing experience. In their haste to return home, many prisoners declared themselves to be fitter than they were, unaware that in doing so they were compromising their chances of being awarded pensions for disabilities attributable to their time in captivity.

Advice given to those waiting to welcome home husbands and sons was, no doubt, well-intentioned, but did no more than scratch the surface of the men's real needs, and suggests that there was little or no perception of the potential for there being any long-term problems arising from the men's captivity. In the era of the stiff upper lip, the emphasis tended to be upon encouraging the men to forget rather than urging them to give voice to their feelings. Newspapers printed brief articles and poems about how to care for the returning servicemen, of which the following extract seems to have been fairly typical:

> **The Prisoner Returns**
>
> LET us not expect too much from prisoners returning; give to them the peace for which they have so long been yearning. He wouldn't want a crowd of strangers waiting for his story, or parties when he is too weary to accept the glory. Simplicity is comfort, unrestricted hours are bliss, progressing towards the things he has forgotten how to miss.
>
> You long to hear, but he may not desire to speak just yet; the past has been so painful you must help him to forget. Give him time for life's adjustment, he has long been out of touch. Give him gentleness and patience, but do not expect too much.

Poem printed in a 1945 newspaper offering advice to the families of returning Far East prisoners of war.

> Let us not expect too much from prisoners returning; give to them the peace for which they have for so long been yearning...
>
> Simplicity is comfort, unrestricted hours are bliss, progressing towards the things he has forgotten how to miss...
>
> You long to hear, but he may not desire to speak just yet. The past has been so painful you must help him to forget.

The advice of the Women's Voluntary Service was equally well-meaning but hardly all-encompassing, and included:

> Don't feel hurt if his fellow prisoners are more important than his family. Remember he will not be able to bear the slightest waste of food. Don't ask him to cook rice.

Only after the intervention of Colonel Philip Toosey, who had maintained an interest in the welfare of former prisoners after their return, was there a recognition of the need for specialist help for the men. This translated into the setting up of FEPoW units at Queen Mary's Hospital, Roehampton, and the Liverpool School of Tropical Medicine (LSTM), and the latter's interest in this field continues to this day.

Whilst some of the sons and daughters of the men whose stories feature here have reached an understanding of what caused their fathers to behave in certain ways, for others, many questions remain unanswered. If there is a comfort, it is surely that which is to be found in the sense of shared understanding that exists

The FEPOW Memorial Building at the National Memorial Arboretum, Alrewas, Staffordshire.

among others whose fathers experienced similar ordeals. In much the same way that only those who endured captivity in the Far East are able to truly comprehend all that that meant, perhaps only those whose fathers were FEPoWs are able to empathise with the difficulties stemming from the legacy of that captivity. Their efforts to understand have been helped enormously by the charitable organisation COFEPOW, dedicated to perpetuating the memory of Far East prisoners of war. Similarly, the Java FEPOW Club 1942 exists to provide camaraderie and support to surviving Far East prisoners of war and also strives to ensure that the FEPoW experience is not forgotten.

These twenty-two men represent but a tiny fraction of those British service personnel who survived Far East captivity despite starvation, disease, ill-treatment, overwork and the neglect of their most basic needs as human beings. It is to their credit that so many of them went on to live happy and fulfilling lives, albeit lives tinged with deep sadness for those of their comrades who did not make it home. For some, those lives were remarkably long, given all that they had experienced. The lives of others were cruelly cut short as a result of their fragile mental health and a range of debilitating physical conditions attributed to their years in captivity. All were indelibly marked by, and unable to forget, the horrific experiences they endured as a consequence of signing up to fight for their country. That fact alone would seem reason enough to ensure that they, in turn, should not be forgotten.

Although it was a comment made by my father that provided the inspiration for this book, further impetus arrived during the course of research when, on a trip to the FEPoW Memorial Building at the National Memorial Arboretum, I glanced at the Visitors' Book. My eyes were drawn to one particular entry, written by a former Far East prisoner of war, one of those whose sacrifices over seventy years ago the building commemorates, and felt humbled by the simplicity of his words.

'Thank you for not forgetting us.'

No words of mine could more powerfully state the case for continuing to remember those who gave so much in the service of their country, and whose lives thereafter were lived in the shadow of a cruel captivity.

***

Select Bibliography

Apthorp, A.A, *The British Sumatra Battalion*, The Book Guild Ltd, 1988.

Audus, Leslie, *Spice Island Slaves*, Alma, 1996.

Baker, Alf, *What Price Bushido?*, Torch Books, 1991.

Banham, Tony, *We Shall Suffer There: Hong Kong's Defenders Imprisoned, 1942–45*, Hong Kong University Press, 2009.

Beattie, Rod, *The Death Railway: A Brief History of the Thailand-Burma Railway*, Thailand-Burma Railway Centre.

Braddon, Russell, *The Naked Island*, Pan Books Ltd, 1956.

Burgoyne, Eric, *The Tattered Remnants*, The Book Guild Ltd, 2002.

Carter, Alan, *Survival of the Fittest*, Paul T. Carter, 2013.

Chater, Les, *Behind the Fence: Life as a POW in Japan 1942-1945*, Vanwell Publishing Ltd, 2001.

Cordingly, Eric, *Down to Bedrock: The Diary and Secret Notes of a Far East Prisoner of War Chaplain 1942-45*, Art Angels Publishing Ltd, 2013

Dunlop, E.E, *The War Diaries of Weary Dunlop: Java and the Burma-Thailand Railway 1942-45*, Penguin, 2009.

Ebbage, Victor, *The Hard Way: Surviving Shamshuipo PoW Camp 1941-45*, Spellmount, 2011.

Hewitt Bro. A, *Craftsmen in Captivity: Masonic Activities of Prisoners of War, Part III*, 1964.

HMSO, CMND 6832 *Government Report*, June 1946.

Loong, Theresa, *Everyday is a Holiday*, documentary DVD.

MacArthur, Brian, *Surviving the Sword: Prisoners of the Japanese 1942-45*, Time Warner Books, 2005.

Martin, Margaret (ed), *Prisoners in Java: Accounts by Allied Prisoners of War in the Far East (1942-1945) captured in Java*, Hamwic, 2007

Michno, Gregory F, *Death on the Hellships: Prisoners at Sea in the Pacific War*, Pen & Sword, 2001

Nelson, David, *The Story of Changi*, Singapore, Changi Publication Co., 1974

Parkes, Meg & Gill, Geoff, *Captive Memories*, Palatine Books, 2015.

Peek, Ian Denys, *One Fourteenth of an Elephant: A Memoir of Life and Death on the Burma-Thailand Railway*, Doubleday, 2004.

Philps, Richard, *Prisoner Doctor: An Account of the Experience of a Royal Air Force Medical Officer during the Japanese Occupation of Indonesia, 1942-1945*, The Book Guild, 1996.

Rawlings, Leo, *And the Dawn Came Up Like Thunder*, Futura Publications Ltd, 1972.

Saddington, Stanley, *Escape Impossible*, Arthur Lane, 1997

Simmonds, Ed & Smith, Norm, *Echoes Over the Pacific: An Overview of Allied Air Warning Radar in the Pacific from Pearl Harbour to the Philippines Campaign*, E.W & E Simmonds, 1995.

Smith, Donald, *And All the Trumpets*, Panther Books, 1958.

Steel, Charles, *Burma Railway Man*, Pen & Sword, 2004.

Stone, Peter, *Hostages to Freedom: The Fall of Rabaul*, Yarram, 1995.

Stubbs, Les & Pam, *Unsung Heroes of the Royal Air Force: The Far East Prisoners of War*, Tucann Books, 2011.

Summers, Julie, *The Colonel of Tamarkan: Philip Toosey & The Bridge on the River Kwai*, Pocket Books, 2006.

Summers, Julie, *Stranger in the House*, Pocket Books, 2009.

Taylor, Ellie, *Faith, Hope & Rice*, Pen & Sword, 2015.

Websites:

http://www.mansell.com/pow-index

http://www.philippine-defenders.lib.wv.us/html/bilibid_prison.

http://www.powresearch.jp/en/archive/camplist

Also:

Imperial War Museum, Sound Collection, audiotapes.

COFEPOW archive material.

Index

Adam Park, 62
Adek, 55
Ahmednagar, 87, 184
Akaster, Capt, 46
Alexandra Military Hospital, 150
Almanzora, SS, 110
Ambon, 107–109
AMES 250, 11
Anankwin, 15
Andes, SS, 71, 87, 158
Apthorp, Dudley, 12
Aquitania, RMS, 192
Argyll & Sutherland Highlanders,
    2nd Battalion, 141–3
Arrow Hill, 46, 161
Athlone Castle, SS, 52
Aungganaung, 15

Baker, Alf, 37
Ballalae, 36–7, 40
Bandoeng, 52, 55
Bangka, 71–2
Bangkok, 25, 48, 93, 101, 117–18, 127, 186
Ban Khao, 46, 161
Ban Pong, 21, 45, 63, 90, 99, 115, 125, 158–9,
    168, 184, 195
Barnes, Eric Gordon, 141–8
Bassett, Lt Col J., 36
Batavia, 52, 55, 79–80, 107
Beckwith-Smith, Maj Gen M.B., 133
Bedfordshire & Hertfordshire Regiment,
    5th Battalion, 183
Bibai, 83
Bilibid, 65
Birdwood Camp, 184
Boei Glodok, 80, 107
Boissevain, MS, 161

British Sumatra Battalion, 12–13
Britannic, MV, viii, 33
Bukit Timah, 29, 44, 89, 158, 184

Carpenter, Lt Col G., 125
Carter, Alan, 81–3
Changaraya, 15
Changi barracks, 20–2, 28, 31, 36, 44–5, 53,
    56–7, 62–3, 77, 89, 98, 100, 115, 125, 132–3,
    158, 166, 184, 192–3
Changi jail, 32–3, 56, 73–4, 199
Chungkai, 45–6, 63, 116, 143, 160–1, 168, 170,
    184, 186
City of Canterbury, SS, 52
COFEPOW, 202
Cordingly, Eric, 193
Corfu, SS, 16, 95, 101, 127, 186
Cox, Fred, 62, 99

D Force, 99, 125
Dainichi Maru, 80, 177–8
Davey, Alfred Frederick, 2, 87–96
Deolali, 132
Docketty, Francis John, 35–42
Doughty, Henry Thomas, 19–26
Duchess of Atholl, HMT, 124
Dunlop, Col Edward 'Weary', 186
Dunstan Hill Hospital, 67, 174

East Surrey Regiment, 2nd Battalion, 61–2
England Maru, 13

F Force, 194
Farrer Park, 166
Felix Roussel, SS, 132, 166
Finlay, Norman McCandless, 61–70
Fitt, Lt Col H.A., 45

Flower, Lt Col, 168
Fort Canning, 113
Fukuoka Camp 15B, 134–5
Funatsu Branch Camp, 143

Gagen, George John, 157–65
Gibbons, Eric, 47
Glory, HMS, 83
Gourock, 1, 43, 79, 98, 106, 124, 176
Gregson, WC O.G., 54
Group 1, 168
Group 2, 184
Group 4, 90

H Force, 193–5
Hakodate, 81, 83
Halifax, 1, 20, 43, 87, 124, 184
Hall, Robert Arthur, 11–18, 199
Hall, William Henry, 97–104
Haruku, 55
Haven, USS, 138
Hellfire Pass, 23
Hlepauk, 13
Hofuku Maru, 64
Humphries, Lt Col H.R., 193, 195

Indian Army Ordnance Corps, 27
Indian Electrical & Mechanical Engineers (IEME), 27
Île de France, SS, 154, 172, 180
Implacable, HMS, 154, 180
Indrapoera, SS, 118
Iruka, 170, 175

J Force, 134
Jaarmarkt, 55
Java FEPOW Club 1942, 202
Java Party 5C, 177
June Mainland Party, 21

Kachidoki Maru, 64
Kachu Mountain camp, 117
Kai Tak Airport, 151

Kallang Aerodrome, 28
Kalibanteng, 54
Kan'buri, 15, 22, 45, 63–4, 90, 93, 99–100, 115, 125, 159, 168, 184, 195
Kannyu, 23
Kempeitai, 12, 72
Keppel Harbour, 52, 56, 87, 132–3, 158, 166
Kinsaiyok, 47, 100, 116–17, 126
Kokopo, 36
Kroeng Krai, 100–101
Kuala Lumpar, 124, 142
Kuala, SS, 12
Kunhnitkway, 15
Kunitamu Maru, 177

Lae, 40
Lang Suan, 186
Largs Bay, HMT, 35, 40
Letter Party S, 158
Letter Party X, 63, 115
Leyte, 65
Lisbon Maru, 153
Liverpool, viii, 1, 19, 25, 33, 49, 57, 75, 87, 132, 158, 161
Liverpool School of Tropical Medicine, 49, 201
Loong, Paul, 179
Lunga Point, USS, 138
Lyceum, 53

McAleese, Andy, 152
McCreath, Capt Henry, 132
Macasura, 55
Mackellar, Lt Col C.E., 158
Madura, 52
Malang, 177
Manila, 65, 83, 138, 154, 171, 180
Marine Shark, USS, 138
Masta Maru, 36
Mayahashi Maru, 107
Medan, 13
Mergui, 13, 25, 127
Mitsushima, 178–9, 182
Mizumaki, 134–5

Moji, 81, 134, 143, 170, 178
Monowai, HMNZS, 75
Morley, Capt, 12
Morris, Rosslyn, 79–86
Morrison, Lt Col C., 63, 115
Moulmein, 13
Mount Pleasant, 132
Mount Vernon, USS, 43, 98, 124
Mundy, William, 107–108
Muntok, 72
Musgrave Park Military Hospital, 154

Nagoya No.3 Camp, 143
Nakhom Paton, 101
Nakhon Nayok, 93, 118
Nee Soon, 98
Negeri Sembilan, 142
Nicholls, William Coates, 71–8
Nishii Maru, 107
Nong Pladuc, 22, 47, 48, 143, 169, 170
Non Pradai, 46
North Point, 150

Okinawa, 138, 180
Oosthaven, 79, 177
Orbita, SS, 49
Orcades, HMT, 19, 176
Orduna, SS, 25
Orizaba, USS, 132
Orontes, SS, 40
Osaka No. 16 camp, 170
OSK Ferry, 56, 109
Overton, Jack, 2, 43–50

P Party, 45
Padang, 12
Palembang, 79–80
Pamekasan, 52
Payalebar, 44
Percival, Lt Gen A.E., 192
Petrie, John Dunlop, 191–8
Phetchaburi, 117
Philps, Dr Richard, 54

Pick, William Harold George, 105–12
Pope, Lewis, 113–22
Prang Kasi, 47
Pratchi, 25, 127
Prechner, Harold Joseph, 1, 51–60, 199
Prince of Wales, HMS, 11
Pudu Jail, 124–5, 142
Pulai Rubber Estate, 124
Purwokerto, 52, 177

Queen Elizabeth Military Hospital, Woolwich, 128, 163, 188
Queen Elizabeth, RMS, 144
Queen Mary, RMS, 83, 138
Queen Mary's Hospital, Roehampton, 57, 102, 128, 138, 201

Rabaul, 36–7, 40, 42
RAF 211 Squadron, 176
RAF 605 Squadron, 79–81
RAF Seletar, 20, 71
Rangoon, 15, 25, 49, 93, 101, 118, 127, 161, 186
Reina del Pacifico, HMT, 184
Rephaw, 15
Repulse, HMS, 11
Rescue, USS, 180
River Mae Klong, 143, 190
River Valley Road Camp, 56, 64, 89, 98, 143, 158, 170, 192
River Valley Road Camp Masonic Club, 192, 196
Roberts Barracks, 28, 98
Robertson, John Stuart, 176–82
Rompin, 72–3
Royal Army Ordnance Corps, 19, 46
Royal Army Service Corps, 43–4
Royal Artillery, 5th Searchlight Regiment, 35
Royal Artillery, 77th (Welsh) Heavy Anti-Aircraft Regiment, 105–107
Royal Artillery, 135th Field Regiment, 97
Royal Artillery, 148th Field Regiment, 157
Royal Corps of Signals, 113
Royal Naval Dockyard Police, Hong Kong, 149–50
Royal Naval Hospital Haslar, 34, 154

Royal Norfolk Regiment, 4th Battalion, 87
Royal Norfolk Regiment, 6th Battalion, 123
Royal Northumberland Fusiliers, 9th Battalion, 131, 134, 166, 170
Rutherford, Robert John, 131–40

Selarang Barracks, 81, 98–9
Semarang, 53
Shamshuipo, 150, 152–4, 156
Shinagawa Hospital, 179
Shonan Maru, 170
Sime Road camp, 195–6
Singapore Straits Volunteer Force, 3rd Battalion, 191
Sobieski, MS, 43, 98
Sourabaya, 36, 52–3, 55, 107
Southampton, 16, 95, 101, 110, 118, 128, 138, 144, 154, 172, 180, 186
Southern Area Fortress Signals, 113
Sussex, HMS, 74, 110
Summers, Julie, 200
Swordy, James, 166–75, 199
Sykes, Maj R.S., 21
Symonds, Albert Edgar, 2, 27–34

Tamahoku Maru, 170
Tampi, 24, 46, 169
Tanah Merah Besar, 11
Tandjong Priok, 79–80, 107
Tanglin Barracks, 44
Tanjong Pagar, 109
Tanyin, 14
Tarsao, 24, 92, 101, 126, 160, 185
Tasikmalaya, 53, 177
Tatu Maru, 13
Taungzun, 15
Tavoy, 13, 92
Taylor, William, 123–30
Tegelberg, HMT, 57
Teia Maru, 143

Tha Khanun, 116, 160
Tha Makhan, 143, 160, 185–6, 189
Tha Mayo, 24, 126
Tha Muang, 24, 92, 126, 160–1
Thanbyuzayat, 13
Thetkaw, 14
Tien Kwang, 12
Tinosa, USS, 134
Tjilitjap, 52, 177
Tjimahi, 55
Tobera airfield 37
Tofuku Maru, 81
Tokyo, 83, 179
Tokyo No. 3B camp, 178
Tonchan, 159–60, 169
Tonchan Spring, 169
Tonchan South, 160, 195
Toosey, Lt Col Philip, 48, 98, 143, 201

Ubon, 48
Uni Kampong, 13

Vendetta, HMAS, 40

Wales Maru, 134
Wang Lan, 168
Wang Pho, 46, 63, 90–2, 100, 102, 125, 169, 185
Wang Takhain, 46, 185
Wang Yai, 46, 47
Wakefield, USS, 87, 158
Warwick Castle, HMT, 79, 106, 132
Watom Island, 38, 42
West Point, USS, 20, 184
Wild, Maj Cyril, 192
Wilson, William Gordon, 149–56
Wyatt, Raymond William Charles, 183–90

Ying Ping, 71–2
Yokohama, 171, 199
Yoma, SS, 177